Unconventional Wisdom

KAREN M. KAUFMANN

JOHN R. PETROCIK

DARON R. SHAW

Unconventional Wisdom

Facts and Myths about American Voters

OXFORD

UNIVERSITY PRESS

2008

OXFORD
UNIVERSITY PRESS

Oxford University Press, Inc., publishes works that further
Oxford University's objective of excellence
in research, scholarship, and education.

Oxford New York
Auckland Cape Town Dar es Salaam Hong Kong Karachi
Kuala Lumpur Madrid Melbourne Mexico City Nairobi
New Delhi Shanghai Taipei Toronto

With offices in
Argentina Austria Brazil Chile Czech Republic France Greece
Guatemala Hungary Italy Japan Poland Portugal Singapore
South Korea Switzerland Thailand Turkey Ukraine Vietnam

Published by Oxford University Press, Inc.
198 Madison Avenue, New York, NY 10016

www.oup.com

Oxford is a registered trademark of Oxford University Press

Library of Congress Cataloging-in-Publication Data
Kaufmann, Karen M., 1959–
Unconventional wisdom : facts and myths about American voters /
Karen M. Kaufmann, John R. Petrocik, Daron R. Shaw.
    p. cm.
Includes bibliographical references.
ISBN 978-0-19-536684-6; 978-0-19-536683-9 (pbk.)
1. Voting—United States.   2. Elections—United States.
3. United States—Politics and government.
I. Petrocik, John R., 1944–   II. Shaw, Daron R., 1966–   III. Title.
JK1967.K38 2008
324.973—dc22 2007043312

9 8 7 6 5 4 3 2 1

Printed in the United States of America
on acid-free paper

Contents

Preface

THIS PROJECT GREW FROM A CASUAL CONVERSATION AMONG FRIENDS in the spring of 2005. Each of us is a political junkie of one ideological stripe or the other, and as we chuckled over some new "conventional wisdom" about the 2004 elections, we began to wonder if there was not some promise in marshaling our collective knowledge (and data) to inject some political science into the conversation. It was not hard to come up with myths and conventional wisdoms in need of clarification; there are lots of them. In fact, the most difficult aspect of the project was narrowing our list and effectively representing what our discipline knows about the subject. In confronting the first hurdle we decided to focus our energies on the most consequential myths and conventional wisdoms, which, not coincidentally, also tend to bother us the most. The second challenge forced us to canvass a broad cross section of political science research—both recent and classic—and to analyze a wide range of data. Over the course of working on this book we were occasionally surprised by where our research took us. Some of the popular conventions are indeed flimsy or patently false. In other cases, things that we had believed to be wrong turned out to have more than a grain of truth.

So while we confirmed that some of what passes for fact in popular political commentary is wrong, we nonetheless gained an appreciation for the news media—especially for those reporters and commentators who have decades of experience in the trenches and a deep commitment to professionalism. There are many fine journalists who do a service to the public by sharing perspectives informed by thoughtful considerations of evidence and history. And while there are a few occasions in this book when we are tough on the media, we do recognize that the proliferation of questionable myths is often understandable and does not necessarily reflect ill-intentioned or sloppy reporting.

Our families and friends have given us endless support during the writing of this project, especially so during the summer of 2007 as the final parts were being pieced together. We thank them all. From suffering through lonely weekends (while we were working) to copy editing various versions of the chapters, Shelly Detomasi-Shaw, Mary Ann Petrocik, and Gadi Kaufmann (our spouses) have been nothing less than exceptional, and we love them for that (and for everything else too!). Dave McBride, our editor at Oxford University Press, made the business side of this project a pleasure, and we extend our heartfelt thanks to him and our thoughtful reviewers. We are also grateful to our colleagues at the Universities of Maryland, Texas, and Missouri for their advice, encouragement, and occasional bad jokes.

In writing this preface, we had an exchange about how best to acknowledge the gratitude we feel for being able to work with one another on this project. The only thing that came to mind is a comment that Sidney Verba made to John Petrocik when he was Verba's student at the University of Chicago. That Verba line, delivered as a quip with a smile is: "Always collaborate. You get to do 1/Nth the work, take all the credit, and none of the responsibility."

The best thing about the quip is the recognition that the exact opposite is the case (and Sidney's smile told you that he knew it, too). In any real collaboration, one's colleagues are always working hard, and each looks to do a little bit more to make it easier for the others. It is impossible to take all the credit because—after talking so much about the ideas and the analysis, measures, and approaches, and writing and rewriting each other's drafts and revisions—it becomes difficult to identify what is uniquely the work of one person. In the end, we are all responsible for this book. We brought the best we could to it and feel like we learned from each other—as we have now for some time.

Karen Kaufmann, John Petrocik, and Daron Shaw

Unconventional Wisdom

Chapter One

Facts and Myths about American Voters: An Introduction

Facts are meaningless. You could use facts to prove anything that's even remotely true.

—Homer Simpson

EVERY ELECTION SEASON COMES WITH AN ABUNDANCE OF MYTHS AND conventional wisdoms that political analysts, self-anointed experts, news anchors, reporters, consultants, and academics use to explain democracy at work. Most election coverage relies on stories about a political process in which success or failure at the polls depends heavily on the clever strategies employed by candidates and parties. The notion that elections are generally won by good campaign strategies and that voters are perennially up for grabs makes for exciting journalism and television commentary, but it often strays afield from what political scientists know about American voters and their behavior. As a matter of fact, most voters identify with one of the two major parties and, when all is said and done, most partisans (even having flirted with defection) come back to their own parties when November rolls around. There are a few exceptional elections in which economic downturns, domestic unrest, and unpopular military engagements are powerful enough to shake even strong party identifiers from their normally steadfast party moorings. All the same, 75 to 80 percent of voters typically support their party brethren on election day.

This consistent finding about the importance of party identification has been tested and contested over the years; but fifty years of data and analysis have left academics with a near consensus about the dominant influence of partisanship on voting, almost exactly as Angus Campbell, Philip Converse, Warren Miller, and Donald Stokes stated in *The American Voter* in 1960. Variables and processes that Campbell and his colleagues did not consider have been incorporated into our accounts of election dynamics, but most of their original insights about party attachments remain integral to how political scientists understand and explain voters and elections.

Still, an attentive consumer of American media would certainly be forgiven for not recognizing the centrality of partisanship. Political commentary usually bypasses stories about partisan voting because they are not seen as particularly novel, sensational, or otherwise newsworthy. In the same way that the editorial criteria used in most news outlets favor the exceptional over the mundane (e.g., plane crashes over safe landings), election coverage generally emphasizes story lines that have dynamic elements or a good dose of conflict. By these standards, reports about reliable partisans lack a good "hook" and get overshadowed by discussions of candidate strategies, likely swing voters, candidate missteps, turnout speculation, and the like.

Election coverage in the mass media often traffics in conventional wisdoms and myths that can skew the public's understanding of voters and what motivates them. The collective misunderstandings that can result from this routine political coverage are more than mere nuisances; they have potentially deleterious consequences for how Americans view democracy and how they understand each other as citizens. Hyperbolic accounts of mass polarization, inaccurate accounts of swing voters, and misleading reports about the consequences of turnout levels, for example, can give rise to pernicious stereotypes, unfounded policy views, and even poorly informed legislative decision making.

We believe that a good deal of what passes for popular political insight is slightly off the mark and in some cases flat-out wrong. Given this, our goal in writing this book is to amend and correct some of the most popular (and suspect) myths and conventional wisdoms that appear and reappear during elections seasons. To this end we identify some of the most important and persistent influences on American voters and election outcomes so that our readers might appreciate the long-term stabilizing forces that shape our political universe. This is the "unconventional wisdom" to which we refer in our title. Most political scientists are well aware of these forces, but popular commentary tends to *underemphasize* them in lieu of more sensational analyses of voters and elections.

Given the news media's proclivity for simple, dramatic story lines and political consultants' incentives to have their ideas advertised by the news media, there is a strong possibility that what passes for insight on CNN and Fox News is unduly shaped by the events of the day. The explanations of politics proffered on television and in newspapers are overly sensitive to unusual events and are rarely checked against an increasingly impressive store of empirical data on electoral politics. Explanations are assumed to be right because they *sound* right even though they are untested and unexamined beyond their initial plausibility. Not only are such examples of "wisdom" a common source of myths and unhelpful conventional wisdom but they also create pointless arguments when there is no evidence—just a lot of opinions. The upshot is an environment where opinions pass as political analysis and where careful assessment is routinely ignored. Without denying there is a place for taste and preference and opinion in politics, we also believe that there is a large area where evidence and analysis trump all opinions. This book is about evidence and analysis. Using fifty years of data about American voters, we clarify and discredit many of the pervasive myths that contribute to popular misunderstandings about who votes, why they vote, and what factors lead to success on election day. We argue that party loyalties form an important and enduring baseline for understanding American elections, and contextual factors, such as levels of presidential popularity, economic prosperity, unpopular wars, and scandals, work in predictable ways to temporarily undermine party loyalties, especially among voters with the weakest party ties.

The notion that party identification and political context jointly determine the outcomes in American elections is not novel, but the important role of party loyalty constitutes one of the enduring "hard facts" about voters and elections. It shapes the larger context within which individual campaigns take place. Beyond emphasizing long-standing factors that influence American voters, we employ hard facts to scrutinize some popular myths propagated by the news media's election coverage. For example, swing voters are a popular topic in a good deal of election coverage. In any given election year, reporters and political consultants typically single out segments of the American electorate and label them as pivotal constituencies. According to much media commentary, mothers constitute a particularly influential swing group (e.g., "soccer moms," "waitress moms," or "security moms"). Fathers can be important too, as "office park dads," "NASCAR dads," and "angry white males" have all had their day in the sun. These colorful incarnations of the swing voter make for engaging stories and occasionally present useful insights, but many are overdone and lack much empirical underpinning. Beyond the question of factual validity, the preponderance of media stories that focus on such politically volatile groups suggests an enormously fluid electorate, where partisanship is less important to the voting calculus than are candidate qualities and clever campaign strategies.

The flip side to volatility and swing groups is division and polarization. By most contemporary accounts, American voters are polarized. Popular depictions of polarization suggest that voters' political differences are so profound that they have physically segregated themselves into Red states and Blue states. But like the entertaining stories about swing voters, the media coverage of polarization can be overly blunt, and it often contradicts other common conventional wisdoms. In particular, the polarization story line is hard to reconcile with the concept of an electorate that is largely up for grabs. After all, if great swaths of voters are susceptible to clever campaign ploys and charming candidates, how can they be so intractably polarized at the same time?

When political commentary ignores the long-term determinants of public opinion and voting behavior, it is relatively easy to disseminate popular myths that go unexamined. For example, the conventional wisdom about American politics consistently maintains that high turnout benefits the Democrats. What this conventional wisdom misses, however, is that the occasional voters who show up in high turnout elections often have weak ties to political parties and are thus among the most likely voters to respond to short-term forces that benefit one party over the other. In years when the political environment favors the Democrats (as it did in 2006), the irregular voters swing disproportionately to the Democrats, but in a political context that favors the GOP, they go to the Republicans (2002).

Once a conventional wisdom or myth gets established, setting the record straight is extraordinarily difficult. Although political scientists occasionally contribute to the swirl of questionable wisdom, on balance our assessments are more accurate. Our strength is not access to better or more information (reporters and political insiders are usually better informed about what is going on); rather, it is that we have the analytic tools and the predisposition by training to make judgments based on facts that span many decades. Unlike journalists who emphasize novelty and newsworthiness, we approach our analysis of American voters from a historical perspective, focusing on long-term trends and established relationships that have been influencing voter behavior for the past five decades. By relying on facts and trends, we avoid much of the ad hoc theorizing so prevalent in political reporting. Further, we are convinced that promoting an accurate portrait of the American voter is more than a mere academic exercise. In an age when information proliferates at the speed of light and when wrong information can have extremely unpleasant consequences, uncovering modern political myths and discrediting those not supported by empirical evidence is, we think, much needed.

Standard Patterns, Myths, and Conventional Wisdoms

We believe that myths and conventional wisdoms arise when those with political insights—academics, consultants, and public intellectuals of various stripes—advance ideas that comport with the professional predispositions of the news media. Ideas, in this sense, are a market commodity. The news media either "buy" them or they don't. Consultants and commentators have a significant incentive to sell their ideas, as there may be a material payoff (i.e., greater notoriety and additional business). Academics and public intellectuals are idea mongers. They may also have material motives, but the biggest incentives of these latter two groups are personal and intellectual: nothing is as rewarding as creating an idea that everybody turns to as an explanation of what is going on. The media pick and choose from among these ideas, giving them voice and credence, and, in so doing, offer analytical frameworks for their audiences.

Standard Patterns as Benchmarks

Fifty years of national surveys have yielded many well-understood regularities in the attitudes and behavior of American citizens. Our certainty and commitment to these regularities softens a bit now and then, but these generalizations—turnout increases with age, most voting is partisan, political activity other than voting is limited to very few, and so on—are parts of our core knowledge, whether we are academics, political junkies, or self-anointed pundits. The wrinkle is that we rarely have the most recent data on these patterns at hand because we "just know" they are true. One goal of this book is to provide accessible data on a wide variety of issues and commonly held beliefs about American politics that may prove useful to political scientists and pundits alike.

The Myths

We have some favorite myths, and they are the focus of the book: Americans vote for the candidate, not the party; late deciders go for the challenger; turnout helps the Democrats; the gender gap emerged because women became more Democratic; swing voters are defined by demography. These myths are standard fare among citizens, students, political commentators, and even some academics. The status of something as a myth worth exploding depends on its importance for an accurate understanding of American mass politics and whether it is quickly and consensually recognized. We stick to topics that are evidently important to the general public and avoid spending much space and energy discrediting myths that are already widely recognized as such (which often persist, nonetheless).

The Conventional Wisdoms

Conventional wisdoms are a little more challenging than outright myths because they necessitate a thorough examination of the details and dynamics that legitimate the wisdom. Our goal here is to help readers *understand*—or *better understand*—the conventional wisdom. Academics and pundits often present pictures of voters or elections that have elements of truth but miss important parts of the story, leading to confusion and distorted understandings. Our focus on the conventional wisdoms is to fill in details. We also want to make clear why, and for whom, a conventional wisdom is right. Some of the conventional wisdoms that we examine include polarization and campaign effects.

Sources of Myths and Conventional Wisdom

Myths and conventional wisdoms have many sources. Some rest on what seem to be age-old observations about people and politics that are almost culturewide constants. The notions that the gender gap emerged because of Republican aggressiveness in foreign affairs or that young voters would participate more if candidates only paid more attention to them are two such common myths. Others depend on historical factoids as well as academic research. A good example (although not one we pursue here) is the standard wisdom about off-year congressional losses by the president's party. As a historical matter, such losses occur. Moreover, academic research has managed to construct some impressively precise models of incumbent party losses.[1] However, we have learned a good deal in the last couple of decades about the factors that produce off-year success by the president's party. Republican gains in 2002 could have been anticipated—and not left the media (and the Democrats) so dumbfounded—if observers had paid more attention to what academics know about the influence of the election environment on candidate recruitment and fund-raising.[2]

But myths and conventional wisdoms become pervasive parts of the society's conventions when the news media, the consultants, and pundits of various types perceive a new pattern or trend and need to explain it. Sometimes these explanations are independent insights by members of the media. Often they are constructions of the mavens who make their living in politics or as public intellectuals on the margins of politics. Suggestions and conclusions from the many hundreds of think-tank researchers, pundits, and public intellectuals become products in the "ideas sector" of politics.

Academics contribute to the idea pool. We often get contacted by reporters looking for an "expert" to quote as evidence of the accuracy of what they want to write. Sometimes academics get called because a reporter is not sure what to write, and a story line develops from our conversation. Sometimes we are called because the reporter is looking for facts and insights about what is happening in a state far removed from the Beltway, such as Missouri or Texas. Individual political preferences, an unquenchable yearning to talk about politics, and (maybe) a desire to see ourselves quoted cause us to peddle ideas to the news media. But academics are typically bit players for the media.

Think-tank researchers, consultants, government officials, and strategists in the various campaigns are the most regular sources for the media. Many are trained as academics. They bring a good deal of expertise to their topics, but they are often active participants in elections and government or closely allied to the participants. The perspectives they bring are those of people who are trying to mobilize "actionable" information. They are weakly or not at all interested in questioning ideas if they think the idea—whatever it is—has any utility for addressing the problem at hand.

We think that academics have an ability to stand back and assess because—when we get our individual preferences on a leash—we can mobilize dispassionate, social scientific research to inform our understanding of electoral politics. Furthermore, we contend that such research is particularly useful as the issues, communication technologies, and underlying populations that animate American politics have become increasingly dynamic. We are not necessarily defending the organization or performance of our profession here. We have shortcomings that stem from our individual and collective preferences. Many academics are quick to proffer perspectives and preferences that are little more than personal viewpoints, some of which can also be self-promoting. Still, our proposition is simple: political science has the tools, methods, and approaches that can and have shed considerable light on issues such as youth turnout, the gender gap, polarization, swing voters, and the role of parties and issues in elections. This book puts them to work on these and other topics.

Political Scientists versus Political Analysts

Political science in the contemporary era often faces a struggle to be relevant—in part, because political expertise is easy to claim, and many insist they are knowledgeable and expert. When a political commentator appears to have a great many facts at hand, the claim seems all the more meritorious, and there are many knowledgeable actors across the American landscape—officeholders, party officials, and consultants, to name a few. They are able to offer what candidates and the news media want and have substantial incentives to do so. Finally, most political scientists lack much incentive to become involved in public political analysis.

It hasn't always been this way. Beginning in the early part of the twentieth century, political science had substantial practical cachet and standing with political journalists and public officials, and many scholars became political figures (Walter Lippmann and Harold Foote Gosnell immediately come to mind). Political scientists became particularly relevant when the study of public opinion and voting became more scientific and engaged immediate political tasks.[3] George Gallup and a handful of others created this relevance when they applied the nascent mathematical science of probability statistics to the study of public opinion and trumped prior popular approaches to predicting outcomes (e.g., the non-scientific surveys of *Literary Digest*).[4]

Although polling may have been the exemplar, the credibility of social science was enhanced by its general willingness to embrace rigorous research designs. For example, in the aftermath of World War II, scholars from Columbia University used repeated interviews of voters from Erie County, Ohio, and later Elmira, New York, to rewrite the book on political persuasion.[5] Their panel design and appreciation of location and social networks led to an original portrait of how voters acquire information and select a candidate. The discipline's professional credibility reached its zenith in the early 1960s with the advent of national surveys of public opinion and documented new insights into citizenship.[6] Political science, not the candidate's campaign or the parties, had the expertise and the motivation to conduct broad, theoretically rich studies of voting behavior over time. Campaigns were (and remain) preoccupied with their own specific race. They did not (and do not) study topics simply to study them; neither do the parties. Political parties were neither permanent nor especially well-developed at peak levels. National parties did not exist in the 1950s and 1960s as they do today. Moreover, the money in politics—especially for public opinion and voting analyses—was nothing like that which we see in the initial decade of the twenty-first century.

But it is not just that political science was better situated than its potential competitors. Endemic in the work of Lippmann, Lazarsfeld, Campbell et al., and Key are two elements that are somewhat lacking in political science today: (1) an appreciation of what constitutes an interesting "actionable" question, and (2) an ability to present a clear argument.

Both features have been less common in political science research since the 1960s, especially because the intellectual maturation of the discipline entailed a growing emphasis on theoretical rigor. It has therefore focused increasingly on conceptual issues without paying much attention to the palpable concerns of ordinary citizens. Furthermore, we have increasingly employed technical methods that are inaccessible to even the well-educated reader. Technical ability, in fact, is often rewarded as a relatively easy way to discriminate between and among ideas. It has also created interest among academics in methodological disputes that are at times too esoteric even for our own peers, let alone the broader potential audience of politicos and voters. Many of the articles in the leading journals and a sizable percentage of university press books are unreadable except for the most motivated and mathematically minded.

But two other developments may have also contributed to the marginalization of political science results. On the demand side of the equation, we have witnessed an explosion in news media attention to politics and elections. Beginning with the syndication of the *Rush Limbaugh Show* in 1988, political talk radio has developed a wide following and has increased the market for politicians, pundits, and ideologues. More recently, the emergence of Web logs ("blogs") has added an additional layer to the milieu of political commentary while also expanding potential markets to include tech-savvy, college-educated Americans. Perhaps most important, the rise of cable news networks—beginning with CNN in 1980—and the simultaneous rise of twenty-four-hour, seven-day-a-week news coverage have created a need for extended and extensive political insight and conversation. The professional norms and biases of the news media are also important: they have a preference for dramatic, confrontational, and less complicated perspectives.[7]

Second, consultants have emerged as a formidable challenge to academics on the supply side of the equation. This development can be dated to the 1960s, although it received a rocket-boost when the 1971 Federal Election Campaign Act (FECA) created funding for new classes of political specialists who could make a living in politics. The FECA provided a blueprint for raising political money, and this—with an assist from increased staffing and mailing privileges in the U.S. Congress—led to the rise of a professional class of campaign specialists in the 1970s. These consultants have incentives to develop and promulgate ideas and stratagems that can be marketed with an eye toward winning clients. The news media offer a prime vehicle for marketing these ideas.

Both supply and demand factors support each other in reducing the contributions of political science. In earlier times, when political science was more accessible, academic research had a direct effect on how campaigns viewed the world. Its impact was evident among students, who presumably graduate and take their ideas with them to the "real world" of politics; intellectually curious candidates and party officials, who might read a book or hear an interview and apply the ideas expressed by a professor; and reporters, who developed relationships with academics and were thus exposed to a broader set of ideas about the way the political world operates. In the contemporary environment, academic ideas are filtered by political consultants who ignore those that do not serve their interests and appropriate those that might do them credit. This is not to suggest that consultants have served their clients or the quality of discourse poorly. But the transmission of research to the showroom of American politics is being filtered by actors who have practical interests that lead to emphases that may not always reflect the nuanced qualifications and results of academic research.

The result of these developments is that political science tends to produce research that is inaccessible or (especially in the view of those outside the academy) irrelevant. Consultants cherry-pick the good ideas and repackage them while simultaneously proffering their own ideas about what makes the electoral world turn. The news media, candidates, and parties debate and select from a variety of these insights, with the most promising being highlighted in election campaigns.

What We Do

This book considers seven broad subjects in the area of voting and elections: party identification, political polarization, swing voting, the gender gap, young voters, voter turnout, and campaign effects. This listing is not meant to be exhaustive, nor is it meant to be a randomly selected representation of all news media coverage of politics. We focus instead on the long-term stabilizing forces in American politics and use these insights to explore a range of contemporary, "hot-button" topics in which the attendant conventional wisdoms and popular myths warrant more scrutiny. Our chapters emphasize empirical exploration of the topics at hand. We rely largely on survey data, usually from the vast archive constructed at the University of Michigan's Interuniversity

Consortium for Political and Social Research. Much of the analysis is original, but we take advantage of the many fine and relevant studies done by other political scientists. Perhaps most important, we aim to leverage over-time data sets, as one of our greatest sources of frustration as consumers of political information is the lack of historical perspective offered in most popular commentary.

In general, the chapters flow from the larger macro issues of partisanship and polarization to more pointed considerations of swing voting, the gender gap, young voters, turnout, and campaign effects. Chapter 2, "Americans Hate to Love Their Party, *but They Do!*" provides a comprehensive overview of the enduring importance that party identification plays in American electoral politics. Americans voters are often quick to assert their political independence from party politics and typically attribute their political choices to a myriad of factors apart from party loyalties. This chapter, using longitudinal data from the American National Election Studies (hereafter ANES), demonstrates the continuing strong relationship between self-reported partisan identification and political behavior. While Americans give political parties lower evaluations than they have in previous decades, voting behavior remains as party oriented as ever. Weak and leaning partisans are more swayed by short-term electoral forces than are self-professed strong partisans, but overall partisanship remains so robust that it effectively stymies third-party movements in the United States.

Chapter 3, "Are American Voters Polarized?" questions the current presumption that American voters are much more polarized than they were in the 1970s, 1980s, and 1990s. Initially, we detail that—among political scientists—there is much debate on the matter. Some argue that voters have become more polarized over time and that this polarization is most evident among the politically aware. Others maintain that elite polarization has not translated into substantial mass polarization; voters are centrist and have been so since at least the early 1970s. Our analyses suggest the electorate has polarized somewhat over the past three decades but that even when split into partisan categories, Republicans and Democrats have more similarities than differences when it comes to their respective issue positions.

The strongest evidence of polarization pertains to feelings that partisans have for parties and candidates. On an affective basis, voters have become more polarized. They like their own parties more and show great aversion to their political competitors. This polarization, however, is not the consequence of reasoned issue differences or ideological fervor; rather, voters rely on their feelings about the groups that comprise the Republican and Democratic parties to make judgments about parties and their respective candidates. We suspect that this affective polarization is the result of an information environment in which notions of good and evil are increasingly used to describe political debates.

Chapter 4, "Who Swings?"examines the myriad of definitions of swing voting and then hones in on the question of who really swings. Our main argument is that there are some common threads to identifying swing voters; nonetheless, the popular view that certain demographic groups are usually swing voters is not borne out by the data. Swing voting appears to be a psychological predisposition, one that is spread across a wide range of demographic and social groups.

The general matter of swing voting leads to a consideration of an exceptionally persistent myth offered in recent elections about late deciders. Most political analysts are unanimous in their belief that late-deciding voters break for the challenger. We find that late deciders are not terribly common in presidential elections (although they are more prominent in a handful of years, such as 1992) and that they tend to break in much the same manner as other voters.

Chapter 5, "Soccer Moms and Other Myths about the Gender Gap," examines the popular myth that attributes the gender gap in party identification and voting behavior to political changes among women. The most common accounts of the gender gap point to women's distinctive economic vulnerability, increasing presence in the workplace, feminist values, and concern over abortion rights as the reasons that they have become the mainstays of the Democratic Party. Much of this chapter is devoted to discrediting this myth; indeed, the increasing movement of white men into the Republican Party comprises the structural foundation of the modern gender gap.

More specifically, we examine fifty years' worth of data on gender differences in attitudes, partisanship, and voting behavior and note the steady movement of men into the Republican Party. We also observe that the most recent changes in the gender gap appear to hinge on short-term fluctuations in the political behavior of women. We conclude this chapter with a brief discussion of the 2004 election, noting new regional patterns in the gender gap that may be consequential in future elections.

Chapter 6, "The Young and the Not-So-Restless Voters," turns to the perennial topic of young voters. Political commentary is awash with assertions about the young. The main claim we deal with here is that young people are an untapped market of votes. While this is true numerically, it is also the case that the attitudinal characteristics of young people make it unlikely they could be mobilized without inordinate resources and a much more compelling issue agenda. We present the voting patterns of the young in comparison to those of some older cohorts. We also explore the popular conception that young people are always liberal and Democrats. Today's eighteen- to twenty-four-year-olds do tend to be more liberal and more Democratic than the rest of the electorate, but in any given time period, young voters generally reflect (even magnify) the trends seen among the remainder of the electorate.

Chapter 7, "The Partisan Bias of Turnout," tackles the topic of turnout and explores the widely propagated myth that higher turnout benefits the Democrats. Not only do political pundits reiterate this "fact" with unyielding consistency, but politicians themselves appear to believe it as well. Legislative proposals aimed at bolstering turnout are typically embraced by Democrats and avoided by Republicans even though higher turnout has no predictable partisan effect. Using over-time data on voter turnout in presidential and congressional races, we illustrate that there is no consistent partisan bias with regard to levels of turnout. High turnout almost always benefits candidates who would likely win anyway. Incremental voters are not renegades who swing elections; rather, they tend to sway with the short-term forces that advantage one candidate over another in any given election.

Chapter 8, "Campaign Effects in the Twenty-First Century," addresses the voluminous and growing literature on campaign effects. From the perspective of popular commentary, campaign tactics and campaign strategies have profound influence over the political choices that voters make. Political scientists, on the other hand, tend to discount this influence. In this chapter we provide a summary of the campaign-effects literature that is largely descriptive, including data on voter attentiveness and receptivity, party outreach, and candidate activities. We also present a distinctive analysis of candidate appearance and TV advertising data from the 2000 and 2004 presidential campaigns. In all, we largely support the political science view that campaign effects are often contextual, conditional, and sometimes evanescent.

Chapter 9 returns to the fundamental themes articulated throughout the book. In particular, we revisit the importance of long-term factors on voters and their choices. We also turn our attention to what we are likely to see in the 2008 elections and beyond. Finally, we return to some of the normative themes advanced here. In particular, we believe that the propagation of myths that have little bearing on the real world has important consequences for the conduct and quality of American elections. For example, popular discourse on swing voters often traffics in stereotypes about groups that are simply not true. The notion that mothers, or NASCAR fans, or waitresses get pushed around by clever campaigns belies the fact that these groups are in no way less thoughtful or more emotion laden than the typical American voter. Similarly, the constant reference to voters as "polarized" contributes to a common understanding of the mass electorate as warring camps, when in fact rank-and-file Democrats and Republicans have much in common. Hyperbolic and inaccurate commentary about our political system denigrates our public discourse and, most important, our faith in our own democratic processes. It is our hope that some cold, hard facts will provide some useful perspective.

Chapter Two

Americans Hate to Love Their Party, *but They Do!*

In the past 50 years independent voters have grown from one-quarter to one-third of the electorate, according to Gallup polls. In California, the number of independent voters more than doubled between 1991 and 2005. The fastest-growing political party in the United States is no party.

—Mark J. Penn, *Washington Post*, March 21, 2006

PARTY AFFILIATION CONTINUES TO BE THE PRIMARY SHAPER OF American electoral politics, despite a common belief—frequently emphasized in media commentary—that party matters relatively little to voters. Public opinion surveys typically reflect discontent with the parties, often as a reflection of unhappiness with current officeholders or events, but partisanship, as we show in this chapter, is alive and well in American politics.

This does not means that Americans are boosters of party government. According to the 2000 American National Election Study (ANES), 23 percent of Americans supported having one party control the Congress and presidency while a majority (51 percent) voiced a preference for divided government. Not only do Americans seem to distrust the notion of unified party government but they also exhibit substantial distaste for the parties themselves. Only 38 percent express a preference for continuing the current Democratic and Republican party domination; almost as many (34 percent) prefer to see new parties challenge the Democrats and Republicans.[1] Not surprisingly, Americans are also unlikely to report basing their voting decisions on party allegiance. Very few (between 6 and 10 percent in recent surveys) report that their candidate choices are dictated by a party attachment; most (sometimes approaching 60 percent but usually around 50 percent) insist that local or national issues determine their choices; another 20 to 30 percent report selecting the better candidate, regardless of party.[2]

Academic research and textbooks have done their part to further the notion that parties are weak influences on voters, candidates, officeholders, and government in general. Election decisions are often presented as candidate-centered at the expense of the parties.[3] Studies of legislative elections (congressional elections in particular) have so consistently trumpeted the importance of incumbency and constituent service that we almost ignore party as an influence in these contests.[4] Candidates, we are told, tout their individuality and service to their constituents and rarely assert virtue in party loyalty. It is common for challengers to criticize incumbents for voting the party line and supporting their party's (or president's or governor's) policies to the detriment of the constituents. It also is not rare for candidates to concern themselves as much with their standing in the mass media as with their reputation among party loyalists. Officeholders are described as focused on reelection, and we expect them to run away from their party affiliation when it advances that goal.[5] The media focus on self-starting candidacies, primary rather than party-selected nominees, individual fund-raising, restrictions on party spending, and the importance of interest group endorsements and support. We cannot, therefore, be too surprised that party is mostly a missing element in the popular understanding of how Americans decide their vote and a contested factor in the popular image of elections and government.

Of course, there are data that make this a reasonable convention—at least at first glance. Expressions of party loyalty have declined and are not high. Consider Figure 2.1, which reports the percentage of the population that thought of themselves as Democrats or Republicans between 1952 and 2004. The downward slope of the line is unmistakable. The proportion

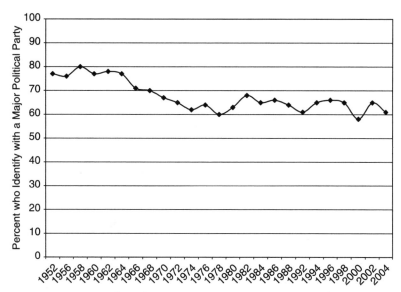

FIGURE 2.1. Party Identifiers, 1952 to 2004. *Source*: ANES from selected years.

who answer "Democrat" or "Republican" to the first part of the standard party identification questions ("Generally speaking, do you usually think of yourself as a Republican, Democrat, an Independent or what?") has declined approximately 15 percentage points since 1964. In the 1950s about 24 percent refused to "think" of themselves as a Democrat or Republican, but almost 40 percent refused this association by 2000 and 2004.

The 1950s were a highwater mark of partisanship by other measures as well. In the 1950s, a 2:1 majority made positive comments about at least one of the parties when they were asked what they liked and disliked about the Democrats and Republicans; barely 25 percent expressed a negative assessment (Figure 2.2).[6] But by 1972, a clear majority was either neutral toward the parties or even found more to dislike than like about them.[7] Partisanship had become a negative phenomenon: many seemed to identify with or support a party because of greater antipathy toward its competitor.[8] These negative partisans were only a marginal majority, but the dramatic change from the positivity of the 1950s was striking. Evaluations rebounded and became more positive by 1990 although the size of the majority that expressed more positive than negative sentiments toward the parties was substantially smaller than it had been in the 1950s.[9]

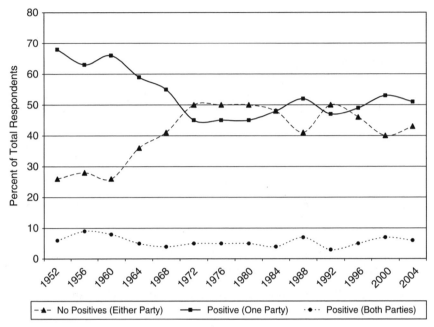

FIGURE 2.2. The Public's Evaluation of Parties, 1952 to 2004. *Source*: ANES from selected years.

The Partisan Electorate

While the notion that the parties are no longer the principal political guidepost of citizens is wrong, broad social and economic changes in the United States have created new sources of information and perceptions of government and politics that are often independent of the parties. "Dealignment"—the abandonment of party allegiance—was a hot topic in the recent past.[10] Furthermore, single-issue interest groups often compete with the parties as a source of voter identity, with distinct ideas about public policy and which candidates deserve our support. But a predisposition in favor of one of the parties—one that is both enduring and precedes the election and candidates at hand—remains a dominant influence on the political behavior of Americans. It continues to shape the perceptions, beliefs, and behavior of the citizenry to a degree that is almost unchanged from what we observed in our first academic national surveys almost sixty years ago.

The purpose of this chapter is to correct a caricature and document the foundational status of the party identification of Americans for most of their political beliefs and behavior. Americans on the whole may not be unbridled partisans, but the often-reported decline in identification with parties and the increase in negativity toward parties are greatly over-emphasized by commentators and analysts. Within the academy, there is a clear agreement that parties matter for voters and within government.[11] Laws governing parties and elections have reduced the influence of party leaders on officeholders, but they remain powerful organizations that are more active and consequential today than they were in the past.[12] The labor-intensive party organizations of the nineteenth and early twentieth centuries have been replaced almost everywhere by complicated party organizations that continue to do the business of parties—identifying prospective candidates and then grooming, nominating, and electing them. And the parties do not disappear at the government building's door. They coordinate the work of the officeholders and control the bureaucracy by the appointment of trustworthy fellow partisans to administrative positions.[13]

Party apparatuses and their influence, however, are not the focus of this chapter. The interest here is what V. O. Key termed the "party in the electorate"—the men and women who are not, on average, attentive or interested in government and politics but are available to vote for candidates of the same party that they supported in previous elections. The predictability of this support is the foundation of the American party system. It allows electoral institutions to be designed with a clear expectation about who will win; it limits the probability that insurgent candidates (George Wallace, John Anderson, Ross Perot) and new parties (the Green Party) will succeed; it provides candidates and campaigns with strong cues about what issues they should raise in their campaign and where likely support can be found.[14] In all, party identification makes electoral politics a predictable feature of the political system because of its powerful influence on voters.

The Meaning of Partisanship and Party Identification

Much ink has been spent on promoting contrasting definitions and conceptualizations of partisanship and party identification. The most common dispute turns on whether party identification should be conceived as a psychological attachment and a social identity or a summary statement of issue preferences.[15] The debate is long standing and unlikely to be resolved because evidence can be marshaled for both conceptions.[16] We do not engage that debate, but it is useful to understand what we are thinking about when we use the term *party identification*.

First, we view it as an expression of preference for one party over the other. The preference may be a social identity or a summary statement about an individual's political beliefs more broadly. We do not believe that this distinction is consequential for recognizing the impact of the preference on a person's political behavior. Second, the evidence indicates that party preference is often formed in the family and through multiple family and social experiences that have weak political content. Individuals learn to think of themselves as a Democrat or Republican because significant figures in their social environment express a preference for one party over the other. Finally, the intensity of the preference varies, and experiences can make the initial attachment to a party more firm or they can weaken it. The initial preference may even change completely, although the bulk of the evidence shows relatively little shifting between the parties in the short run.[17]

The key fact about this preference is that at any given time it represents an expression of support for one of the parties that subsequently influences behavior and other attitudes. People who think of themselves as (for example) Democrats are inclined to vote for Democratic candidates and contribute time and money to Democratic campaigns (although not many Democrats, Republicans, or Independents give money or time). They are also inclined to view the public statements of Democrats as more credible and to have views on public issues that are more like the views of others who call themselves Democrats. Moreover, the intensity of this preference is meaningful. Those who strongly embrace it are less likely to behave in an inconsistent way: a person with a strong preference for the Democrats is less likely than someone with a weak preference to vote for a Republican and less likely to hold political views that are inconsistent with what Democrats normally believe about public policy issues. In addition, they are more likely to be interested in and knowledgeable about public affairs.

The associations are not perfect, but they are very strong. Party preference is the predisposition that shapes political behavior and attitudes more than any other predisposition or preference we have measured. This fact makes it a foundation for most of the citizenship-relevant behavior of Americans.

This chapter documents the continuing importance of partisanship for voters in three distinct sections. The first part establishes the attachment that Americans have to the parties. The second section documents the influence of party identification on vote choices. The third and final section illustrates its influence on aggregate election patterns.

Undiminished Partisanship

The top line in Figure 2.3 documents that a willingness to express a preference for either the Democratic or the Republican Party has diminished little over the past fifty years. The difference between Figures 2.1 and 2.3 is that the latter classifies partisans as those who answer "Democrat" or "Republican" to the first of the standard party identification questions ("Generally speaking, do you usually think of yourself as a Republican, Democrat, an Independent or what?") or who admit to thinking of themselves as "closer" to the Republicans or the Democrats in the follow-up probe.[18] If we regard only those who call themselves Democrats or Republicans in response to the first question as partisans (recall Figure 2.1), then partisanship has declined substantially. But if we regard the willingness of most Americans who first call themselves Independents to acknowledge that they feel closer to one of the parties, then partisanship has barely changed in the last fifty years.

Party support declined slightly after 1964 to a low of about 83 percent by the late 1970s, when it began a largely uninterrupted resurgence. By the end of the 1980s the fraction of the citizenry declaring themselves supporters of the Democrats or Republicans had effectively reached the level of the early 1950s. The balance of Democrats and Republicans has changed. Democrats outnumbered Republican supporters by about 20 percentage points until the late 1970s. The Democratic advantage in party preference is about half that number today (see Figure 2.3). The overall level of support for the parties, however, is virtually the same as it was during the benchmark decade of the 1950s.

Identifiers and Supporters

Many students of the electorate (including more than a few political scientists) have treated those who respond to the first part of the

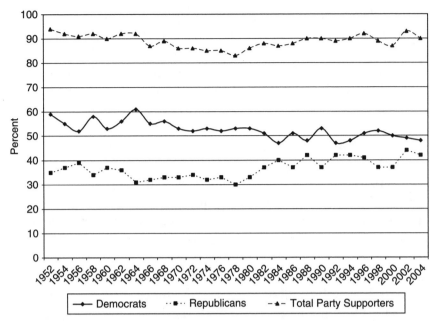

FIGURE 2.3. Party Supporters, 1952 to 2004. *Note*: Democrats, Republicans, and Total Party Supporters include strong, weak, and leaning partisans. *Source*: ANES from selected years.

party identification question by choosing "Independent" as though they have no preference between the parties. That is not the right interpretation, and it explains the difference between an apparent decline of partisanship in Figure 2.1 and the almost unchanged percentages in Figure 2.3.

Most of those who first assert that they are independents immediately acknowledge that they feel "closer" to one of the parties. The important fact about those who acknowledge this closeness is that they behave like partisans and evaluate candidates like partisans.[19] Two pieces of data document their substantial partisan preference. Table 2.1 allows a comparison of those who first call themselves Independents but then acknowledge being closer to one of the parties (labeled "Leaners"—the conventional term—in the table), with Democrats and Republicans who choose a party preference immediately.[20]

The voting behavior of each group of Democrats and Republicans— the strong identifiers, weak identifiers, and the leaners—is partisan. Throughout the fifty-year period, the strong partisans stand out, with

TABLE 2.1. The Voting Choices of Leaners and Identifiers

Election Years	Strength of Democratic Party Identification			Strength of Republican Party Identification		
	Strong	Weak	Leaner	Leaner	Weak	Strong
1952–1960	88	65	72	9	9	1
1964–1972	84	63	67	19	24	6
1976	91	74	72	17	23	4
1980–1988	88	66	70	18	13	6
1992–1996	93	74	70	17	15	3
2000	96	85	72	13	16	2
2004	97	83	84	10	11	2

Note: Table entries equal the percentage of each category who voted for the Democratic candidate.
Source: ANES from selected years.

approximately 90 percent or more voting for the candidate of their party.[21] Democratic leaners voted for Democratic candidates at almost the same rate as weak identifiers (an average of 72 percent over the fifty years of the table). Republican leaners averaged only a 15 percent Democratic vote, while weakly identified Republicans averaged a 16 percent Democratic vote. The almost indistinguishable voting choices of leaners and weak identifiers of the same party demonstrate that leaners are highly partisan, even if their first response to the party identification question is to call themselves independent.[22]

Other ways of looking at leaners tell the same story. Table 2.2 reports each group's thermometer assessment of the parties and the presidential and vice-presidential candidates in 2000 and 2004.[23] The thermometer ratings, of course, summarize many different assessments: policies, diffuse ideological perceptions, personal qualities (in the case of candidates), and real and perceived group affiliations. The average thermometer difference between weak and leaning Democrats is slightly less than 4 degrees, with weak identifiers almost always slightly "warmer" toward the Democratic Party and Democratic candidates and slightly "colder" to the GOP and Republican candidates. The Republican leaners

TABLE 2.2. Feelings toward the Parties and Candidates

	Democratic Identifiers			Neither	Republican Identifiers		
	Strong	Weak	Leaner	Neither	Leaner	Weak	Strong
2004							
Bush	25	43	36	51	71	78	91
Cheney	26	43	38	46	59	64	77
Republican							
Party	27	46	42	49	62	71	83
Average	26	44	39	49	64	71	84
Kerry	77	65	65	51	41	38	25
Edwards	77	65	63	53	47	44	34
Democratic							
Party	83	73	65	55	48	45	32
Average	79	68	64	53	45	46	31
2000							
Bush	40	48	47	56	68	70	80
Cheney	46	52	49	53	61	62	74
Republican							
Party	38	44	46	51	62	70	79
Average	41	48	47	53	64	67	77
Gore	79	67	64	53	43	47	33
Lieberman	70	61	60	50	46	52	43
Democratic							
Party	84	73	64	52	44	46	32
Average	78	67	63	52	44	48	36

Note: Table entries are average thermometer scores (0 to 100).
Source: 2000 and 2004 ANES.

are no less partisan in their evaluations: weakly identified Republicans are warmer toward the GOP and its candidates than the leaning Republicans by slightly less than 4 degrees. By contrast, leaning Republicans and Democrats are an average of 21 degrees apart on the thermometers.

So how should we understand the leaners? We have known for a long time that Americans, especially the middle class and the better educated, are inclined to call themselves independent and assert an unbiased judgment of the candidates.[24] This inclination to call themselves independents and to acknowledge a party preference only after a bit of probing is more a matter of self-presentation than an accurate statement about how they approach elections and make judgments about candidates, the parties, and politics in general. Leaners are partisans, and Figure 2.3 tells the appropriate story about Americans: a majority (more than 85 percent) is partisan and although that proportion declined noticeably after the late 1960s, it never dropped very low and gained back most of what was lost by 1990.

Things, of course, have changed. The contemporary news environment is invariably critical of public figures. That has an impact on views of parties and party figures. It creates contradictory considerations about the parties and candidates and leaves voters more willing to recognize the shortcomings of their preferred party. As a result, the early twenty-first century may not be the golden age of parties that historians believe existed at the end of the nineteenth century, but the best evidence we have is that some 85 to 90 percent of Americans feel close to or identify with the Democrats or the Republicans. This preference has a significant impact on voting and elections.

Partisanship and Voting

Figure 2.4 illustrates how strongly party identification influenced the vote choice during the last half century. The top figure reports the lowest and the highest Democratic presidential vote for each category of identifiers for every presidential election from 1952 through 1988. The narrowness of the range illustrates the consistency of vote choices despite the differences that existed among the candidates and the political situations of the elections. Inter-election differences in the voting choices of each class of identifiers (strongly identified Democrats, for example) pale compared to differences between Democrats and Republicans. Also, nothing has changed recently. The relationship between the vote and expressed party preference was higher in 2000 and 2004 than it was in previous elections, as a comparison of the two figures makes clear.[25]

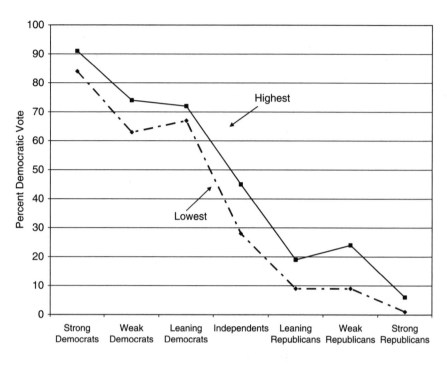

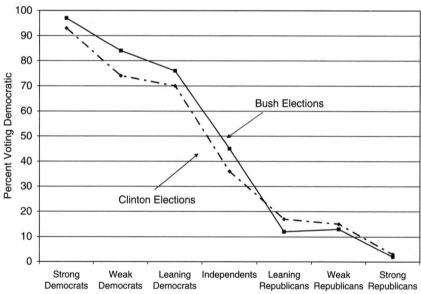

FIGURE 2.4. Party Identification and Presidential Voting. *Note*: The top chart reports the lowest and the highest Democratic presidential vote cast for each category of partisan identifiers for the time period spanning 1952 to 1988. The bottom chart compares the average rates of Democratic voting by category in the Clinton (1992 and 1996) and Bush (2000 and 2004) elections.

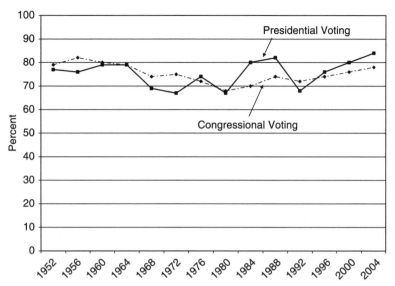

FIGURE 2.5. Party Voting in National Elections. *Note*: Lines represent percentage of partisans voting for their own party candidates. *Source*: ANES from selected years.

Similarly, the aggregate level of party voting is high and varied hardly at all from 1952 through 2004. Figure 2.5 reports the pattern, graphing the total share of the vote that is contributed by Democratic identifiers who vote for the Democratic presidential or House candidate and Republican identifiers who voted for the Republican candidate.[26] Some minor variations have occurred: party voting declined after 1964, reaching its lowest level in 1972 and 1980, after which it increased (with a slight dip again in 1992). Since 1992 it has remained slightly below the watermark set in the 1950s for congressional candidates, but party voting for the presidency is, on balance, as high as ever. In general, party loyalties are as consequential today as they were half a century ago. Any erosion in party voting has been minimal and there is no evidence of a decline in the future.

Short-term Forces and Party Voting: Identifying a Normal Vote

Rates of party voting are high but do differ among elections because party predispositions can be reinforced or eroded by circumstances of the moment. Examining this variation not only confirms the importance of partisanship but also allows us to create an estimate of how different groups of partisans vote when the situation is more or less "normal." Party voting is at its highest level when the candidates are typical representatives of their party and no exceptional issue or event is on the public's agenda. It is lower—sometimes much lower—when one or maybe both candidates are atypical of their party or the issues and events of the moment cut across party lines to the detriment of one of the parties. Elections contested in an environment of domestic and foreign policy failures or malfeasance by the incumbents almost always cause many partisans of the incumbent party to vote for the other side while it reinforces partisans of the out-party. An election held during "good times" has the opposite effect: partisans of the in-party are motivated to vote their party affiliation, uncommitted voters disproportionately support the "ins," and defections from partisans from the out-party will increase the incumbent's majority.

These outcomes are not easily predicted, to the occasional embarrassment of the savants who try to do it.[27] Going into the Bush-Gore election in the fall of 2000 the perception of economic good times led many observers to predict a substantial popular vote majority for Gore. As we come into the 2008 elections, dissatisfaction with the continuing American military involvement in Iraq is widely predicted to ensure a Democratic victory. Predictions can fail, however, for many unanticipated reasons. But prediction failures notwithstanding, the direction of the vote swing between adjacent elections corresponds to changes in the issue environment and the differential appeal of the candidates. The swing is sufficiently regular and orderly—and centered on the partisanship of the voters—to permit generalized predictions about changes and the outcome of elections across election environments.

Consider Figure 2.6, which provides a graphic representation of this process. The line labeled "competitive" is the average of the vote for John Kennedy and Jimmy Carter. The elections were expected to be competitive and were narrowly won—and not marked by any overwhelming set of issues or popular concerns. The "Good Democratic Year" reports the vote for Lyndon Johnson in 1964, when the popular perception of Barry Goldwater as too conservative led to a Democratic win across the board. The "Good GOP Year" reports the Democratic vote in 1972, when George McGovern was widely viewed as outside the Democratic mainstream.

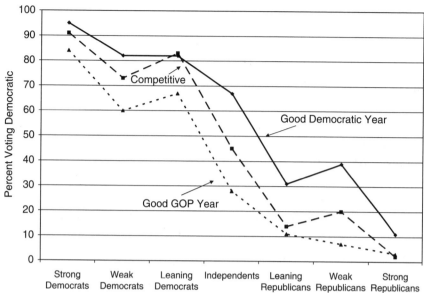

FIGURE 2.6. Party Identification and Election Forces. *Note*: Lines represent percentage voting for the Democrat in each of the party identification categories. *Source*: ANES from selected years.

The lopsided Democratic win in 1964 was created by Democratic identifiers voting for Johnson more heavily than they had in the competitive contests; independents moved an average of 22 points toward Johnson compared to their Democratic vote in the balanced elections of 1960 and 1976; Republicans defected at much higher rates. The good Republican year of 1972 is a mirror opposite of the good Democratic year of 1964: Republican identifiers were slightly more loyal; independents voted for Richard Nixon; Democrats defected. In both cases, it is the weaker partisans of the disadvantaged party and independents who are responsible for most of the movement between these election types.

There are two features to note in Figure 2.6. First, all classes of identifiers—strong identifiers, weak identifiers, leaners, and independents—respond to the short-term tide presented by the election environment. Partisans vote more heavily for the candidate of their party when the environment of the election reinforces their predisposition and less heavily when the tide of the election makes their candidate or the issues he represents less attractive. Second, the shift is moderated by the strength of the individual's identification. It is smallest among those who express the strongest party attachments and greatest for those with weak—or no—party loyalties.

The pattern in Figure 2.6 is typical of how varying levels of party attachment correspond to levels of party voting. Because these patterns are fairly regular, they allow us to formulate predictions about how each group will vote when the election environment favors the Democratic candidate, when it favors the Republican candidate, and when it is more or less balanced. Table 2.3 reports the results.[28] The numbers are percentages representing the expected Democratic vote when the short-term forces in the election significantly favor the Republican Party and its candidates, are neutral, or favor the Democrats. The "vote swing" column is the absolute value of the difference between the Democratic vote when the short-term force favors the Democratic Party compared to when it favors the Republicans.

The size of the swing depends on the intensity of the identification and the party preferred by the voter. When the environment of the election shifts from pro-Democratic to pro-Republican, the vote choices of strong identifiers change about 12 percentage points. Weak and leaning Republicans respond to a similar short-term force with about a 16-point shift in their vote. Independents, weak Democratic

TABLE 2.3. Short-Term Forces and Changes in the Vote

	Average Democratic Vote When Short-Term Forces Favor the:			
	Republicans	Neither	Democrats	Vote Swing
Strong Democrats	79	87	91	12
Weak Democrats	58	70	80	22
Leaning Democrats	57	70	80	23
Independents	37	51	59	18
Leaning Republicans	21	28	37	16
Weak Republicans	19	26	35	16
Strong Republicans	12	15	24	12

Note: "Vote Swing" is the numerical difference between rates of partisan voting when short-term forces favor one party over the other.
Source: Petrocik (1989).

identifiers, and leaning Democrats are the most responsive. We should emphasize, however, that changes in political context do not affect all voters the same way: party attachment matters. While Democrats may react as much as independents to short-term forces, their expected vote is quite different. Approximately 80 percent of weak and leaning Democrats will vote for the Democratic candidate when short-term forces favor the Democrats, while only 59 percent of independents are expected to vote for the Democrat. When short-term forces favor the GOP, we expect a 57 or 58 percent Democratic vote among Democrats but only about 37 percent support for the Democrat among independents.

The vote of each class of partisans when the short-term forces are in balance (the "neutral" column in the table) is particularly important, as it defines the "normal" vote (expressed as a Democratic percentage in the table). A "normal election" in the first decade of the twenty-first century will produce a 53 percent Democratic win in the national electorate. In this "normal" election, 51 percent of independents vote for the Republicans and approximately 70 percent of weak and leaning identifiers vote for the candidate of the party with which they identify (with Republicans displaying slightly more loyalty). About 87 percent of the strong Democrats vote Democratic and slightly fewer strong Republicans (85 percent) support the candidate of their party.

This loyalty, not absolute but very substantial, stabilizes American politics by placing a ceiling on the support that third parties and insurgent candidates are likely to receive.[29] Laws and practices burden the efforts of third parties, but the commitment of most voters to the major parties provides an additional, powerful barrier to candidates and movements separate from the major parties. In fact, if voters did not have the kinds of loyalties they do for the existing parties, there likely would be election structure changes that permit more opportunities for new parties. But given these loyalties, there is minimal pressure for elites to change the laws, and the existing parties provide a barrier to insurgent movements of every sort. Consequently, whatever the nation loses by having an electorate committed to the traditional parties and unresponsive to innovative party movements, it may also gain with a built-in resistance to the kinds of left and right radical movements that have often been serious contenders for national office in other countries.

The vote for Wallace in 1968 and Perot in 1992, whatever one might think of them as presidential prospects, illustrates how partisan attachments

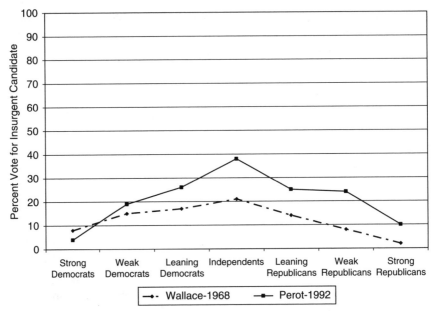

FIGURE 2.7. Support for Insurgent Presidential Candidates. *Source*: ANES from selected years.

depress the opportunities for insurgent candidacies (see Figure 2.7). Perot did better among Republican than Democratic identifiers in 1992. His take from Republicans was greater overall and across all levels of party attachment (for example, Strong Republicans were more likely to vote for Perot than Strong Democrats). Wallace, on the other hand, did better among Democrats. Strong Democrats were more likely to defect to Wallace than Strong Republicans. The most noteworthy feature of the graph, however, is not the Democrat-Republican differential between the elections but the relationship between responsiveness to these insurgents and the voter's strength of identification. Strong identifiers were the least likely to defect, followed by weak identifiers, then leaners.

An electorate in which a large majority is attached to the parties presents a formidable barrier to insurgents. In 1968 and 1992, Wallace and Perot presented strong candidacies early in the election year. Perot, in particular, led in the national polls in the spring of 1992. Partisanship aside, he was subject to aggressive attacks and personally did things that undermined his candidacy. Still, it is worth noting that Perot received almost 40 percent of the votes cast by pure independents.

In an electorate in which independents are the norm rather than the exception, it seems quite possible that an appealing insurgent candidate could become the plurality winner in a three-person contest. Figure 2.7 is a reminder that the many election law hurdles that impede third-party and insurgent candidates are reinforced by the predisposition of partisans to be uncertain or doubtful about the merits of independent candidates. In a mass electorate that is not highly involved in public affairs—the condition of the American electorate—party loyalties provide stability across elections and a barrier to insurgency and change.

The Normal Vote as a Baseline

But insurgent candidacies are rare and usually partisanship is not called upon to protect the major parties against them. In normal times, partisanship only moderates the impact of the election environment on the two-party vote. Candidates use this knowledge of how different groups of party identifiers normally vote to evaluate strategies and campaign themes. Observers and analysts use this same baseline to formulate an explanation of the election result. For example, because we can determine how many of each type of partisan there are in a legislative district, it is possible to calculate an overall expected vote by simply weighting the size of each partisan group by the vote they cast when short-term forces are in balance (the "neither" column in Table 2.3) to get an expected total. A district that has 10 percent Strong Democratic identifiers, 30 percent Weak Democratic identifiers, 20 percent Leaning Republicans, and 40 percent Strong Republican identifiers has an expected GOP vote of about 59 percent.[30] A Republican who wins with 62 percent is getting about the vote we would have expected from the district's partisanship; he or she has no unusual personal appeal to the voters beyond partisanship. A campaign survey that finds a Republican ahead with 54 percent, in contrast, shows the candidate is "under-achieving." The effect of an issue on the vote can be similarly examined.[31] A comparison of the vote or vote intention among those who want a different way to finance health care in America with the baseline expected vote allows a candidate (or observer) to identify whether opinions about health care financing may be having an influence on the vote.

Similarly, comparisons between the observed vote and expected vote of demographic groups make it possible to understand what is happening (or happened) in an election. Every campaign plan begins by asking who is voting for whom. The specific question for a campaign is usually whether support from a group matches the vote that is expected given its partisanship.[32] Answers to such questions allow campaigns and observers to proffer suggestions about whether a campaign is doing well or why it was won or lost. In all of these cases, the partisanship of the individuals, because it can be converted to an estimated vote, provides an otherwise missing benchmark.

Academic analysts may not always think this way, but it is the principal way that candidates, strategists, and even journalists think about campaigns. Anyone who has participated in a discussion with campaign strategists about whether an issue is helping or hurting understands that the strategist needs to be able to compare a vote intention with an expectation. The candidate wants to know whether he is getting "his vote" from various segments of the electorate. The journalist who is reporting this to the rest of us wants to be able to assess how things are going, regardless of what the campaigns might be reporting to him. Some examples follow.

Incumbency as a Partisan Phenomenon

The major component of an incumbent's success is the partisanship of the voters in the district. Since almost all legislative districts are drawn with the underlying partisanship of the voters as the central consideration, the foundation of every incumbent's security is a district that includes enough voters of his or her party that no likely issue or top-of-the-ticket-induced tide will produce defeat.[33] The partisanship of the district has powerful second-order effects as well. The minority party's candidate, viewed as certain to lose, usually receives few of the resources (money and strong support from party leaders) needed to mount a serious challenge in a district with a strong preference for the opposing party.[34] The most talented candidates of the minority party avoid a campaign in such hopeless districts (an outcome that Jacobson and Kernell described as the *strategic politician* phenomenon).[35]

Just how much of a voter's support for congressional incumbents has been a direct function of partisanship is apparent in Figure 2.8, which

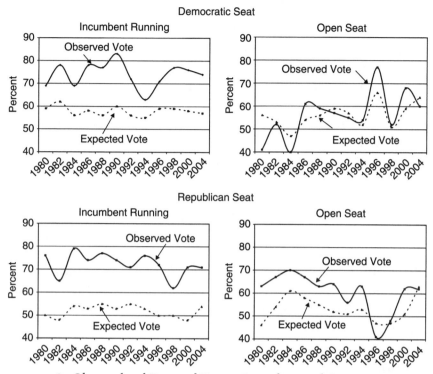

FIGURE 2.8. Observed and Expected Vote in Incumbent and Open Seat Races. *Note:* Expected vote is based on authors' calculations and is explained in note 15 of this chapter. *Source:* ANES from selected years.

compares the difference between the reported House vote and the vote that would be expected if party identifiers had cast a normal party vote. Each graph plots two lines: the reported vote of the respondents and the vote that might have been expected given the respondents' partisanship in the absence of short-term forces (the "normal vote"). The top graphs present data for Democratic seats and the lower ones present data for Republican seats.[36]

Overall, voters supported incumbents more than their party preference would have led us to expect. Their vote for incumbents averaged about 16 percentage points more than expected (upper-left figure), while voters in Democratic open seats cast a vote that was 2 points *less* (on average) than their partisanship predicted (upper-right figure). Put differently, voters in Democratic seats were approximately 18 points more likely to support the Democrat when he (or she) was the incumbent. The pattern is virtually identical for races in GOP seats. Voters supported Republican incumbents about 19 points more than expected given their party identification (lower left) but only 5 points more when the seat was open (lower right).

The evidence that partisanship shapes the vote regardless of incumbency is in the expected vote values for Democratic- and Republican-held districts. A majority of the respondents in incumbent and open-seat races have a party preference that matches the party of the current or previous officeholder. Voters in districts represented by a Democrat seeking reelection (the upper-left graph) had an average expected vote of 57 percent Democratic. Open Democratic seat districts (upper right) had a party identification that yielded a 54 percent expected Democratic vote. Voters in districts where a Republican sought reelection (lower-left graph) had an expected Republican vote of 54 percent; those in districts where a Republican was retiring (lower right) had an average expected GOP vote of 53 percent. In brief, incumbents and would-be successors in open-seat races were supported by electorates of partisan supporters: partisanship is the basis of incumbency.

Planning a Congressional Campaign

Partisanship is, of course, also the stuff of election planning for every campaign. Table 2.4 presents data from a congressional campaign in which the Democrat was the incumbent.[37] The Republican challenger in this congressional district was facing a formidable task. With 40 percent of the vote among probable voters he had to identify groups to whom he could appeal for support to overcome the 20-percentage-point deficit. His campaign plan settled upon six target groups based on the political history of the district, the "potential" appeal of the candidates (as it was perceived by those planning the campaign), and the issues in the election. A majority of blacks and younger voters in the university town in the district were expected to vote for the Democratic incumbent. The Republican challenger sought to win a "share" of votes among these "hostile" groups and heavy support in other portions of the electorate. The difficulty faced by the Republican challenger is apparent in a comparison of (1) the target percentage needed from each group in order for him to win (according to his strategists) with (2) the vote he might expect given the partisanship of the groups.

TABLE 2.4. An Expected Vote and a Congressional Campaign Plan

	Vote Intention in January	Expected Party Vote	Campaign Target
Whites			
Suburban Areas	74	54	80
Industrial City			
Younger voters	44	41	60
Older voters	38	40	50
University town			
Younger voters	25	35	40
Older voters	67	47	70
Blacks	2	17	5
Total	40	42	50 (+)

Note: Table entries are the percentage Republican.

At the time of the survey, he was receiving overwhelming support from the most Republican segment of the district (whites in the suburban areas) and an unusually heavy vote among older white voters in the university area. The candidate and his advisors had decided that a win was possible if they could increase their support among several of the groups presented in Table 2.4. The plan was too optimistic. The campaign's target percentages for some groups substantially exceeded the Republican vote that was likely from the party identification of voters in the group (column 2 of the data). Barring the introduction of a spectacular issue, it is hard to believe that a candidate could drum up support that exceeded the underlying normal vote of the groups by such wide margins. The Republican lost with 44 percent of the vote. According to a late survey (in which the estimated vote for the Republican candidate was 46 percent), his share of the vote among older whites in the industrial portion of the district slightly exceeded the normal vote. He fell about 5 points short of the normal vote of younger whites in the university area.

The Evaluation of Issues Effects with the Normal Vote in 2004

Personal qualities (strong, decisive, weak, experienced, and so forth) were the most common reasons for liking or disliking George W. Bush or John Kerry in 2004. Discrete issue comments largely fell into four categories: moral and value references (hereafter also referred to as cultural issues), social welfare issues, matters dealing with economic policy, and foreign policy and defense references (including terrorism). Foreign policy and defense references were the most common comments about the candidates, reflecting, one might surmise, the facts of our military involvement in the Middle East and the national emphasis on terrorism and security. Cultural issues were a particular strength for Bush. Kerry, by comparison, was much more likely to be viewed in terms of social welfare concerns. Foreign policy references were usually offered as part of a positive assessment of Bush.

There was a connection of these assessments with the vote. The first data column of Table 2.5 reports the expected Republican vote of the individuals mentioning each issue type in their evaluations of the candidates.[38] The second column reports the Bush vote associated with these different mentions, and the third reports how much that vote exceeded what should have been expected given the voters' partisanship. Bush's majorities among voters who evaluated the candidates in cultural issue terms exceeded the partisan vote by approximately 6 percentage points. It exceeded the partisan vote among those mentioning economic and foreign policy issues by 5 and 2 points, respectively. Bush's losses were concentrated among those who mentioned social welfare issues in evaluating the candidates or the parties. Among these voters, Bush's

TABLE 2.5.   Evaluation Dimensions and the 2004 Presidential Vote

Type of Issue Mentioned	Expected Vote	Reported Vote	Gain/Loss
Cultural	55	61	6
Social Welfare	36	27	−9
Economic	51	56	5
Foreign/Defense	52	54	2

Note: Table entries are the percentage vote for Bush.
Source: 2004 ANES.

vote was only 27 percent (column 2)—a full 9 percentage points below the party identification baseline of 36 percent.

Conclusion

Everett Carll Ladd set up his assessment of Robert Putnam's thesis about declining social capital with this anecdote:[39]

> I was waiting in line....And a voice boomed out: "So what do you think of 'Bowling Alone'?
>
> It was a distinguished colleague, not in the social sciences, who had just finished reading a commentary on...Putnam's work. It wasn't exactly the spot for an extended seminar on America's "social capital." I replied briefly that while I agreed entirely with Putnam (and many others) that the health of a country's associational life and individual participation in civic affairs is of vital importance, I didn't think Putnam was right in claiming that the data show civic decline. "Well, I don't know about the data," my friend replied, "but what he has to say feels right to me, right here." At that he gently patted his abdomen.

Putnam's story captured a social convention—a "feeling"—about a decline in social involvement in America.[40] Ladd's analysis, by contrast, emphasized that whatever changes had occurred in the society's sense of community, there had not been a decline in the associational networks that Putnam had identified as the cause of an eroded sense of community in America. But many—perhaps most—Americans live with a sense that community has declined, no matter what Ladd documented. An attentive American with an interest in public affairs might have a reaction to this chapter that is similar to Ladd's colleague.

Like Ladd, we think that the evidence we present is clear and persuasive. And we suspect there may be insight from the *Bowling Alone/ Ladd Report* dialogue that explains why Americans feel that parties matter little to voters despite overwhelming evidence to the contrary. In addition, we think the full story is complicated and deserves analysis that we cannot offer here. We do, however, offer three ideas about why Americans might be uncomfortable with their partisanship and (erroneously) doubt that it matters any more.

The first is that they have become accustomed to appeals that are not partisan. In the more distant past, the labor-intensive focus of campaigning was almost exclusively a narrow-casting exercise. Appeals were directed at likely supporters, and the other side only saw a slice of what was going on. Fifty years ago a billboard might have read "Make it Emphatic, Vote Straight Democratic." You don't see that today. Modern campaigns seem to be broadcasting exercises in which appeals are made that cannot be limited to core supporters, and the people who run campaigns rarely try to polarize voters along a party divide.[41] Candidates, party strategists, and the specialists who run modern campaigns do not emphasize their party association because they believe they will do better if they do not. The minority party candidate in any locale can use broadcasting technology to improve his prospects. It doesn't take the majority party candidate long to adopt this as a counterstrategy, especially with a national culture that prizes individual decisions over group loyalties. Candidates, as a result, have become unusually good at marketing themselves outside of the framework of appeals to partisanship. The effect of decades of experience with campaigns in which party is not emphasized is the erosion of a public sense that party matters.

Second, we suspect that the watchdog posture of the modern mass media has had an effect on our sense of partisanship. Whatever their individual political preferences, reporters and publishers, for business reasons and in response to professional norms, adopt a stance of belligerent neutrality toward both parties and all candidates. It is rare that ulterior motives and shortcomings in performance and policy are not the stuff of a political report, and campaigns are typically reported not as clashes of policy and principle but as maneuvers by the competitors. We should not be surprised that this kind of information environment erodes the culture's sense of party attachment. In the past, a more partisan press reinforced party loyalty because it created a personal and group information environment in which Americans heard only supportive good news about their party and only about the shortcomings and machinations of the opposition.[42]

Third and finally, the complexity of issues that parties and candidates address today makes it more difficult for the "big-tent" party and candidate coalitions of the past to be maintained without leaving many partisans uncomfortable with their party. Special interest groups (to which we all either belong or feel some sympathy) constantly press the parties and candidates and announce their failures to follow through on presumed commitments. A pro-life Democrat with traditional social views can be as uncomfortable with his party as a pro-choice and small-government Republican when the GOP talks about a right-to-life amendment. Those differences were more manageable in a time when the parties and campaigns—indeed politics overall—were less national. The transformation of the parties in the 1970s and 1980s has reformulated the coalitions but did not even begin to eliminate the differences that exist among ostensibly like-minded fellow partisans. Many Americans may feel uncomfortable with the postures of their parties and their candidates. It may temper our willingness to announce a strong a priori commitment to the parties. This discomfort with our coalitional two-party system, however, seems more than balanced by the nation's feelings toward polarized parties and the politics they require (as we describe in the chapter on polarization). The result is that parties enjoy a loyal electorate and an election system in which partisanship is the central fact of campaigns, turnout, electoral swings, and issue differences among Americans.

Chapter Three

Are American Voters Polarized?

The divide in American politics is about more than the ideological dis-
tance between the two parties. Right now, red staters and blue staters
live in two different political universes.

—E. J. Dionne, *Washington Post*, March 14, 2006

WHILE AMERICAN VOTERS EXPRESS CONSIDERABLE DISDAIN FOR
the two-party political system, they are still fairly loyal members of their respective parties, as we show in Chapter 2. And while
popular election commentary pays relatively little attention to the
enduring importance of party identification, journalists and pundits are
nonetheless (and somewhat paradoxically) fascinated by the notion that
the American electorate has become polarized. Polarization is a hot topic
in the media because, from their perspective, it often entails political
conflict of the most visceral kind. The Red state–Blue state metaphor
that has become so popular among political commentators involves
more than partisan disagreement; in its most extreme incarnation, it
represents a clash of values and worldviews pitting traditional religious
and moral beliefs against modernism and moral relativism. Given the

frequency with which polarization is depicted as an epic battle between good and evil, it is not terribly surprising that it has captured the imagination of journalists, consultants, and scholars alike.

In this chapter we take a closer look at the question of mass polarization. On the one hand, there is much credible evidence that Republicans and Democrats have become more distinctive in their political views over the past three decades. On the other, we show that the opinion differences between rank-and-file party members are still fairly slight; partisans continue to be more moderate than party elites and also tend to agree with one another more often than they disagree. Polarization exists, but its magnitude is greatly exaggerated and represents a description of American voters that deserves significant clarification.

Responsible Parties: A Double-Edged Sword

In 1950, the American Political Science Association produced an influential report that called for more responsible political parties.[1] According to this report, the two major parties lacked discipline and programmatic coherence, and in the absence of responsible parties, our democracy was presumably at risk.[2] In the wake of this report there was considerable hand-wringing over the lack of a vital party system. Strong, ideologically coherent parties were viewed as an essential component of a good democracy, and their absence led many political observers to lament the programmatic incoherence of the Democrats and Republicans and the overall impotence of the political system.

Parties, however, began to demonstrate greater institutional strength beginning in the late 1970s, and elites in both parties became more ideologically divided.[3] Nowhere was this more pronounced than in the chambers of the Congress where straight-line party voting increased at exceptional rates.[4] Even at the level of the mass electorate, ordinary citizens (long noted for their general lack of political sophistication) became more partisan in their vote choices[5] and showed growing levels of ideological consistency.[6]

The much-anticipated emergence of strong parties, however, was not uniformly hailed. In fact, following the ascendance of the Republican majority in the Congress after the 1994 elections, pundits and scholars voiced increasing concern over the lack of compromise and harsh partisan rhetoric that accompanied reinvigorated party organizations. After the bitter resolution of the 2000 presidential election, political commentators frequently used the phrase "polarization" to describe the new state of American politics.

By this account, the American public had become increasingly divided into warring camps that could be identified as much by geography as by politics.[7] The popular "Red state–Blue state" metaphor suggested that liberals and conservatives not only disagreed on political matters but that they also had organized themselves on competing terrains.[8] The unspoken (but often implied) subtext to this story was that the political divide between Republicans and Democrats was so palpable and personal that partisans chose to physically segregate themselves from all but their ideological brethren.

Polarization: Definitions and Debates

Popular emphasis on polarization is a relatively new phenomenon, emerging from the closely contested 2000 and 2004 presidential elections. Media descriptions of it evoke notions of intransigent rival groups who live in different states and hold vastly different views on a wide range of political matters. Furthermore, the pundits and academics who apply the notion of a "polarized public" to the mass electorate seem to imply a citizenry who increasingly hold extreme views. Especially during election years, Americans are routinely described as polarized, suggesting that not only is the public much less moderate than in years past but that centrist politicians will not be able to satisfy the ever more ideologically distinct opinions of Republican and Democratic identifiers.

Some political scientists have been quick to point out that the public, per se, is not polarized. On most issues of the day, they have found public opinion to be quite centrist and moderate.[9] By their reckoning, party leaders, officeholders, and activists are the polarization culprits. The Republican and Democratic parties take increasingly noncentrist positions on many important issues, creating ideologically extreme choices for a generally moderate voter base. Moreover, when parties take unyielding, lopsided positions on salient political issues of the day (e.g., abortion, immigration, foreign policy, taxes, gay marriage, etc.), attentive partisans adjust their political orientations to mirror their increasingly divergent elite cue-givers.[10]

While most political scientists are well aware that the public at large is not polarized, many still argue that *party identifiers* (especially *strong* identifiers) have become more polarized across a variety of issue domains. Dividing the electorate into competing camps of partisans, studies suggest that the attitudes of the Republican and Democratic rank and file have become both more internally consistent with party platforms and progressively divergent from one another over time.[11]

Longitudinal analyses of party identifiers and their views provide sound evidence that, on average, Republicans and Democrats are farther apart on many issues than they were two or three decades ago. Some of this change can be attributed to the realignment in the South; as conservative white southerners, once mainstays of the Democratic Party, systematically moved into the Republican Party, the ideological coherence of the Republican and Democratic parties improved.[12] But the effect appears to be more than a by-product of party realignment. The opinions of party adherents also changed in response to polarizing elites.[13]

This chapter blends these emphases into a more complete portrait of policy divides among Americans. Our finding is straightforward: mass partisan polarization on most political issues remains modest. Taking both the averages and the distributions of partisan views into account, we find considerable overlap in opinion between Republicans and Democrats on a vast array of issues. Where Republicans and Democrats differ most is not on questions of abortion, social welfare spending, defense spending, or taxes. They are most polarized with regard to their feelings about the political parties and their candidates. From 1988 to 2004, partisans increasingly held strong aversions to their competitors in spite of overlapping opinions on most political issues. To the extent that policy views remain largely centrist while feelings about parties and candidates continue to be ever more distinctive between partisan camps, polarization in the American setting is largely an affective phenomenon. Republicans and Democrats perceive one another in an increasingly adversarial light, but amid all the overheated rhetoric, partisans generally fail to notice that their opinions on most political issues are more similar to one another than they are different. The hyperbolic debate associated with contemporary U.S. politics often conflates good and evil with Red states and Blue states, with Republicans and Democrats, and particularly with Republican and Democratic leaders. Moderates within both parties are decried on talk radio and cable television as traitors to the cause. Yet, ironically, moderate legislators and executives are arguably more in tune with mass opinion than are the evangelists on the Right and the Left.

Measuring Polarization

In its most common use, the term *polarization* is invoked when parties or their members take opposing sides on an issue or an election.

When the majority of voters in southern states choose Bush and the majority of voters in northeastern states choose Kerry, the media and political commentators see polarization. When the nation gives the popular vote to one candidate and the electoral college goes to another, this too is reported as evidence of mass polarization. Polarization has become the catchphrase for all sorts of partisan disagreement and for heightened electoral competitiveness, but these characterizations are simply too broad.

On the one hand, mass polarization points to the divergence of party identifiers on important political issues. When Democrats and Republicans become ever more dissimilar and their respective views trend toward the extremes, this pattern reflects parties that are polarizing. Popular agreement may exist because party members are middle-of-the-roaders, with most clustering at some midpoint between an extreme liberal and extreme conservative viewpoint. But extreme preferences, in and of themselves, are not the equivalent of polarization. Polarization is rooted in the notion of partisan disagreement, not necessarily extremism. For example, Americans are not polarized on the question of whether abortions should be legal in the case of rape (87 percent support abortion in this circumstance).[14] Democrats are slightly more supportive (91 percent versus 83 percent of Republicans), but the vast majority of both party's members support legal abortions under some set of circumstances. The percentage of Democrats and Republicans who oppose abortion under all circumstances is relatively small—9 percent and 17 percent, respectively. And while the minority of Americans who oppose abortion in all circumstances may feel strongly about their views and may be greatly irritated that so many of their fellow citizens disagree, their minority viewpoint (or opinion intensity) does not define polarization. Polarization describes a distribution of partisan opinion, and on these issues—and many others—Americans are not polarized.

The proponents of polarization, especially those in the popular culture, ignore these distinctions. Polarization may describe the views of political activists, but the mass public is almost never polarized. There are differences, but they are not huge; and on most matters, public opinion does rest in the middle of the policy spectrum. In terms of self-professed ideology, for example, moderates make up almost one-half of the population; conservatives constitute approximately 30 percent and self-identified liberals about 15 percent. The same basic pattern of centrist opinion can be seen on a wide array of public issues. Whether abortion rights, domestic spending, prayer in school, or civil rights, a plurality of Democrats and Republicans will pick middle-of-the-road positions to the extent they are offered as an option.

Nor are election results automatic indicators of polarization. If one candidate is slightly preferred to another and wins by a slim margin, this points to *competition* but not necessarily to polarization. Candidates may represent extreme choices, but close electoral outcomes do not tell us whether the nation is polarized. It is not entirely clear what a polarized electoral outcome would look like inasmuch as in most national elections voters choose between two major party candidates and often pick the one they perceive to be the most moderate.[15] In fact, the best evidence indicates that when voters are given a "choice not an echo," they opt for the echo.[16] If voters tend toward moderation and if candidates actively temper their campaign messages in an effort to "play to the middle," then the notion of a polarized electorate is counterintuitive indeed. In multiparty systems one might argue that a polarized electorate is one where a majority of votes are cast for the most ideologically strident parties. In the context of American politics, however, there are few opportunities to really assess the ideological extremism of the voting public.

Patterns in Issue Polarization

Most political science accounts of public opinion conclude that the average issue positions of Democrats and Republicans have diverged in recent decades, particularly on those issues most associated with the parties and their governing agendas.[17] According to Layman and Carsey (2002a), the increasing prominence of cultural issues in the political realm has resulted in growing party polarization on a number of issues. Their theory of "conflict extension" argues that even as the parties' coalitions grow increasingly divided on the relatively new cultural issues such as abortion and gay rights, party polarization on older policy agendas such as social welfare and race may also increase. From this perspective, increasing ideological coherence among political elites (such as the president and members of Congress) is communicated to the mass public, and attentive partisans are those most likely to adjust their views to conform to new party orthodoxy. Less sophisticated partisans and political independents exhibit lower levels of political knowledge and less ideological consistency in their issue positions.[18]

Layman and Carsey's studies, and others like it, focus on the individual-level processes that lead to partisan change. They offer important contributions to our understanding of political communication and how it affects the views of mass partisans, but in general, political science has had little say about the real magnitude of these changes. Even if party members are moving apart on certain issues, does this really mean that parties are polarized and that citizens have much less centrist views than before?

While most political scientists have not grappled with this question directly, Abramowitz and Saunders (2005) are an important exception in making an explicit case for why polarization is politically consequential. Looking largely at data from the 2004 presidential election, they argued that "active partisans" make up approximately 28 percent of voters and that active partisans are indeed polarizing. It is clearly beyond the scope of our expertise to say whether 28 percent of voters is a lot (or a little), but it does seem that if 28 percent are polarizing a great deal, then another 72 percent are polarizing a little bit or not at all. In fact, the general consensus among most political scientists is that knowledgeable and active partisans are polarizing to a much greater degree than the remainder of voters. Our analyses corroborate this insight and go further to suggest that overall levels of polarization, especially as characterized by the popular media, are greatly exaggerated.

The patterns in Figure 3.1 clearly show that shifts in mean partisan opinion over time have been quite small and that popular claims regarding mass polarization have been overstated. The charts show trend data for six survey questions that pertain to public opinion on race, abortion, the proper scope of government, defense spending, and the role of women in U.S. society. The trend lines illustrate the average opinion on these six issues for Democrats and Republicans spanning the time period from 1980 to 2004.[19] The data come from the ANES conducted during presidential election years. All of the questions that we use to construct these time series are identical; thus, changes in opinion cannot be attributed to changes in the questions. Finally, all of the questions are scored from most liberal to most conservative so that higher scores reflect more conservative views.

A number of features are immediately clear. First, the average Republican or Democrat holds fairly centrist views. While Republicans are consistently more conservative than Democrats, both sets of partisans hold views close to the middle. For example, on the question regarding

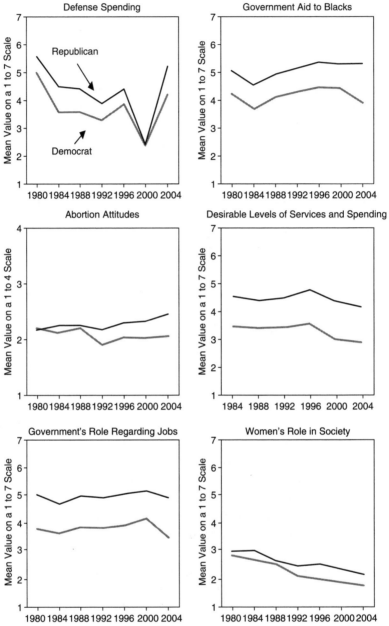

FIGURE 3.1. Mean Partisan Opinion on Various Political Issues. *Note*: Lines represent mean values for Democratic and Republican respondents. Each graph is scaled to reflect the range of possible answers. Partisan respondents include self-identified strong party identifiers, weak party identifiers, and those who lean toward one party or the other. *Source*: ANES from presidential election years 1980–2004.

whether the government should ensure that all Americans have jobs, Democratic responses fall close to the midpoint ("4") of the 7-point scale for the entire time series up to and including the year 2000. Predictably, Republicans are consistently more conservative and score in and around "5" for the entire series. To the extent that partisans have become appreciably more polarized on this issue, it appears to have been a rather recent phenomenon with Democrats moving to the left in 2004.

Over the course of this time series, Republicans and Democrats tended to differ most on questions that pertain to the size and role of the federal government; yet, even in the case with the largest partisan difference—desired levels of services and spending—the mean scores for both groups hover around the center of the scale. There is little evidence that partisans "polarized" on questions of the social welfare state; Democrats and Republicans became ever so slightly more liberal in 2004, but the trend for both parties was nearly identical. The abortion issue illustrates the largest change between Republicans and Democrats. Even so, there remain substantial numbers of moderates in both camps. The notion of a polarized electorate, as described in popular commentary, evokes visions of extremely conservative Republicans and similarly liberal Democrats, but the respective views of party identifiers do not appear to cluster at the extremes of these scales. Even when Republicans and Democrats disagree, the difference between them is certainly not the gulf that popular rhetoric implies.

These trend lines emphasize how modest the changes in partisan attitudes really have been over this twenty-four-year time period. In spite of the heated rhetoric about partisans and their unyielding extremism, Republican and Democratic party identifiers have not become polarized camps when it comes to their general policy sentiments. This is not to say that political scientists who promote the polarization thesis are wrong; we readily concede that partisan changes across time are statistically significant and that sophisticated partisans drove this phenomenon. Our point is that these changes are not necessarily *politically* significant, especially when taking into account that neither set of partisans strayed too far from the center. If legislators mirrored the general views of the American public, political debates should be between those in the center and those sitting center left or center right. To the extent that political struggles are played out between the far left and the far right, this is an elite phenomenon somewhat unrelated to the typical views of American voters.

Polarization and Political Symbols

While partisans are not sharply divided over matters of policy, they are divided on their feelings about the parties and their candidates. As illustrated in Figure 3.2, party labels and party candidates evoke much larger partisan differences than do policy issues. The charts in Figure 3.2 were generated using party and candidate thermometer ratings over the same 1980 to 2004 time period.[20] Unlike policy questions that require considerable political sophistication to answer, thermometer scores ask for people's feelings, and they are typically interpreted as a measure of affect. The patterns demonstrate predictable results. Republicans like the Republican Party and the Republican presidential candidate more than Democrats; Democrats similarly favor their own. The Democratic Party thermometer ratings are fairly consistent over this time period with the Republicans hovering at the 40-degree mark and the Democrats staying around 70 degrees. By contrast, the Republican Party thermometer ratings showed a rather clear pattern of increased polarization between 2000 and 2004, with Republican ratings creeping up while Democratic ratings dropped. The patterns for candidate ratings are quite comparable to the party ratings. Of particular note, George W. Bush appears to have generated considerable movement in the mean thermometer scores, with a Republican increase of almost 10 degrees and an equivalent decline among Democrats. Across all of the thermometer ratings, feelings about Bush have generated the greatest amount of party polarization.

The relative distance between Republicans and Democrats in their evaluations of parties and candidates is considerably greater than their respective policy views. At one level, this should be expected because the policy questions used in these surveys do not explicitly mention party positions. Knowledgeable voters are more aware of party orthodoxy and, as a result, are most likely to reflect the values of party elites. The relative policy distance between well-informed Republicans and Democrats is always greater than the distance between average citizens who pay much less attention to politics. The thermometer ratings clearly primed partisanship as a basis for evaluation, enabling less-aware partisans to pick sides; but even here, strong partisans were more likely to hold extreme views than weak partisans.

Comparing the partisan gap in policy views to the relative difference in affect toward political parties and their candidates illustrates an important point about polarization. To the extent that the American

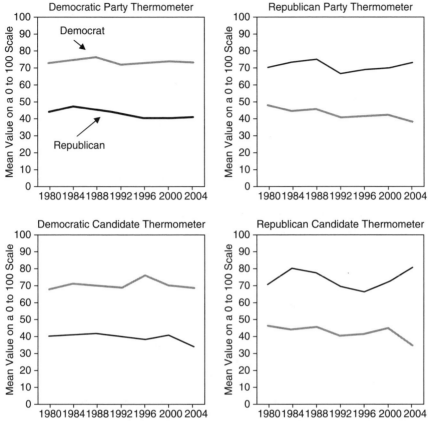

FIGURE 3.2. Mean Party and Presidential Candidate Thermometer Ratings over Time. *Note*: Lines represent mean values for Democratic and Republican respondents. Each graph is scaled to reflect the range of possible answers. Partisan respondents include self-identified strong party identifiers, weak party identifiers, and those who lean toward one party or the other. *Source*: ANES from selected years.

public is polarized, they are more influenced by the symbols than they are by the substance of political life. Polarization is not really a function of policy disagreement but rather a demonstration of increasing partisan intensity, consistent with the trends in voting behavior we discuss in Chapter 2. Beyond this, it seems quite clear that polarization—the concurrent movement of Republicans and Democrats toward more extreme views—is a very recent phenomenon. It is really between 2000 and 2004 that partisans appear to have polarized, and while this may foreshadow future polarization, the movement is far too short-lived to be considered a trend.

A Different Perspective on Polarization

While it is common practice in political science to compare means as a measure of group differences, relying on averages alone may not paint a complete picture. If public attitudes are evenly arrayed across the range of opinion, the mean will be the midpoint of the distribution. If public opinion is clustered around the midpoint, with relatively few extreme views, the mean will still be in the middle. In these two examples, the means will be similar, but their standard deviations will be quite different. The standard deviation is the statistic that tells us how tightly clustered opinions are around the average. It provides important information about how public opinion is distributed and the extent to which party identifiers largely agree or disagree with one another. The following section looks at the question of polarization from a somewhat different vantage point using the distribution of partisan opinion to explore the extent to which Democrats and Republicans overlap in their political views from 1980 to 2004. By incorporating the variance associated with partisan policy views into the prior analysis, Figure 3.3 shows a good deal of similarity in the political viewpoints of Republicans and Democrats.

The bar diagrams in Figure 3.3 compare the overlap in Republican and Democratic policy views. Each bar takes the average opinion (for Republicans or Democrats on a given issue) and adds one standard deviation on either side of the mean to illustrate the range of views found within a large majority of partisans.[21] By placing Republicans and Democrats side by side, it is easy to see how much the policy views of most partisans overlap. On average, Democrats are a little more liberal and Republicans a bit more conservative, but on questions of abortion and defense spending far more partisans overlap than disagree. Even on the social welfare issues where mean differences are the greatest, considerable partisan overlap weakens popular claims of a polarized public. While partisan elites may struggle to find common ground in their legislative lives, the American public suffers no similar fate. This analysis clearly shows that public views are neither extreme nor diametrically opposed. Simply, Americans are generally moderate (even when grouped by party) and not particularly divided on most political issues.

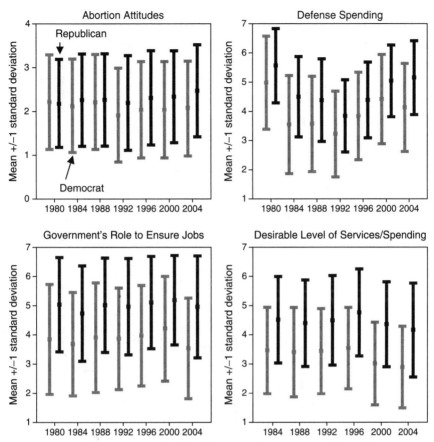

FIGURE 3.3. Public Opinion Overlap between Democrats and Republicans over Time. *Note*: Bars indicate mean values with one standard deviation on each side of the mean. *Source*: ANES from selected years.

While Americans may find ample common ground in the realm of political attitudes, they are considerably more at odds over their feelings about the parties and their candidates. Using the same basic method employed in Figure 3.3, the bar charts in Figure 3.4 assess the overlap in positive or negative feelings that Republicans and Democrats hold toward the parties and their respective presidential candidates. Taking the distribution of candidate and party thermometer ratings into account, it is clear that Democrats and Republicans have divergent views. In contrast to the notable common ground in the policy views of Republicans and Democrats, there is relatively little overlap over the course of the entire

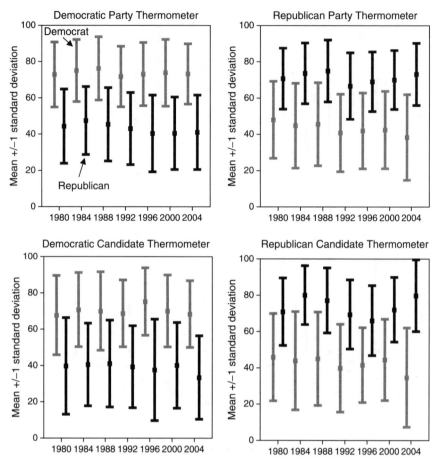

FIGURE 3.4. Partisan Overlap in Party and Candidate Evaluations over Time. *Note*: Bars indicate mean values with one standard deviation on each side of the mean. *Source*: ANES from selected years.

time series when it comes to party and candidate thermometer ratings; this is especially true with respect to the Democratic Party thermometer. From the Reagan era to the Clinton era, Republicans found little to like about the Democratic Party. Democrats and Republicans showed a bit more commonality in their feelings about the Republican Party, although by the end of the time series Democrats became more negative toward the Republicans, and the overlap diminished.

The trends in the candidate thermometer scores provide the strongest evidence in support of polarization; there was virtually no overlap between Democratic and Republican opinions regarding George W. Bush in 2004 and only slightly more regarding John Kerry. This suggests that among a large majority of Democratic and Republican identifiers, almost none shared similar views about the two major party candidates. For most of the time series the overlap between Republicans and Democrats is small. During the 1980s, Republicans were closer to Democrats on their opinions of Democratic candidates, and during the 1990s Democrats were more aligned with Republicans on their evaluations of Republican candidates. There was little evidence of overlapping opinion in 2004, and, as mentioned earlier, this appears to have been an exceptional year in terms of party-based voter polarization. History may render this election epiphenomenal or, alternatively, it may represent the beginning of brave new world in American politics. In either case, recent evidence of polarization is really limited to the affective orientations of American voters. The antipathy that partisans feel toward one another powerfully overshadows the underlying mass consensus on most issues, even those thought to be most divisive.

Sources of Polarization

Popular wisdom and scholarly analysis agree that voters are polarizing in response to elite cues. By this account, as party elites stake out ever more distinctive and intractable policy positions, politically aware voters increasingly come to adopt more extreme issue attitudes, hold more aversive feelings toward their partisan competitors, and become progressively more partisan in their voting behavior. While the overall magnitude of issue polarization is dampened by the fact that less aware partisans remain largely unmoved by elite policy cues, party members—even the less politically sophisticated ones—still demonstrate considerable polarization in their feelings toward the parties themselves and their respective candidates.

We can examine this by using the 2000 and 2004 ANES to explore potential explanations for polarization. In particular, we can determine whether polarization is being driven by issue opinion differences between party members or by more general affective orientations toward the groups that make up the Republican and Democratic parties. Using thermometer ratings, we measure individual-level polarization by taking the mathematical difference between how party identifiers rate their own parties versus how they rate their political opposition. For example, one Republican may give her party a score of 90 and give the Democrats a 10, yielding a difference of 80 degrees between the two. If another Republican were to give his party a 60 and the Democrats a 40, this constitutes a smaller difference—only 20 degrees. Our analysis (reported in Table 3.1) equates higher difference scores with more polarized views.[22]

We begin with the assumption that strength of partisanship will likely be a strong predictor of polarized views toward the candidates and parties. Strong partisans, by definition, have more intense ties to the parties and their candidates than do weak and leaning partisans. Given the strong affective basis of partisanship,[23] we expect to find a positive correspondence between polarized feelings and partisan intensity. Simply put, we expect self-identified strong partisans to have more polarized views of the parties (and their relative merits) than do weak and leaning partisans. All the same, we consider the possibility that even strong partisans who hold extremely favorable views of their own party may not necessarily have extremely unfavorable views of their political rivals.

Because we believe that polarization is predominantly rooted in affective orientations toward the parties that are largely devoid of issue content, we also investigate the extent to which individual feelings toward liberals, conservatives, and the various constituent groups associated with the Republican and Democratic parties may be strongly connected to polarized views of parties and candidates.[24] In particular, we expect that partisans who feel particularly close to the groups highly associated with their own party (or who feel hostile toward those in the opposing party) are more likely to hold polarized views than are those who do not.

Finally, given the contention that partisan policy views have become more polarized over time, we investigate whether extreme political opinions on questions of social welfare, race, abortion, and gay marriage predict polarized ratings of the parties. In light of the prominence that the Iraq War played in the 2004 election, we also explore the extent to which strong approval or disapproval of the war may have influenced voter polarization by including it in our list of 2004 issues.

Findings

The findings from our analysis of Democrats and Republicans are reported in Table 3.1. Our primary test is whether polarized views

TABLE 3.1. Explaining Polarized Views toward Political Parties, 2000
and 2004

	2000		2004	
	Democrats	Republicans	Democrats	Republicans
Unique influence of:*				
Issue attitudes	4%	3%	6%	4%
Affect measures	14	21	19	17
Shared effects	3	6	11	18
Total variance explained by all 3 sets of factors**	21%	30%	36%	39%

Note: Table entries are the percentage of variance in individual-level party polarization explained by issue attitudes and measures of affect. The percentages were generated using the data from the statistical models in Appendix Table 3.1.
*The unique influence of issue attitudes and affect toward parties is the unique variance explained by each set of factors independently from one another.
**Total variance refers to the total explained variance in each of the models.

toward the political parties are a function of conflicting issue positions, partisan intensity and strong feelings about the groups that make up the parties, or both. The data in Table 3.1 detail the unique influence that issue opinions and affective orientations toward the parties have on whether one is polarized. We report the percentage of variance in party polarization that is explained by each set of factors. Larger percentages indicate stronger relationships to polarized attitudes.

For example, the 2000 analysis (shown on the left side of table) provides considerable support for our argument. Among Democrats, only 4 percent of party polarization was explained by issues whereas 14 percent was explained by feelings toward the groups that make up the Republican and Democratic parties. The pattern was even more pronounced among Republicans, with issues explaining 3 percent of the variance in party polarization compared to 21 percent explained by affective orientations.

A similar pattern was found in 2004; among Democrats, issue positions explained 6 percent of the variance in party polarization, while affect explained a much larger 19 percent. For Republicans, issue opinions explained only 4 percent of the total variance in party polarization whereas affective orientations toward the parties (partisan intensity and feelings toward Democratic and Republican constituent groups) explained 17 percent.

On balance, these findings validate our general thesis that issues matter less to polarization than do more general group attachments and aversions. Popular accounts of party polarization seem to give too much weight to abstract ideologies and policy views. Polarization is partly an issue and ideological phenomenon—but not for most Americans. Their feelings about the candidates and parties are not dictated by ideas about the relative merits of individualism and egalitarianism or small government versus large government. Polarization, rather, results from the intensity of feelings that voters have for groups and symbols associated with the parties and candidates. Issues matter to some voters and to some degree for many voters, but, in general, the role that issues play in generating polarization pales in relation to more general affective orientations toward the parties and their candidates.

Increasing partisan intensity—even if it has little basis in policy opinion—has very real implications for how voters behave. Party loyalty at the ballot box has increased over the past two election cycles, most likely as a direct result of this affect-based polarization. All the same, popular accounts of voters as polarized camps who share little in the way of values and policy preferences are off the mark. Republicans and Democrats may hold each other's parties in low regard, but they nonetheless share similar views about important public policies. This underlying consensus is what gets lost in the heated rhetoric about polarization.

Are Americans Becoming More Polarized?

The preponderance of scholarly evidence demonstrates that the distance between the average policy views of Democrats and Republicans has grown over the past three decades. Partisan voting behavior is also on the rise. However, while we are certainly *becoming* more polarized in a relative sense, it is less clear that we *are* polarized, especially when it comes to our political views. On balance, most partisans have centrist views; Republicans are still more conservative than Democrats on most political issues, but neither party's mass base holds extreme viewpoints. If anything, the data we present in this chapter suggest that as of 2004, partisans were still fairly moderate and that they agreed more often than they disagreed.

The reciprocal ill will that Republicans and Democrats have for one another's candidates and parties constitutes the strongest evidence for polarization. Partisans have become ever more divided in their assessments of themselves and their political competition. Differences over policy explain some of this divide. Polarization, however, is not simply a reasoned difference of opinion. Positive feelings toward one's party brethren and strong negative affect directed toward political rivals are at the root of partisan polarization.

Demonizing one's political opponents is nothing new to American politics, but in the information age, where we have almost limitless bandwidth and a near infinite number of political commentators to fan the flames of popular discord, the American public's growing disregard for its political adversaries casts a contentious shadow over the future. At its core, American voters remain firmly grounded in the center of the policy spectrum, yet political compromise often remains elusive. It would be naïve to believe that strident political rhetoric will become more conciliatory over time. All the same, the "politics as blood sport" frame that has become so pervasive ignores a simple fact: on most things political, Americans hold a broad and largely moderate consensus.

Chapter Four

Who Swings?

Mabel Schley, 82, and Shawn Henslin, 30, have few things in common. She enjoys dispensing advice to her 12 children and 14 great-grand children. His idea of a good time is having a beer with friends at a sports bar. But they share this: Both are the sort of independent minded "swing" voters, not loyal to any political party, who are key to whether President Bush can claim a second term.

—Susan Page and Jill Lawrence, *USA Today*, October 30, 2003

Nowhere has the manufacture of swing voters been more evident than in the intramural argument over the future of the Democratic Party. Both Republicans and Democrats perennially debate the relative merits of placating the party base versus reaching out to the center. What distinguishes the Democrats is that they can't even agree on what the center is.

—Jonathan Chait, *American Prospect*, July 1, 2002

OUR GENERAL THESIS IS THAT LONG-STANDING PREDISPOSITIONS, such as party identification and political context, determine the behavior of most voters. This, in turn, produces fairly predictable election outcomes. But when the party identifications of voters and the events of the day are not so one-sided, predicting winners and losers is less certain. Long ago, those who studied and practiced politics observed that close elections are often decided by a subset of voters who could "swing" to either party's candidates.[1] Beyond this simple observation, however, there is very little consensus about how many "swing voters" there are, what they look like, and what influences their behavior.

Political operatives, consultants, and the news media have charged into this chasm of doubt with unusual vigor. The result, in our view, has been the development of at least two myths about swing voting. First, swing voters supposedly have certain demographic characteristics. In fact, there is usually a significant amount of back-and-forth between consultants every two years on the question of "who are the swing voters?" Second, most experts assume that swing voters break for the challenger over the incumbent since they already know the incumbent and have (presumably) been unimpressed. Beyond these conventions, we find very little empirical evidence concerning how many swing voters are out there and the circumstances under which they influence election outcomes.

In this chapter, we take aim at swing voting and the attendant gaps in our knowledge. Initially, we find it is extremely difficult to define the swing voter population. We offer a new empirical definition, which shows that although swing voting was common and important in the 2000 and 2004 presidential elections, it seems to have declined since the late 1960s. Second, we examine swing voters in search of particular dispositions or demographic characteristics that define them. We demonstrate that psychological factors are more powerful determinants of swing voting than is any particular group membership. Third, we present evidence from presidential elections to dispel the myth that swing voters always break for the challenger.

Classic Conceptions of Swing Voting from Political Science

The idea that certain voters are more likely to be persuadable than others is not new. Studies conducted by sociologists from Columbia University in the 1940s found that voters from mixed social backgrounds were the most likely to either (1) abstain from voting or (2) have variable preferences.[2] Large national survey analyses conducted by political scientists from the University of Michigan in the 1950s and 1960s offered a slightly different perspective, suggesting that voters with multiple (and cross-cutting) social identities are more likely to develop conflicted attitudes and, therefore, fluctuating vote preferences.[3] From the rational choice perspective, voters near the median of the ideological spectrum are swing voters—if candidates behave rationally,[4] they will congregate at or near the median voter, presenting voters with a difficult decision calculus that, in turn, should produce both ambiguity and volatility in vote preferences.[5]

In considering these seminal perspectives, we see a core problem. There is little acknowledged connective tissue among the different concepts advanced by political science or between these and the layman's notion of swing voters. For the layman, a commonsense definition of swing voting would concentrate on those whose candidate preferences tend to be variable and whose decisions will ultimately determine the outcome of the election. Indeed, practitioners incorporate this conception into their strategies for identifying swing counties and precincts; they define the swing vote as the difference between the high and low vote percentages obtained by a party's candidates across some number of recent elections.[6] But political science has committed to neither a single term for—nor a common definition of—voter preference volatility.

The News Media and Swing Voting

In the absence of any strong, consistent definition or understanding of swing voting, those for whom politics is a living have relied on practical surrogates and descriptive measures to make sense of voter volatility. Most obviously, many in the news media equate swing voting with the lack of commitment to a party candidate. That is, reporters and pundits believe that anyone who says she does not know for whom she is voting is a swing voter. This conception is reflected in the methodologies employed by news media–sponsored public opinion surveys. The Gallup Organization, for example, asks people (1) for whom they will vote, (2) whether there is a chance they will vote for another candidate, and (3) how strongly they support their candidate. Anyone who is undecided *or* might support their nonpreferred candidate *or* only moderately supports their preferred candidate is classified as a swing voter. Similarly, the Pew Center for People and the Press classifies all undecided respondents (as well as those who support a candidate but say there is a *chance* they will vote for another candidate) as swing voters.

In the 1992, 2000, and 2004 presidential elections, the percentage of undecided—or swing—voters was often greater than the margin between the Republican and Democratic candidates, leading reporters and pundits to assume that the swing vote would be decisive. This assumption was evident in the media attention paid to swing voters. For example, *USA Today* ran a story on swing voters on October 30, 2003—over one year before the 2004 presidential election.[7] They also posted a swing vote analysis on their election Web site. In the spring of 2004, National Public Radio aired a half hour show on swing voters.[8] The online *NewsHour* posted a primer on swing voters on its "Politics 101" Web site in September 2004. In both 2000 and 2004, ABC, CNN, and MSNBC convened focus groups of swing voters to gauge reactions to the nominating conventions, debates, and last-minute campaign maneuvers. Between September 7 and November 6, 2004, at least twenty-five segments on MSNBC's *Hardball with Chris Matthews* included a mention of swing voters.[9]

In 2004, coverage of swing voters was leavened with stories about turnout; the new popular wisdom maintained that mobilizing partisans and enhancing turnout were more important to the Bush and Kerry camps than was persuading the undecided. In fact, reports from early 2004 emphasized an unusually high percentage of voters who had already made up their minds. Still, the closeness of the race was enough to perpetuate the conventional wisdom that winning swing voters was critical for capturing the White House.

Equally important, the news media often seek to identify broad, demographically coherent groups as "swing" groups. Every election since 1988 has seen one or more groups proffered up as a "swing" group whose vote decision will determine the election. Reagan Democrats, angry white males, Latinos, soccer moms, waitress moms, wired workers, Catholics, rural voters, and many others have all had their moments in the spotlight. As noted in the *Washington Monthly*, 2004 produced "Sex and the City" voters, office park dads, NASCAR dads, security moms, the Stern gang, and freestyle evangelicals. NASCAR dads alone were the focus of stories by *USA Today*, the *CBS Evening News*, MSNBC, *Time*, *The Nation*, the *BBC News*, and newspapers from the *San Francisco*

Chronicle to the *Arizona Republic* to the *Indianapolis Star* to the *New York Times*.

The appeal of painting election dynamics in terms of these groups is obvious: the idea that there are millions of swing voters introduces impossible complexity, whereas grouping them according to two or three characteristics makes things more comprehensible. This is especially the case if the group can be represented by an archetype, preferably one from pop culture, because it helps news organizations explain politics to their audience.

Political consultants also understand the power of simplifying swing voters into coherent groups. In fact, it was consultants who first began to pair groups with slightly higher than average levels of indecision (or persuadability) with cutesy labels as a way of marketing their ideas about how to win elections. The result is that today's pollsters and consultants constantly compete to identify (and label) the group whose preferences are most critical to the next election.

The news media may not have a theory of swing voting, but they often have expectations about how swing voters will behave. In general, and especially in 2004, the news media expected swing (undecided) voters to break for the challenger. This expectation is part of the received wisdom of political consultants, which draws on their experience from legislative races. The underlying logic is simple: elections are referenda on the incumbent, and those who are ambivalent about backing the incumbent during the fall campaign usually vote for the challenger on election day.[10]

This idea is consistent with some of the research in political psychology and has empirical backing. In 1989, Nick Panagakis analyzed results from 155 surveys—most from the late 1980s—conducted during the last week before an election. He found that in 82 percent of the cases, undecideds "broke" for the challenger.[11] Panagakis concluded:

> Incumbent races should not be characterized in terms of point spread. [Suppose] a poll shows one candidate leading 50 percent to 40 percent, with 10 percent undecided....Since most of the 10 points in the undecided category are likely to go to the challenger, polls are a lot closer than they look—50 percent to 40 percent is likely to become 52 percent to 48 percent, on election day.

In 2004, Chris Bowers found that while there were some signs that the incumbent rule might be weakening in state and local races, it had even stronger support in presidential elections. In twenty-eight surveys involving presidential elections, Bowers claimed that 86 percent show undecideds breaking mostly to the challenger. Similarly, Guy Molyneux (2005) averaged "the final surveys conducted by the three major networks and their partners" in the last four presidential elections featuring an incumbent and found that "on average, the incumbent comes in half a point below his final poll result....In every case, the challenger(s)... exceed their final poll result by at least 2 points, and the average gain is 4 points."

Finally, Mark Blumenthal (2004) pointed out an intriguing pattern in the Gallup Poll's final vote projections (see Figure 4.1, which adds 2004 to the data):

> In the presidential elections since 1956 that featured an incumbent, the final projection of the incumbent's vote exceeded the incumbent's actual vote six of eight times....On average, Gallup's projection of the incumbent's vote has averaged 1.3 percentage points greater than the actual result. Obviously, without seeing the raw results we can only speculate, but this pattern suggests that Gallup has allocated too many of the undecided over the years to incumbents.

In 2004, the prediction that swing voters would break for the challenger caused some bloggers and pollsters to propose that surveys showing

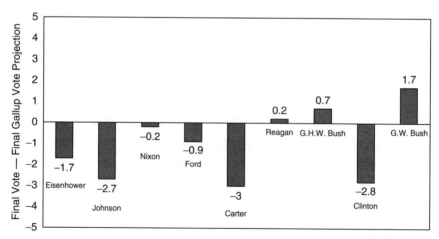

FIGURE 4.1. How Swing Voters Affected the Incumbent's Presidential Vote. *Note:* Bars represent the difference between the incumbent's share of the actual vote and the Gallup Poll's final projections. Negative numbers mean that the actual vote was less than the predicted vote. *Source:* Gallup Polls from selected years.

George W. Bush leading John Kerry by several percentage points should be characterized as a within the margin of error *lead for Kerry*. No mainstream news media took this advice, but the discussion caused many to believe that Kerry would win the election despite trailing in almost all of the preelection polls. Moreover, the Gallup Poll ended up allocating 80 percent of undecided voters to Kerry in making their final vote projection.[12] We believe that more analysis needs to be done before these sorts of leaps reasonably can be made.

While swing voters and swing groups make for entertaining television viewing and newspaper reading, there are obvious deficiencies in our understanding of this phenomenon. For starters, there is no common definition or metric for measuring swing voting or swing groups. This means that the news media parrot the often ill-defined and occasionally banal demographic explanations of political consulting companies. This tendency to grope around for a plausible swing group is especially troublesome because it is unclear that there is any coherent sociology to swing voting. It may be, for example, that swing voting is driven by psychological attributes that are scattered across any and all politically relevant groups. This raises the very real possibility that both campaigns and the news media are seriously off track in their efforts to sensibly interpret voting dynamics. Because news coverage focuses much of its attention on the attitudes and behavior of these individuals, the fundamental equation of swing voting with "undecided" respondents in surveys and the accuracy of group-based conceptions of swing voters is worth examining in some detail.

A Second Look at Political Science and Swing Voting

There are both methodological and theoretical reasons to doubt that undecided voters are necessarily swing voters. When one considers the method by which we measure vote choice, we see that whether someone is "undecided" in a sample depends upon both the actual incidence of "indecision" and the strategy of the pollster. For example, pollsters who ask a straight vote choice question, without identifying the candidates by party or pushing undecided respondents to say which candidate they "lean" toward, will yield a relatively higher percentage of undecided voters. Furthermore, the norm for preelection polls (and certainly those immediately prior to the election) is to push voters to declare a vote choice.

Theoretically, the equation of swing voters with undecided voters is even more dubious. Some respondents who do not state a candidate preference for a pollster are almost sure to vote a certain way or to abstain. The first group would include strong partisans who have yet to engage fully with the campaign but—when they do—are extremely likely to vote with their party. The second group would include those who are genuinely uninterested in politics and are thus unlikely to ever engage with the campaign. It is also the case that some voters who express a preference for one candidate are likely to swing back by election day. Again, this group would include partisans who have yet to be mobilized by either issues or party outreach. It is true that the disjuncture between swing voters and undecided voters should close as the election nears, but it remains, nonetheless.

If undecided voters are not necessarily swing voters, what can we recommend as a superior measure? Looking again to political science, two research strands strike us as being particularly instructive: one focuses on "party switchers" while the other focuses on "floating voters." The proposition that the electorate is comprised of "stand-patters," "new voters," and "party switchers" is a central point of V. O. Key's *The Responsible Electorate* (1966). This idea has its roots in some of the early political science survey research work[13] and conceives of shifts in the major party presidential vote as a product of the preferences of new voters and the relative proportion of partisans who defect from their party's nominee in a particular race. Party switchers are synonymous with this second possibility. Key (1966) estimated that party switchers constituted between 11 and 22 percent of the electorate. In addition, he argued that these voters were making a rational choice based on perceived differences between themselves and their party. This point was picked up by Boyd (1985), who examined the Reagan elections and found that 15 percent of the electorate "switched" votes between 1980 and 1984, mostly due to evaluations of the candidates and appraisals of the economy.

To the extent that party switchers from one election are more likely to defect in another, they strike us as synonymous with swing voters. But two subtle differences between these concepts stand out. First, most practitioners (and probably more than a few political scientists) would classify someone who seriously considers voting against their party's candidate as a swing voter. The fact that they ultimately vote in accord with their party identification does not mean they are like every other partisan. Second, a voter who supports the party's candidate in the current election but has defected in the past is not the same as a reliable partisan voter. More generally, we believe that measures of swing voting ought to include the previous behavior of individuals and groups to inform our understanding of their potential for "unusual" behavior in an unfolding election. We want to be able to identify those voters who may surprise us on election day. Otherwise, swing voting is nothing more than a post hoc, descriptive notion.

In contrast, "floating voters" are defined as those voters who are most susceptible to shifting back and forth between the parties during campaigns.[14] Although the term has a pedigree predating University of Michigan political scientist Philip Converse, his treatment is considered seminal. Particularly influential is his contention that voters whose preferences vary over the course of an election campaign are likely to be both relatively less attentive and less partisan. More recently, John Zaller (2003) revisited the floating voter, arguing that these voters were distinguished, even defined, by their relatively low levels of political information. As such, he found that they disproportionately rewarded presidential successes in foreign policy and aggregate national economics (and conversely, punished failures) and that they were acutely responsive to the ideological positions of the candidates.

As we consider swing voting, the main limitation of the "floating voter" literature is that it insists on observing changes in candidate preferences in a given campaign cycle. The problem is that preference consistency may simply be an artifact of when surveyors happen to interview a respondent or, alternatively, it may mask real ambivalence that a voter has about her choice.[15]

The question of whether swing voters look like party switchers, floating voters, or neither strikes us as an empirical matter. In this vein, it is important to note the differences between "floating voters" and "party switchers." "Floaters" change their preferences during the campaign and are affected by short-term forces and elite cues conveyed by the news media. Although they move in response to the candidates' espoused ideologies, they are not ideologues; indeed, they are neither especially interested nor involved in the politics of the day. On the other hand, "switchers" cast votes out of line with their party identification and tend to do so because they prefer another candidate's credentials or positions or because of some highly salient issue. These voters defect based on a rather detailed and exceptional understanding of current political information.

A New Definition of Swing Voting

As we seek an improved definition of swing voting—one that allows us to consider its frequency and whether certain blocs constitute "swing" groups—let us begin by simplifying. One of the main sources of confusion with respect to swing voting is specifying the individual-level manifestation of what is viewed by campaign practitioners as a district or county level phenomenon. We therefore start with the theoretical assumption that every individual has a probability of voting for a particular party in a generic election. Swing voters are defined as those whose probability of voting for one of the two major-party candidates in a generic election is close to 50 percent. In other words, swing voters are those who are almost equally likely to vote for the Democrats or the Republicans because they have no history of strong party loyalty to either.

Our initial task, then, is to estimate the probability that a given individual will vote Democratic by examining his actual behavior over some subset of elections.[16] Ideally, we would want individual-level voting data for the same office over time, accompanied by detailed attitudinal and demographic information (more on this shortly). Traditional stand-alone surveys are of limited use in this regard as they measure attitudes and behavior at a single point in time and, at best, ask respondents how they voted in the last election. The ANES panel surveys, however, offer a promising alternative. Following their 2000 pre- and postelection survey, the ANES reinterviewed respondents in conjunction with the 2002 midterm and 2004 presidential elections. The 2000 to 2004 panel study provides us with estimates of individual voting behavior spanning three presidential elections (1996, 2000, and 2004) for 840 respondents, along with data on a wide array of other factors.[17]

In addition to the 2000 to 2004 panel study, the ANES conducted a similar panel from 1972 to 1976, which provides us with estimates of individual presidential voting behavior for 1968, 1972, and 1976. These data provide an excellent opportunity to compare both the magnitude and correlates of swing voting over the span of the post–New Deal party system.[18] In particular, we can ascertain the extent to which the groups that reputedly drove the restructuring of the New Deal coalition over social issues in the 1960s and the 1970s actually did so and whether they continue to vacillate with respect to presidential voting preferences.

Because we wish to hold the office constant here—this is what distinguishes swing voting from ticket-splitting—we focus on presidential elections. As suggested above, the time frame is a matter of convenience, although the panels encompass six elections with maximal variance in the outcome—one decisive Republican victory (1972), one decisive Democratic victory (1996), and four close races (1968, 1976, 2000, and 2004).

We use the summation of an individual respondent's votes across the three elections of the panel to estimate the underlying probability of a partisan vote and to identify swing voters. This process is straightforward: anyone casting three consecutive party votes is identified as a party voter, anyone abstaining in all three elections is a nonvoter, and everyone else is a swing voter. Thus, voters who abstain or vote third party in one or two elections are swing voters, as are those who oscillate between the major-party candidates across elections. This variable (whether one is or is not a swing voter) is the central factor we explore in our subsequent analyses.

Given our conception and measurement of swing voting, it is important to observe that swing voting ought to be affected by both voter and candidate dynamics. For example, swing voting is relatively likely if one of the following occurs:

- The costs of voting change for a specific voter from one election to another (leading to entrance or exit from the electorate).
- A voter changes her mind on one or more important issues (leading to a different metric for comparing candidates).
- A voter changes his mind about which issues are most important to him (again, leading to a different basis for comparing candidates).
- A voter's preferences are close to the median (leading to difficulty in choosing between candidates who campaign on moderate positions).

Swing voting is also relatively likely in the following circumstances:

- The parties nominate candidates who offer different issue positions from their predecessors (leading to possible new considerations when comparing candidates).
- The parties nominate candidates who emphasize different issues from their predecessors (again, leading to a different metric for comparing candidates).

Even more fundamentally, we link swing voting directly with oscillations in individual-level party vote choice for a single office across election cycles. This conception has implications for which factors we think will drive swing voting. Despite the credible case made by Key (1966) and others that engaged voters are more likely to pick up on issue and candidate details and swing accordingly, we expect that politically unengaged people will be more likely to respond to the varying agendas and candidate positions that occur across presidential elections.

How to Explain Swing Voting

In addition to clarifying and measuring swing voting, we are also interested in the attitudes and characteristics that might influence it. We proceed by grouping a wide range of potential explanations into three separate categories, each rooted in a separate strand of the voting literature. Two of the three categories emphasize political and demographic characteristics. The other emphasizes the psychological factors *interest* and *engagement*.

The first set of potential explanations for swing voting looks to groups whose departure from the Democratic Party's New Deal coalition has been offered as a rationale for the heightened competitiveness of the post–New Deal system. In other words, we measure the degree to which swing voters are members of groups whose long-standing partisan predispositions have shifted over the past forty years. This category includes Catholics, union household members, white southerners, westerners, seniors, college graduates, higher income household members, and (to a much lesser extent) Latinos and Jews. We also include African Americans, who have presumably moved even more strongly toward the Democrats, and men, whose votes have become more Republican.[19]

In the second category we include groups who are "cross pressured" by multiple and conflicting social identities (e.g., wealthy women or poor evangelical Christians). The critical idea behind this category, derived from the Columbia studies, is that some voters are (for example) more likely to favor one party on economic issues but the other party on social issues. Many of the groups tagged by the media and political pundits as swing groups fit nicely under this heading. Hence, into this category we place those in the middle class, those with some college, suburbanites, and rural dwellers, along with soccer moms, waitress moms, and office park dads.[20]

The third category uses psychological factors—political interest and political knowledge—to explain swing voting. This draws on Converse's notion that the most persuadable voters are those who are engaged enough to be exposed to the political debate but are the least resistant to political messages. For presidential elections, exposure ought to reach the lowest rungs of the information ladder, so the expectation is that the least informed are the most likely to be swing voters. Although we are most interested in individual-level psychological predispositions, we do test for the possibility that certain groups are disproportionately likely to have these predispositions. Thus, we examine political independents, the young (under thirty years of age), the less educated, the less affluent, and those who otherwise express lower levels of political interest and engagement.

Our expectation is that swing voting will be most affected by psychological attributes while membership in specific groups will be significantly less influential. This expectation is less strong for the 1968–1976 data, however, because the Democratic Party was more demographically and ideologically heterogeneous then than in the later period. Various subsets of the Democratic coalition had opposing opinions on salient political issues of the day—namely, civil rights, women's rights, and the Vietnam War.

Of course, it is possible that sociological and psychological factors work together. For example, it might be that more informed and interested soccer moms are relatively likely to be swing voters. Thus, we allow political information to interact with group membership so that we might estimate the influence of engagement on swing voting within and across groups. Given our preference for psychological explanations of swing voting, we are somewhat skeptical of interactive effects. If they exist, however, we would expect that informed members of groups with strong historical attachments to a particular party should realize even deeper commitment to the group's party preference (e.g., informed African Americans for Democrats). For groups who lack strong historical party attachments or who have been heavily targeted by both major parties, we expect that heightened information could lead to party defections.

What about Issues?

It is reasonable to question the absence of issue positions in our models of swing voting. In our view, issue and candidate dynamics drive the *direction* of swing voting in a specific election but have only an indirect effect on *who* is a swing voter. For example, swing voters voted for Ronald Reagan in 1984 but turned around and voted for Bill Clinton in 1996. So while their vote choices were blown by the prevailing political winds, swing voters *looked* the same in these disparate elections. Put another way, political context tells us how swing voters behave in a given election but sheds little light on the underlying nature of swing voters.[21] We assume broader dynamics are dominant here—particularly those involving party system reactions to new issues and cross pressures that are at the core of these analyses.

We assert that swing voters form a distinct group whose membership is roughly consistent from election to election. We believe that the underlying probability of voting Democratic or Republican is conditioned by the parties' positions on the dominant issues of the era. For example, someone who is liberal on social welfare issues but conservative on social issues—the preeminent issues of the post–New Deal party system—is likely to have a Democratic vote probability of about 0.5 (assuming she cares equally about both issue dimensions). We have similar expectations for someone with a mixed background encompassing divergent political views. In this way, issues are fundamental to our understanding of swing voters. But psychological predispositions and sociopolitical identities are prior to issue positions; as such, we believe they will best explain swing voting.

How Many Swing Voters Are Out There?

Political commentators often talk about swing voters and their potential impact on a given election, but there have been few recent attempts to estimate the real number of swing voters in the electorate. Table 4.1 shows that 24 percent of Americans qualify as swing voters based on their behavior in the presidential elections of 1996, 2000, and 2004. The electorate seems loosely divided into quartiles, with one-fourth voting straight Republican (26 percent), one-fourth voting straight Democratic (27 percent), one-fourth not voting (23 percent), and one-fourth swinging. A more detailed examination demonstrates that 53 percent of Americans voted a straight party line over these three elections and another 19 percent voted mostly along party lines (11 percent voted two of three Republican, 8 percent voted two of three Democratic).[22] Only a

TABLE 4.1.   Estimates of Swing Voting in Presidential Elections

	1968–1976	1996–2004
Three Presidential Votes		
Collapsed		
Straight Republican	30%	26%
Straight Democratic	15	27
Nonvoter	12	23
SWING	*44*	*24*
Detailed		
Straight Republican	30%	26%
MOSTLY REPUBLICAN	*21*	*11*
Straight Democratic	15	27
MOSTLY DEMOCRATIC	*13*	*8*
MOSTLY INDEPENDENT	*1*	*2*
Mostly Nonvoter	12	23
1 REP., 1 DEM., 1 IND.	*9*	*3*
CASES	*902*	*826*

Note: Italic smallcaps numbers indicate swing voter categories.
Source: 2000–2004 and 1972–1976 ANES Panel Surveys.

tiny fraction of the electorate voted mostly independent (2 percent) or Republican, Democratic, and independent (3 percent).

From this perspective, swing voting is not a scarce commodity. More important, given the incidence of swing voting in the electorate and the even distribution of party-line voters (26 percent Republican to 27 percent Democratic), swing voters were critical to deciding recent presidential elections. Clinton in 1996 and Bush in 2000 and 2004 *had* to carry swing voters to win.

Given the context of the 1968–1976 presidential elections—in particular, a strong third-party candidate in 1968 and an extraordinarily weak major-party candidate in 1972—it is unsurprising that the level of swing voting across this cycle would be high. Still, the 44 percent swing voting estimate in Table 4.1 represents a significant proportion of the electorate.[23] The distribution of voters is even more surprising—30 percent voted straight Republican across these elections, whereas only

15 percent voted straight Democratic. A full 9 percent voted for independent, Republican, and Democratic candidates over these three elections (presumably, the lion's share of these supporting Wallace, then Nixon, and then Carter). Note also the relatively low proportion of nonvoters: 12 percent, compared to the 23 percent in the 1996–2004 data.

The impact of swing voters on election outcomes in 1968, 1972, and 1976 is therefore complicated. Although there were more swing voters in these elections, the distribution of party-line voters was less balanced. Thus, unlike these more recent elections, one could win without carrying a majority of swing voters during the late 1960s and early 1970s. More generally, the data support the perception that this was a transition period in American politics: at the tail end of the New Deal party system—a system characterized by Democratic dominance—Republicans had crafted an advantage in presidential elections.

In sum, the data indicate that swing voters were important in 2000 and 2004 not only because the vote was so close but also because they constituted almost one-fourth of the total eligible electorate. By our estimation, swing voters are a critical part of contemporary elections despite the powerful pull of partisanship (see Chapter 2) and the polarization of attitudes toward the parties and their candidates (see Chapter 3).

Who Is a Swing Voter?

Notwithstanding the popular fascination with soccer moms and office park dads, we generally expect that contemporary swing voters are relatively less interested, less engaged, and less informed about politics. Figure 4.2 comports with our expectation. Comparing each group's swing voting rate to the national mean of 24 percent, political independents were the only one of our groups with a higher than average swing rate in the 1996, 2000, and 2004 elections. In fact, most of our groups had swing voting rates significantly below the national average: African Americans (12 percentage points less likely to swing), Hispanics (−11), those from middle-income households (−10), suburbanites (−7), college graduates (−6), church attenders (−6), Democrats (−6), those under thirty years of age (−6), married people (−5), seniors (−4), and southerners (−3).

Recall that we also expect social group identities to be more relevant for swing voting in the 1968–1976 elections. Figure 4.3 bears this out,

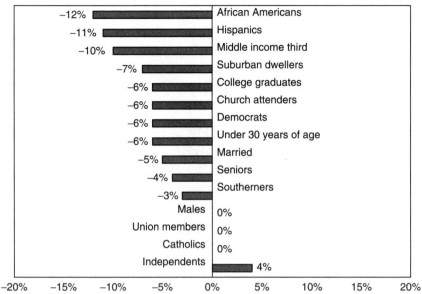

FIGURE 4.2. Swing Voting Rates for Various Groups, 1996 to 2004. *Note:* The baseline is the overall average swing voting rate of 24 percent. Positive numbers indicate a higher than average swing voting rate, and negative numbers indicate a lower than average swing voter rate. Calculations are based on the statistical analyses in Appendix Table 4.1. *Source:* 2000–2004 U.S. National Panel Surveys conducted by the ANES.

clearly demonstrating that independents were not the only wellspring of swing voters in those elections. People under thirty years of age (10 percentage points more likely to be swing voters), southerners (+9), Democrats (+6), Catholics (+4), and union household members (+3) had swing voting rates above the national average of 44 percent across these races. Furthermore, these tendencies are consistent with the common perception that the white South was particularly volatile during this time period, as race and civil rights issues cross-cut established ties with the Democratic Party in 1968 and 1972, only to be temporarily reaffirmed with the candidacy of native-son (and born-again Christian) Jimmy Carter in 1976.

Do these core findings hold up to more rigorous testing? For both 1996–2004 and 1968–1976, we estimated statistical models of swing voting to ascertain the independent and conditional effects of these social group and attitudinal factors.[24] For 1996–2004, our analyses

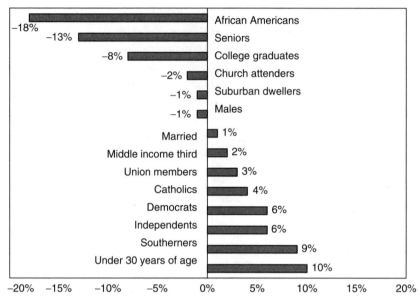

FIGURE 4.3. Swing Voting Rates for Various Groups, 1968 to 1976. *Note*: The baseline is the overall average swing voting rate of 44 percent. Positive numbers indicate a higher than average swing voting rate, and negative numbers indicate a lower than average swing voter rate. Calculations are based on the statistical analyses in Appendix Table 5.1. *Source*: 1972–1976 U.S. National Panel Surveys conducted by the ANES.

indicate that political independence and political information are critical in predicting swing voting.

Our expectation is that informed members of *core* party groups are less likely to swing, and this is partially borne out by the 1996–2004 model. While we found that informed union members, informed high-income individuals, and informed Catholics were all very slightly *more* likely to swing, informed African Americans and informed white southerners were, nonetheless, *less* likely to swing.

Our expectation that informed members of *targeted* groups are most likely to swing is often (but not always) the case. For example, informed suburbanites, informed members of middle-income households, informed younger voters, and informed Latinos were all more likely to be swing voters whereas informed waitress moms, informed office park dads, and informed soccer moms were very slightly less likely. However, these patterns are based on marginally significant results—in statistical terms—and thus ought not to be over-interpreted.

For the 1968–1976 elections, information and political independence dominate the model, with the former limiting swing voting and the latter driving it. Of the two, however, political information is the dominant influence. In other words, once information levels are accounted for within groups, the unique effect of independence goes away. Our analysis also shows that informed African Americans, white southerners, those in the top-income third, informed college graduates, and uninformed office park dads are less likely to swing whereas informed people under thirty years of age, informed westerners, and informed office park dads are more likely to swing.

In short, attitudes such as engagement and partisanship are the most powerful predictors of swing voting. Sometimes, however, the effect of these factors depends upon the social identity of the vote and the relationship between particular social groups and the parties. What we do not find is much evidence supporting the notion that soccer moms, waitress moms, or office park dads were swing voters in the 1996–2004 elections.[25]

Do Undecided Voters Break for the Challenger?

We turn now to the specific contention that swing voters break for the challenger. To consider this myth empirically, we follow the lead of the news media—setting aside our strong theoretical objections—and treat undecided voters as swing voters.[26] While the preliminary data are formidable, we contend there are strong reasons to disbelieve the conventional wisdom. First, the dominant characteristic of undecided voters (however ascertained) is not their party identification or demographic profile. It is, rather, their tendency to be less interested, less involved, and less motivated. Compared to those with solid candidate preferences, they are disproportionately likely to stay at home on election day. Table 4.2 examines undecided voter behavior in elections from 1948 to 2004 and shows that almost one-fourth of undecided voters do not vote.

Second, despite the analyses cited earlier, the received wisdom about undecided voters breaking for the challenger has not been systematically analyzed for presidential elections where information (especially about the challenger) is more readily available to rank-and-file voters.

TABLE 4.2. How Undecideds Voted, 1948 to 2004

	Voted Challenger Party	Voted Incumbent Party	Voted Other	Didn't Vote
1948	22%	44	1	33
1952	49%	38	0	13
1956	29%	52	1	18
1960	51%	33	2	14
1964	48%	39	2	11
1968	33%	42	9	16
1972	52%	29	1	17
1976	40%	33	3	23
1980	42%	27	11	24
1984	37%	38	2	24
1988	44%	27	1	28
1992	24%	27	31	18
1996	31%	31	16	22
2000	46%	29	5	20
2004	18%	25	0	57
Average	38%	34	6	23
Average (incumbents running for reelection only)	34%	35	7	25

Source: 1948–2004 ANES pre- and postelection surveys.

Again, consider Table 4.2, which demonstrates that undecided voters do *not* break decisively one way or the other. The overall average is 38 percent for the challenger, 34 percent for the incumbent, and 6 percent for third-party candidates. For years in which an incumbent president was running for reelection, the averages are 34 percent for the challenger, 35 percent for the incumbent, and 7 percent for third-party candidates.[27] With 25 percent not voting, this indicates that one would need either a huge pool of undecided voters or an anomalous outcome to sway the average total vote more than a point.

Of course, this analysis does not consider that some of the undecided voter pool consists of respondents who were interviewed in early

TABLE 4.3. How Late Deciders Voted, 1948 to 2000

	Voted Challenger Party	Voted Incumbent Party	Voted Other
1948	14%	83	3
1952	64%	36	0
1956	32%	67	1
1960	70%	27	3
1964	54%	46	0
1968	49%	43	8
1972	68%	29	3
1976	54%	42	4
1980	56%	29	15
1984	47%	50	3
1988	47%	50	3
1992	35%	29	36
1996	33%	42	25
2000	40%	55	5
2004	38%	53	0
Average	47%	45	7
Average (incumbents running for reelection only)	42%	48	10

Source: 1948–2004 ANES. "Late deciders" are those who say they decided on their vote during the last week before or on election day.

September. These people may have made up their minds shortly thereafter rather than in the last few days of the campaign. Table 4.3 focuses squarely on voters who say they decided in the last two weeks of the campaign. From 1948 to 2004, an average of 47 percent of late deciders voted for the challenger and 45 percent voted for the incumbent. Focusing only on races with an incumbent seeking reelection, 42 percent voted for the challenger and 48 percent voted for the incumbent. Again, the data provide absolutely no empirical reason to assume that an incumbent polling below 50 percent is doomed.

So what is wrong with the common belief that undecided voters break for the challenger? Part of the answer is methodological: most analyses compare poll results to the vote. The conclusions drawn from this kind of analysis partly reflect how undecided voters break, but they also include a good measure of polling error and changes that resulted from real shifts in the preferences of committed voters. Figure 4.4 adopts this more traditional (and, in our view, flawed) approach to analyzing undecided voters, comparing the final vote with Gallup Poll surveys from (1) the day before the election and (2) the week before the election. The data indicate a minor tendency for incumbent vote share to slip on election day. A slightly more significant tendency is for the challenger to gain support in the last two weeks before the election. But again, even these data do not establish the fact that undecided voters break one way or the other.

Part of the answer is also undoubtedly substantive: people who say they are undecided have not necessarily decided against the incumbent president. Given the amount of information available in presidential campaigns, it is certainly plausible that a voter might have serious misgivings about a president and still prefer him to the challenger.

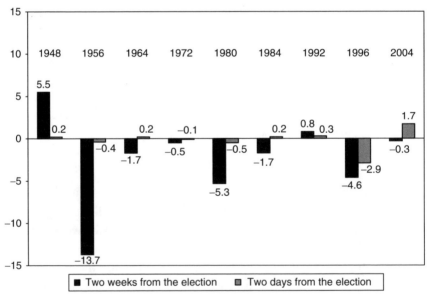

FIGURE 4.4. Do Undecided Voters Swing to the Challenger? *Note*: Bars represent the difference between the president's share of the two-party vote and the Gallup Poll estimates. Negative values mean that the actual vote was lower than Gallup predictions two weeks and/or two days before the election. *Source*: Gallup Polls from selected years.

But perhaps the most important part of the answer is that undecided voters are not where our attention should be focused. As suggested in Table 4.2, many undecideds are actually consistent nonvoters. Furthermore, some of the undecideds who do vote are actually reliable partisans who are simply late in coming home. This reinforces our perspective that undecideds are loosely synonymous with swing voters only when there is a chance they will vote and when their preferences are not tethered to a strong party identification. That is, when all partisans pledge to show up at the polls and declare their support for their party's nominees, we can be certain that undecided voters do not include wayward partisans who will be mobilized on or before election day. In all other instances, undecided voters include a good measure of habitual abstainers and reliable partisans.

Further Discussion of Swing Voting

Taking into account all of the data, three important points emerge. First, the propensity of individual voters to swing across some subset of presidential elections increases with political independence, political disengagement, and (to a lesser degree) the interaction between certain demographics and political disengagement. Group identities, important for swing voting in the 1968–1976 elections, were much less so in the 1996–2004 elections. We think it is especially important to observe that the swing groups offered by consultants and the news media over the last few cycles only occasionally measure up as such. Soccer moms, Latinos, and rural voters were simply not swing voters.

Second, conventional news media accounts of swing voting—most of which focus on undecided voters—do little to help us understand presidential election dynamics. This is partly because the methods for identifying undecided voters are unduly influenced by sampling error and partisan mobilization. The undecided are not necessarily swing voters; some are partisans, some are nonvoters, and others are truly persuadable.

Third and finally, although swing voting declined from 1968–1976 to 1996–2004, 24 percent of Americans remained swing voters. This is not to say that one-quarter of the electorate ignores partisanship while voting; rather, we find that across a range of recent presidential elections approximately one in four voters will occasionally deviate from party-line behavior. This number is, in fact, quite consistent with our estimates from Chapter 2 since only about 15 percent of voters stray from their partisan moorings in any particular year. In recent elections, however, the even distribution of Republican and Democratic party-line voters ensured that swing voters decided the outcomes. But this fact has produced an ironic reaction. While political consultants readily acknowledge the practical importance of swing voters in contemporary election campaigns, many also believe that these voters are difficult to reach and even tougher to win over.[28] They argue that swing voters tend to locate in the middle of the political-ideological spectrum, meaning that persuading them to support a specific candidate is best accomplished by championing moderate, mainstream issues and policy positions. It is difficult, however, to grab headlines or fire passions with enthusiastic moderation. In addition, by laboring to tempt swing voters to the polls, a candidate runs the risk of alienating his base. This perspective has led some professionals to question the wisdom of chasing such an elusive quarry.[29]

This raises the issue of whether swing voters are worth the trouble. The robust relationships between swing voting and political independence and political disengagement suggest that campaigns may actually be well advised to scale back their efforts to reach out to swing voters. Campaigns have limited resources and the commitment necessary to reach independent, inattentive swing voters may be prohibitive. Moreover, such outreach might well be swamped by larger events or circumstances (the prevailing wind that tends to dominate swing voter impressions). This logic has not been lost on recent presidential campaigns. The 2004 Bush campaign, for example, spent 50 percent of its advertising and contacting budget on "persuadable" voters; in 2000, they spent 75 percent.[30]

On the other hand, how can a presidential campaign ignore 24 percent of the electorate? Furthermore, recent innovations such as "micro-targeting" voters[31] with particular appeals based on survey results might put strategists in a position of contacting those who are persuadable with great precision. One could, in fact, argue that micro-targeting represents the triumph of those who emphasize individual attitudes and psychology over group-based, aggregate approaches to campaigning.

Whatever the strategic implications of our analysis, the larger point remains: if we are going to talk about swing voting, let's get it right. Swing voting appears to be produced by a distinct set of attitudes—lack of political engagement and information—which are spread out across social groups. Focusing on swing groups therefore fundamentally mischaracterizes the phenomenon. Moreover, by highlighting specific swing groups, pollsters and pundits encourage candidates to focus disproportionate amounts of time and energy on the issue concerns of a small segment of the electorate. Strategic behavior is unavoidable in a system such as ours, but on this occasion the extra attention lavished on swing groups is not only normatively disturbing but also makes little practical sense.

Chapter Five

Soccer Moms and Other Myths
about the Gender Gap

Swing voters and polls, while a far cry from cream-colored ponies and crisp apple strudels, are a few of lazy campaign reporters' favorite things. In the past few days, "security moms" have become all the rage with the political press corps, who have promptly elevated these moms to the top of the swing voter heap—all based, we must say, on a smattering of recent (and often conflicting) polls.

—Liz Cox Barrett, *Columbia Journalism Review*, September 22, 2004

MOTHERS HAVE BEEN REGULARLY TOUTED AS SWING VOTERS IN recent presidential elections, and the notion that various kinds of mothers are more fluid in their partisan attachments than are other groups of voters is a mainstay of popular election commentary. In particular, the security concerns of women were a theme of the 2004 election because various preelection polls indicated that women were more concerned with national security than were men. As the gender gap varied over the course of the campaign, "security moms" became the swing voter célèbre of the election season, seized on by many media stories despite limited evidence that they existed in numbers or behavior not seen in previous elections.[1] This attention to the voting behavior of women was not new, however. The gender gap has been a source of political interest for many decades, and the conventional wisdom surrounding the gender gap is that women "caused" it.

Stories about soccer moms and security moms tend to sensationalize rather than enlighten the public about how men and women differ in their political beliefs and behavior. By implication, they overstate accounts of gender solidarity at the ballot box and reinforce stereotypes of macho men and compassionate women, all the while disseminating a version of American politics that variously confuses and misleads the public about the actual nature of gender differences. Men are more politically conservative than women across a variety of political issues. Women do identify with the Democratic Party at higher rates than men and have done so since the mid-1960s. Given the current intensity of party competition and the razor thin margin of victory in recent presidential elections, many political pundits and scholars alike have argued that women's votes decide election outcomes; to the extent that male voting is presumed to be normative, female deviations from this standard are seen as particularly consequential.

This chapter aims to clarify the character, sources, and recent consequences of the political gender gap. We begin by revisiting the durable conventional wisdom that changes in the party preferences and voting behavior of women are responsible for the gender gap. Many popular accounts suggest that the growing political difference between men and women resulted from women moving into the Democratic Party. In fact, the opposite is true. The structural foundation of the modern gender gap is a direct result of white men moving from the Democrats to the Republicans.

The Contemporary Gender Gap

The gender gap refers to the male-female difference in party identification and voting behavior. As a practical matter, the contemporary gender gap (with women on the Democratic side of the ledger) began in 1964 with

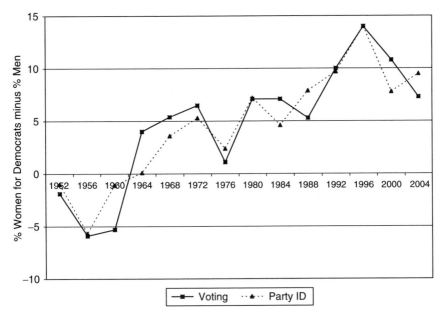

FIGURE 5.1. Gender Gap in Presidential Voting and Party Identification, 1952 to 2004. *Note:* The gender gap in voting and party identification is calculated by subtracting the percentage of men who vote for or identify with the Democratic Party from the percentage of women who do. *Source:* ANES from selected years.

the Johnson-Goldwater election (see Figure 5.1).[2] During the 1960s and early 1970s, the gender difference in vote choice and party identification averaged approximately 5 percentage points. The gap effectively disappeared in 1976 in the wake of the Watergate scandal but rebounded to its prior level in the 1980 election. It grew slightly during the decade of the 1980s but jumped into double digits beginning with the Clinton presidency. The gender gap was approximately 10 percentage points in 1992 and hit a high-water mark of 14 percentage points in 1996.

As the data clearly show, the political cleavage between men and women that began more than forty years ago has grown into a significant and enduring political division. Its size does not rival that of racial differences or even the partisan gap between the religiously devout and the secular; nonetheless, substantial differences between the party and candidate choices of men and women most certainly have electoral consequences.

Since Clinton's reelection in 1996, the gender gap in presidential voting has declined; the party difference between men and women was approximately 10 percentage points in 2000 and fell to 7 points in 2004. The 2004 vote gap was only half the size that it had been eight years earlier, and while one hesitates to make too much of this single point in a larger time series, a sustained contraction of the gender gap (with more women in the Republican camp) would pose rather dire implications for the future of the Democratic Party and, conversely, a great boon to the Republicans.

Early Thinking about the Gender Gap

While a gender gap has been visible in voting since the beginning of the ANES time series (and was probably there before but did not receive much attention from observers), it did not become a focus of scholarly inquiry until media polls trumpeted it in the 1980s.[3] Early research conducted on voting behavior during the Reagan administration posed a number of possible explanations for the gap between women and men. With few exceptions,[4] women were the focus of this research and were considered to be the causal force behind the gap. One popular account for the partisan differences between the sexes focused on use-of-force issues in American foreign policy and the buildup of the military during the early Reagan years. Martin Gilens (1988), for example, found attitudes regarding defense spending to be the most powerful issue predictors of Reagan's presidential approval and, after noting that women were less supportive of defense spending, argued that this was a major source of the gap. Several studies maintained that male-female differences on these and similar issues were at the heart of lower rates of GOP support among women.[5] Later analyses that tested this proposition more directly did not confirm this conventional wisdom,[6] but it remained strong—and does to this day.

The reason for these contrary results about the importance of foreign policy and military spending attitudes for the partisan gender gap probably reflects the diminished salience of defense spending and foreign policy in the post–cold war era, when most of the null findings about foreign policy views were published. American involvement in Afghanistan and Iraq as well as the terrorism environment of today may reinvigorate the salience of foreign policy and international conflict issues—giving them more importance for the gender gap now than we observed in the 1990s.

A second argument attributed the gap to domestic policy and per-ceived Republican hostility toward social welfare spending. Francis Fox Piven (1985) argued that women during the 1980s were more reliant than men on the social welfare state generally and that their relative economic vulnerability placed many women at odds with the domes-tic budget-cutting priorities of the Republicans.[7] This interpretation has received a good deal of support by studies done during and after the Reagan presidency.[8] Men are consistently more conservative than women about the appropriate size and scope of government, and the correlation between social welfare opinion and party identification or vote choice is consistently more robust than any other factor, often by a multiple of two. As a consequence, most accounts of the gender gap place strong emphasis on the important role that social welfare attitudes play in sustaining it.

A third set of explanations for the gender divide was attributed to Rea-gan's opposition to the Equal Rights Amendment (ERA), abortion rights, and the feminist movement generally.[9] This explanation, while intuitively appealing, has not generally fared well when subjected to rigorous testing. Feminist values correspond somewhat equally to voting behavior for men and women, providing no evidence that feminism was more politically important to women than men during this period.[10] Questions of abortion and women's rights are two issue domains where gender differences gen-erally do not exist; thus, in order for these issues to animate the gender gap they would need to be disproportionately important to one gender or the other. Another popular myth attributes the gender gap to female concerns over the abortion issue, but as we demonstrate in this chapter, there is little empirical support for this conclusion.

In short, the first generation of gender gap research disproportion-ately looked to the attitudes, sensibilities, and circumstances of women to explain a growing male-female political divide. It was a reasonable perspective. These scholars, many writing in the long shadow of the women's movement, presumed that monumental changes in the lives of women—increasing workforce participation, rising divorce rates, grow-ing numbers of single head-of-household families, mounting economic vulnerability, rising group consciousness, and so on—were the source of partisan change. But they are accounts more easily described as myths than documented explanations. Moreover, as we noted at the start of this chapter, it was not women who were dramatically changing their party affiliations; it was men.

Where Did the Men Go?

As intuitively appealing as women-centric explanations for the gender gap may be, they belie the simple fact that the gender gap was created by the movement of men to the Republican Party. The proportion of women shifting to the Democrats has been comparatively modest; by and large women have retained the party identification and voting profile of women from fifty years ago.

Fifty-eight percent of adult women identified themselves as Democrats in 1952, and 53 percent identified themselves as Democrats in 2004, a net decline of 5 percentage points in Democratic support over fifty-two years. In contrast, 59 percent of men identified with the Democrats in 1952, and this number fell to 43 percent by 2004—a 16-percentage point change (see Figure 5.2). Some scholars writing in the mid- to late 1980s argued that women were moving in the same direction as men, only at a slower rate.[11] Given the benefit of hindsight, however, the dip in Democratic Party identification among women in the 1980s reversed course in the 1990s. By contrast, male support for the Democrats underwent an almost uninterrupted decline to 1988, after which it remained largely stable, varying from 43 to 45 percent.

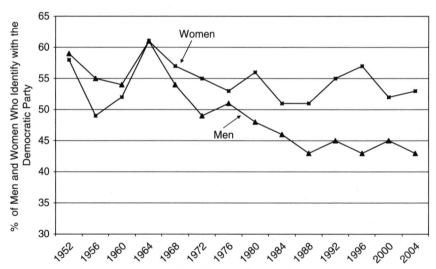

FIGURE 5.2. Democratic Party Identification by Gender, 1952 to 2004. *Source:* ANES from selected years.

In contrast to much of the early research on the gender gap, recent scholarship acknowledges that partisan change among men constitutes the long-term structural foundation of the gap we see today.[12] The male realignment that precipitated the gender gap, however, is still only part of the story. From 1988 to 2004, male partisanship remained remarkably stable, yet the gender gap continued to expand and contract; thus, *recent changes in the gender divide appear to be caused more by movements among women than men.*[13]

Over the sixteen-year period from 1988 to 2004, women's identification with the Democratic Party increased 6 percentage points during the first eight years and then gave back about half of this gain by 2004, at which time approximately 53 percent of women identified with the Democrats. The trend for men is largely invariant over the same period; 43 percent of men favored the Democrats in 2004. If one looks solely at white voters (who represent the overwhelming contributors to partisan change), the pattern of female variability over this sixteen-year period is even more pronounced. Democratic Party identification among white women increased a full 10 percentage points from 1988 to 1996 and then receded by 4 points over the next eight years (Figure 5.3). By 2004, 46 percent of white women considered themselves to be Democrats.

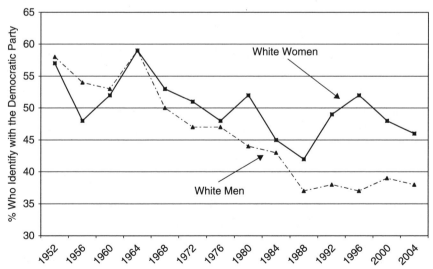

FIGURE 5.3. Gender Differences in Party Identification among Whites. *Source*: ANES from selected years.

By contrast, the percentage of white men who identified with the Democratic Party fluctuated within a 2-point range from 37 to 39 percent. The rapid decline in Democratic Party identification among white men from 1964 to 1988 (22 percentage points), followed by the pronounced stability over the subsequent sixteen years, strongly suggests a partisan realignment among American men that is quite separate from the pattern among women. In particular, the resurgent Democratic support from women during the 1990s implies some differences in the way that men and women have responded to contemporary American politics.

Gender Differences in Political Attitudes and Priorities

There is a broad consensus that gender differences in political views provide an ongoing foundation for the partisan divide between the sexes.[14] Beyond gender differences in political opinions, discrepancies in the priorities that men and women attach to given issues can either exacerbate or mitigate the magnitude of the gap. The relative prominence of political issues changes from year to year, but if the importance that men and women attach to these issues moves in unison, the gender gap should stay constant. If men and women care about very different sets of issues, the gap should be more variable and certainly more complicated to predict.

Most research on the gender gap finds that gender differences in political opinions in combination with the relative importance that men and women place on various issues influences the overall size of the gender gap.[15] Thus, year-to-year differences in the relative magnitude of the gender gap can result from male-female differences in political views, gender differences in the relative salience of these issues, or a combination of both.[16]

Issue Salience and Issue Opinions among Men and Women

In the aggregate, gender differences in political opinion are quite stable over time. Men are more conservative than women on most social welfare matters; they prefer less government to more services and are generally less supportive of government spending on social programs.[17] The average differences between men and women on social welfare spending issues tend to be modest, about 5 to 8 percentage points. Women are generally more pessimistic about the national economy and their personal finances,[18] and these differences typically fall in the 5-point range. The largest gender discrepancies in public opinion typically surround matters of gay rights, where women are approximately 10 percentage points more liberal than men.[19] Conversely, women and men are notably like-minded on questions of abortion, women's rights, and race/minority-related policies.[20] Men historically report higher levels of support for military interventions, use of force, and defense spending.[21] The relative female distaste for the use of military force remained evident in 2004: women were more critical of the Iraq War as 62 percent of women reported that the war was "not worth it" versus 56 percent of men with this view. In all, considerable evidence suggests that while public opinion across a variety of topics ebbs and flows, differences between the political views of men and women are quite stable over time.

The data in Figure 5.4 represent the average female and male responses to four identical questions—on defense spending, social welfare spending, abortion attitudes, and the desirability of government aid to minorities—asked in the past five ANES surveys. Higher values represent more conservative responses. The graphs indicate that even

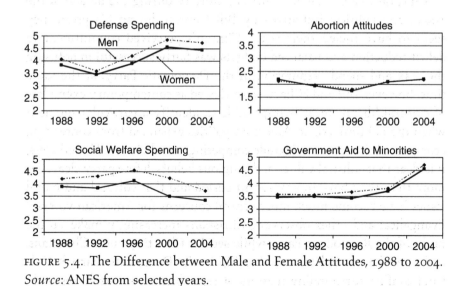

FIGURE 5.4. The Difference between Male and Female Attitudes, 1988 to 2004. *Source*: ANES from selected years.

when overall mean values rise and fall (like the increasing conservatism on defense spending and government aid to minorities), the differences between men and women remain largely unchanged. Simply, men and women *have not* become more polarized over political issues during the past sixteen years; therefore, fluctuations in the gender gap during this period are most likely a result of changes in the relative importance men and women place on various topics of the day.

Gender Politics and the Culture Wars

Since the New Deal realignment, political divisions have been anchored to contrasting viewpoints regarding the appropriate size and scope of the federal government. Traditionally, the Republicans were the party of small government, low taxes, and fiscal conservatism. Conversely, Democrats wore the mantle of big government and social welfare liberalism. Class divisions were a notable feature of the American party system; Republicans were wealthier, better educated, and largely Protestant while the Democratic Party housed the less well-to-do as well as religious and racial minorities. These sweeping generalizations continue to describe the parties, although the Republican Party today is more demographically diverse than it was even thirty years ago, and the Democratic Party is smaller.

Cultural issues grew in political notoriety during the decade of the 1990s, and political initiatives by Bill Clinton during his presidency seem to have fueled their rise.[22] Clinton's perceived commitment to deficit reduction and balanced budgets was fairly successful in defusing the "tax and spend" reputation of the Democratic Party; at the same time, however, Bill and Hillary were viewed as contemporary exemplars of cultural liberalism. It is impossible to identify a particular moment when the political axis in American politics expanded from contending economic philosophies to include competing moral visions. Nonetheless, it is clear that cultural values and religious beliefs define party cleavages more than they have in any recent period and that cultural and moral issues have become much more central concerns for American voters.[23] Evangelical and other observant Christians increasingly make up the ranks of the Republican Party while secular Christians, non-Christians, and nonbelievers bolster membership in the Democratic Party.[24] Cultural conflict surrounding matters of reproduction, scientific research, women in society, gay rights, religion and public schools, and the separation of church and state more generally have risen to prominence and have become powerful mobilizing issues on both the right and left. In this regard the Clinton era was particularly notable, as for the first time since the New Deal realignment, the most significant and defining differences between the Democrats and the Republicans were their cultural policy positions. For this reason, cultural issues were politically front and center to a much greater degree during the 1990s than they had been in prior years.

Some of the gender gap, according to conventional wisdom, is a product of this new party issue divide. By this argument, women are, more than men, concerned with cultural issues such as abortion and women's rights. Women have been the beneficiaries of progressive policies to a greater degree than men (especially white men). So, to the extent that group interests find their way into the political calculus of men and women, the enhanced salience of cultural issues is a plausible explanation for changes in female partisanship during the recent era.

Issue Salience and the Gender Gap—1998 to 2004

The similarity of male-female opinions on abortion suggests an argument about how cultural issues might have contributed to the gender gap: the prominence of cultural issues was a potent short-term force during the 1990s and, as a result, the respective salience of these issues for men and women may have changed. To assess this notion, the following pages examine the relative importance of cultural attitudes vis-à-vis other political values during the past five presidential election years. Our main interest is to quantify the relative salience of particular political issues over this time period and to see whether cultural issues have become increasingly important for women, as is often assumed in the media and popular commentary.

The design of the test is straightforward. We divide these five elections into two time periods (1988 to 1996 and 1996 to 2004) and conduct our analyses for the two periods separately.[25] If issue salience is a factor, one would expect to observe a growing or declining correspondence between various types of political opinions and party identification over the course of these two time periods.[26] The relative "effects" we report in Figures 5.5 through 5.7 represent the degree of rightward movement on the party identification scale when one moves from the most liberal to the most conservative position on a given question. For example (in Figure 5.5), the effect of social welfare conservatism on male partisanship in 1988 is approximately 4 points on the 7-point scale. This means that holding all other issue attitudes constant, a man with the most conservative views on the social welfare state probably will be in the high range of party identification (most likely a Republican) whereas a man who holds the most liberal views on social welfare will be in the lower part of the range (almost certainly a Democrat). In the same year, however, the relative effect of abortion views on male partisanship was relatively weak, only .38 on the same 7-point scale. This suggests that, all else being equal, a man with pro-choice abortion views is only slightly more likely to identify with the Democratic Party than is one with pro-life opinions.

In the baseline year, 1988, we find that social welfare attitudes (opinions regarding the appropriate size of government, whether the

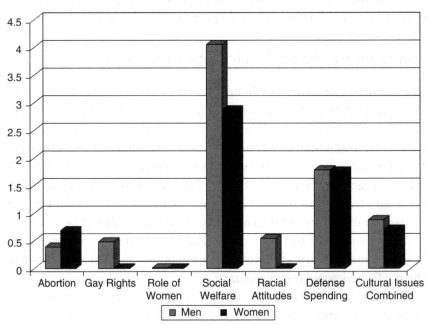

FIGURE 5.5. Issue Salience and Party ID, Men and Women in 1988. *Note:* Bars represent the total effect that issue attitudes have on self-reported party ID as respondents move from the most liberal to the most conservative position on the various issues. The party ID scale ranges from (1) Strong Democrat to (7) Strong Republican. The effects are generated by the analysis found in Appendix Table 5.1. *Source:* 1988 ANES.

government should provide health care, and whether the government should guarantee jobs) are the most salient concerns when it comes to party identification (see Figure 5.5). Social welfare attitudes are important to both men and women but are more consequential to men. Opinions regarding defense spending also influence party affiliation, albeit less so than social welfare concerns. Cultural issues such as abortion views and opinion regarding laws to protect gays from discrimination also correspond with party identification, although the magnitude of these relationships is small. Opinion on the appropriate role of women (whether they should be in the workforce or are better off staying home) appears to have no effect on partisan attachments.

Our analysis of changing issue salience over time indicates that some cultural values do grow in relative importance for women (Figure 5.6). The relationship between party identification and preferences on gay rights and the role of women gets stronger from 1988 to 1996. By contrast,

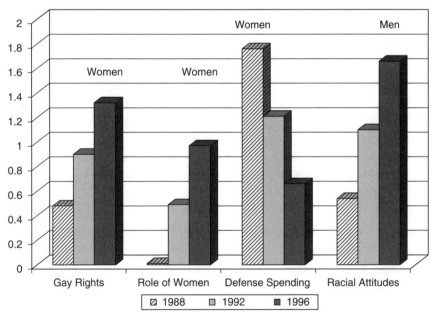

FIGURE 5.6. Changes in Issue Salience, 1988 to 1996. *Note*: The chart shows significant increases and decreases in issue salience based on the analysis in Appendix Table 5.1. All other issues (not shown in this chart) were constant in their relative salience to party ID for both men and women from 1988 to 1996. *Source*: ANES surveys from 1988, 1992, and 1996.

abortion opinion, the crown jewel in the culture wars, is positively associated with party identification for both men and women but does *not*
become increasingly important to either over time. Simply put, partisanship is no more closely linked to abortion attitudes in 1996 than it
was 1988, and this is true for both men and women. The relationship
between party identification and social welfare opinion is very strong
in 1988 but stays constant over this time period. Opinion on defense
spending is also important in 1988 but shows a significant decline among
women by 1996. What this suggests is that between 1988 and 1996,
women place greater weight on questions of social equality (gay rights
and women's rights) and less emphasis on defense spending when it
comes to their attachments to the political parties. Over this same time
period racial considerations become more important for men, but none
of the other issues change in their relative salience. In sum, two cultural
issues become more important, and defense spending opinion becomes
less important for women. For men, cultural issues remain constant
while racial issues become increasingly salient.

By 1996, the disparate importance of cultural issues between men and
women is clearly evident (see Figure 5.7). If one compares the size of
the social welfare effect with any individual cultural issue, social welfare
beliefs far outweigh cultural issues in their relative importance to party
identification. However, if one adds the individual effects of the three cultural issues together ("cultural issues combined"), the cumulative effect
of cultural attitudes for women in 1996 is double that of the effect for
men. Furthermore, the collective effect of women's cultural issues on
party identification is only slightly less than the respective influence of
social welfare attitudes. In all, the culture wars do appear to have influenced the politics of women during the late 1990s; however, the popular
notion that women politicize their abortion attitudes to a greater extent
than men is *not* borne out by these data. By 1996, the difference between
men and women on abortion is trivial. Overall, however, when the relative importance of cultural attitudes is taken into account collectively,
women do appear to place more emphasis on questions of social equality
than do men in making their party identification calculus.

The findings from the 1996 analysis also reveal gender salience differentials with regard to defense issues. Defense spending is more salient
to men than to women in 1996, and its importance to men continues to
grow throughout the remainder of the period. For women, the relative
importance of defense spending attitudes declined in the 1990s and does

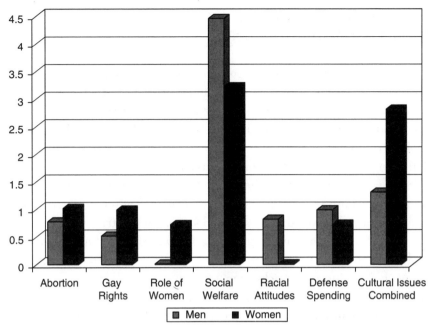

FIGURE 5.7. Issue Salience and Party ID, Men and Women in 1996. *Note*: Bars represent the total effect that issue attitudes have on self-reported party ID as respondents move from most liberal to most conservative positions on the various issues. The party ID scale ranges from (1) Strong Republican to (7) Strong Democrat. The effects are generated by the analysis found in Appendix Table 5.1. *Source*: 1996 ANES.

not appear to rebound later. Apart from the increased salience of defense spending among men, there are no other significant changes in issue salience for men or women between 1996 and 2004.

In sum, social welfare attitudes appear to matter more for men than for women—and considerably so. This is consistent with prior studies of the gender gap and strongly suggests that the political difference between men and women is still largely rooted in divergent opinions over the social welfare state and the relative priority that women and men place on social welfare issues. For a brief period in the early 1990s, cultural conflict influenced the politics of women more than men, moving them in the direction of the Democratic Party. Since 1996, however, the relative importance of cultural values has not changed for men or women. As such, the culture war perspective provides no explanation for the receding gender gap during the Bush years.

The Gender Gap in 2004: Security Moms or Southern Belles?

The 2004 presidential race had some features that may help to explain recent shifts in the appeal of the Republican Party to women. As we noted at the beginning of this chapter, media coverage during the 2004 presidential contest attributed much of the declining gender gap to "security moms" and their heightened concerns over national safety. This gendered account of the presidential contest had the same carpool-driving women who tipped the scales for Clinton in 1996 swinging to Bush in 2004 out of fear for the future of their children in a dangerous and unpredictable world. It was a good story, but not true.

As we demonstrate in Chapter 4, security moms (and moms in general) are not swing voters. Furthermore, findings from the 2004 ANES show that mothers with children at home were no more concerned with security issues than were their non-mother female counterparts. More to the point, mothers did not support the Bush candidacy in 2004 in greater proportions than they had in 2000 (see Figure 5.8): among women who have children under the age of eighteen living with them at home, 49 percent voted for Bush in 2000 and 48 percent voted for him in

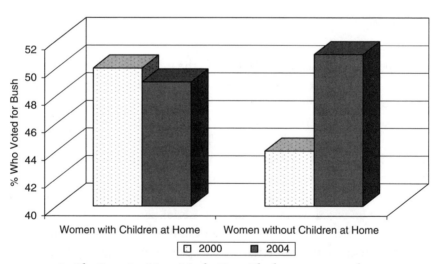

FIGURE 5.8. The Security Mom Myth. *Note:* The bars represent the percentages in each category that voted for Bush. *Source:* 2000 and 2004 ANES.

2004.[27] In terms of Republican gains among women, Bush made inroads among women without children at home, receiving 51 percent in 2004 compared to only 44 percent of their vote in 2000.

While pundits propagated the security mom myth, a far more interesting story was evolving; the gender gap among whites in the South was collapsing in 2004. Southern women, once considered the mainstays of the modern gender gap,[28] were voting for the Republicans. While the partisan gender gap between white southern men and women was a full 11 percentage points in 2000, it had fallen to only 5 points by 2004.

More dramatic still, the presidential vote gap in the South hit its lowest point in forty years (see Figure 5.9). Southern women chose Bill Clinton over Bob Dole by a 17-point margin in 1996 (compared to men) and preferred Al Gore to George Bush by 9 points more than men did in 2000. By 2004, southern women favored the Republican Bush by a margin of 2 percentage points over the men.[29] The plummeting (perhaps reversing) gender divide between white men and women in the southern states was not mirrored elsewhere. Outside of the South, the male-female difference in the presidential vote stayed much the same. Thus to understand the shrinking gender divide, it seems essential to look to the South.

Southern women are characteristically more conservative than women who live outside of the South (which is also true for men); this

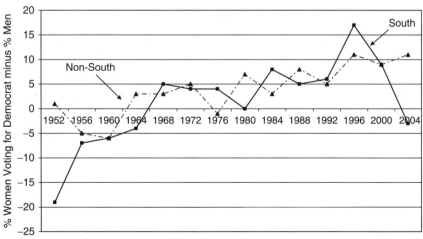

FIGURE 5.9. White Gender Gap in Presidential Voting, South versus Non-South. *Source*: ANES from selected years.

is particularly the case with regard to cultural issues such as abortion attitudes and gay rights. Southern women are consistently more liberal than their male counterparts on social welfare issues, however, and this difference has sustained a gender gap among white voters in the South since 1968. In spite of these differences, southern white women favored George W. Bush in record proportions in the 2004 contest. The lack of Democratic support from southern women is particularly striking in contrast to other groups. Partisan voting overall was extremely high in 2004. Among self-identified white Democrats, 88 percent of southern men, 90 percent of non-southern men, 91 percent of non-southern women, but only 75 percent of southern women cast their votes for John Kerry. Conversely, southern Republican women were the most loyal of all Republican identifiers, casting 98 percent of their votes for Bush.

Of the many plausible reasons that southern women may have disproportionately shifted to the GOP candidate in 2004, one stands out in conventional accounts of the 2004 vote: Iraq.[30] To the extent that southern women were more supportive of the war than other women, this could potentially explain the relatively high Democratic Party defection rate among southern women in 2004 as well as the reversal of the gender gap. The data in Figure 5.10 show the gender and regional differences in response to national security concerns and opinion about the war. While the gender gap on the question of Bush's handling of the war was roughly equal in the South and elsewhere (6 points versus 8), the southern gender gap regarding whether the war was "worth it" and whether or not the United States is less secure was only 2 points and 1 point, respectively. Outside of the South, the discrepancy between men and women on these issues remained substantial—11 points regarding the war and 9 points on the question of national security. While women in the aggregate did demonstrate somewhat lower levels of support for ongoing military operations in Iraq, the regional differences between women were considerably larger than most of the gender differences. Southern women were 17 percentage points more approving of Bush's handling of the war than were non-southern women; they were 15 points less likely to say that the Iraq War is not worth the cost; and they were 10 points less critical of the state of national security than were their non-southern counterparts.

Furthermore, while statistical analyses of the 2004 vote reveal that southern women were no more or less likely than their non-southern

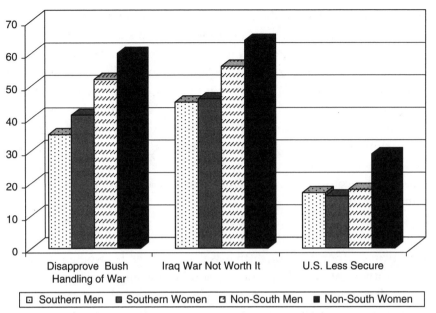

FIGURE 5.10. White Opinion on War Issues, Gender and Regional Differences. *Source*: 2004 ANES.

female counterparts to base their vote choice on the Iraq War and security concerns, these issues were nonetheless important to both groups of voters, independent of party identification.[31] Southerners (men and women) supported the Iraq War to a greater degree than people living outside of the South. The combination of smaller gender differences in the South and greater focus on war-related issues may help to explain at least part of the declining gender gap in 2004.

Religion and the Gender Gap

Another possible account for the southern decline in the gender gap centers on the role that religion and religious affinity may have played in the 2004 election. George W. Bush was not the nation's first religiously devout president; his predecessor Bill Clinton was a lifelong Southern Baptist. During the Clinton presidency, the southern gender gap was actually larger than the male-female difference in the remainder of the country. Southern women simply liked Bill Clinton and supported him in much greater numbers than their male counterparts. During the Bush presidency, the gender gap in the southern states contracted considerably. This was particularly true in the 2004 contest when Bush, an overtly religious person, ran against John Kerry, a northeastern Catholic who, until the later stages of the campaign, made few religious references. Also, Bush's first term was sensitive to the concerns of his religious and evangelical constituency. Cultural issues were often prominent symbolically and in policy decisions (a pro-life stem cell policy and vocal opposition to gay marriage, for example), and he appointed two socially conservative Supreme Court justices in John Roberts and Samuel Alito.

It seems plausible, therefore, that religious considerations drew southern women to the Republican Party in 2004. Southern women felt a particular affinity for Bush that was not shared by women living in non-southern states.[32] In particular, southern women were much more likely than non-southern women to express the belief that President Bush "cares about people like me." It is certainly possible that some of this affinity may have been rooted in their shared identity as southerners and as people of faith.

Among southern evangelical Christians in 2004, there was a trivial gender gap in the vote: southern evangelical women preferred Bush by almost 1 percentage point more than their male counterparts.[33] Outside of the South, however, the gender gap among evangelical Christians was considerably higher (7 percent) and comparable to the overall national gender gap. Southern evangelical women were more pro-Bush than evangelical Christian women in the non-South and were more Republican that their nonevangelical counterparts everywhere. Particularly notable: the Democratic defection rate for southern evangelical women exceeded 30 percent, almost twice the 18 percent defection rate for southern evangelical men. Democratic defection rates among evangelical Christians in the non-South were also quite high (23 percent and 24 percent for men and women, respectively) but not nearly as lopsided as among their religious brethren in the South.

Conclusion

The realignment of white men to the Republican Party began in 1964 and reached its current balance in 1988. For the subsequent sixteen years, the Republican Party made no additional inroads into hearts and minds of male voters. Over this same period, however, female partisanship was considerably more variable. Cultural, defense, and foreign policy-related issues were often cited as factors that tipped the scales for the Democrats—or, as in 2004, against them—among women.

By and large, the high levels of partisan loyalty demonstrated by southern men, non-southern men, and non-southern women illustrate the continuing importance that party attachments play in American electoral politics. The unusually high defection rates among southern women might appropriately be interpreted as an election-specific reaction to Bush and his particular appeal to southern women. As discussed in Chapter 2, party defections generally result from short-term forces that favor one party over the other. Particularly attractive candidates or unusually salient issues can be powerful short-term forces that lure otherwise stalwart partisans away from their party candidates in any given year. Southern women were disproportionately attracted to Bill Clinton in 1996 and similarly drawn to Bush in 2004. While we hesitate to engage in too much unfounded speculation, these patterns seem to suggest that southern women may have a particular affinity for fellow southerners, especially Christians. They also suggest that short-term forces cut both ways; sometimes they benefit the Democrats and at other times they benefit the Republicans. And when they benefit neither party particularly, party members usually find their way home.

Chapter Six

The Young and the Not-So-Restless Voters

Campaign strategists believe that if mobilized, the 24 million young people eligible to vote could turn the election for either major candidate. But young people, the conventional wisdom goes, don't do politics.... But this year, people keep saying, things are going to be different. They already are. More organizations are working to engage and register young voters than ever.... Most groups say they are nonpartisan, and by law none can tell anyone to register with a particular party. While conservative groups are certainly involved in targeting young voters, there seems to be an especially energetic response on the left.

—Evelyn Nieves, *Washington Post*, July 4, 2004

The Democratic majority in 2006 was also bolstered by support from voters ages 18 to 29. Almost all of these voters fall into the category pollsters call "millenials" or "Generation Y." In contrast with the previous generation, they prefer Democrats over Republicans and the

center-left over the center-right....The millenials can be expected to
bolster a new Democratic majority.

—John Judis and Ruy Teixeira, *American Prospect*, June 19, 2007

THROUGHOUT THIS BOOK WE HAVE EMPHASIZED CONTINUITY AND stability in elections as we consider some of the more hyperbolic claims about phenomena such as swing voting and the gender gap. But what can we say about change? Are there foreseeable changes on the political horizon that may shift the partisan balance of power in future elections? This chapter focuses on young voters and specifically considers whether the current crop will change the dynamics of American politics by adding age-distinctive opinions and party preferences to the mix on election day. Popular wisdom about young voters falls into two broad categories; one has to do with turnout (and that given the right candidate or issues, they can be mobilized in much greater numbers) and the other has to do with their liberal views and presumed future allegiance to the Democrats. We are less sure of these "facts" than are many consultants and reporters. Our expectations are straightforward. We believe that the "millenials" (also called "Generation Y") are somewhat more liberal and pro-Democratic than their predecessors. Like generations before them, the key issues and leaders of the contemporary period have left a significant imprint on their political preferences.[1] In particular, young voters (hereafter defined as eighteen- to twenty-four-year-olds) are more Democratic in their partisanship than are most other generations, save the New Dealers. In the long-term, *if* young voters were to retain their relative preferences for the political parties, they would contribute disproportionately to the ranks of the Democrats. But young voters are known for their weak partisan ties, and history has shown us that levels of party affinity can change over time. In addition, the young vote at much lower rates than other age groups. And while hope springs eternal every election season that young voters will rise up and participate in proportions that match their elders, there are simply not many good reasons to expect this to happen. The hard fact about young voters is that they participate less—not because candidates don't cater to them but because they are less interested in politics, they are less committed to their parties, and the costs associated with voting are higher for them than for older citizens. While political commentators may continue to point to young voters as untapped wellsprings of party support for the Democrats, they typically underperform when it comes to participation on election day.

Why Study Young Voters?

There is substantial evidence that mobilization is a powerful source of long-term electoral change, and that new voters, especially the young, are particularly consequential.[2] In the relatively short term of a decade or so, newly naturalized citizens can have a considerable effect on the balance of power within the party system.[3] Chronic nonvoters who join the ranks of the participators can also have an impact. But naturalized citizens are usually few in number and chronic nonvoters are hard to pull into the ranks of participators.[4] Those who are coming of age, however, are numerous (by virtue of age alone, there will be 16 million new eligible voters in 2008) and have the demographic profile and motivations that are characteristic of voters. They are, for example, more educated than their elders, more adept at gathering the political information— election dates, polling locations, and candidate positions—necessary to vote, and more likely to be imbued with the values and viewpoints about government and society that make people want to take a position and vote for candidates who promote it. Furthermore, the young may have interests in issues that are strongly generational and disproportionately prefer the party that comes closer to their cohort's position. Add to that a generational facility at scouring the Internet for information and using e-mail to transmit such information to others in their age group, and it is possible to imagine a distinctive generation that can overturn many conventions.

Working against this potential influence is the typically low turnout rate of younger voters. American elections generate among the lowest turnout rates in the democratic world, and the young are the least likely to vote. As shown in the quotations above, this indifference generates frequent public expressions of *angst* among the news media and academics at every presidential election for several reasons:

1. There is a widespread assumption that younger voters have distinct political sensibilities and priorities.

2. These sensibilities and priorities are assumed to disproportionately favor the Democratic Party and its candidates.

3. The mobilization of these voters could therefore swing a close election.

In this sense, young voters are perceived to be very much like traditional nonvoters—liberal and likely Democrats. But the logic here is different. Whereas typical nonvoters are assumed to be liberal by virtue of their lower socioeconomic status, younger voters are assumed to be liberal by virtue of their position in the life cycle. Younger citizens (whether they vote or not) are residentially mobile and typically single. They do not pay property taxes nor do they have children in the public schools. One might reasonably expect them to be less interested in tax-and-spending issues (which might shape a GOP perspective), more interested in lifestyle issues, and more inclined to apply progressive norms and values (which tilt them toward the Democrats).

To the three sources of angst about the young listed above, we would add a fourth: voting is a learned activity and if younger voters do not acquire the voting habit in their formative political years, the nation may acquire a generation of nonvoters who, as they age, will further depress the nation's low rate of political activity. It is almost certain that the voting rates of Generations X (born between 1963 and 1977) and Y (born between 1978 and 1992) will increase as they marry, have children, and take on mortgages.[5] But their respective turnout levels may have to increase dramatically to reach the turnout rates of previous generations that passed through the same phases of the life cycle.[6] And while lower turnout rates might not have significant effects on election outcomes (see Chapter 7), they can raise questions about the legitimacy of the party system, elections, our laws, and governmental institutions in general.

Studying the Impact of New Voters

This chapter examines turnout rates and issue preferences across age cohorts from 1980 through 2004. Our findings largely confirm the standard view in political science and practical politics that turnout among young Americans is anemic. We then compare the attitudes of younger and older voters across different generations to examine the potential for electoral change. Younger voters do not much like the parties or care about elections. So while they have recently been voting more Democratic than their older brethren, young voters are at best reluctant participants in U.S. elections. This creates the classic chicken-or-the-egg dilemma: campaigns are less likely to target their outreach at young voters, who are then less likely to participate and more likely to be diffident about the candidates and their parties.

Why the Young Are Reluctant Voters

As university professors, not an election goes by in which we do not receive an inquiry from the student newspaper (and local and national papers) asking about the youth vote. In particular, we are asked why young people don't vote and what the parties and candidates could do to increase their turnout. The implicit assumption among those asking the questions is intriguing: politicians are not addressing the issues that young voters want to hear about. Presumably, if the candidates would only come to Austin and College Park and Columbia to outline their plans to increase funding for Pell Grants, young voters would flock to the polls.

Most political science research, however, points in a different direction. A long line of studies suggest that the young are, at best, reticent voters.[7] Moreover, this actually makes quite a bit of sense theoretically. Let us assume that young voters are rational, and let us further assume that they vote when they perceive benefits of voting to be higher than the attendant costs. As we pointed out earlier, younger voters are more likely to be residentially mobile—to rent apartments rather than owning homes. They have to reregister to vote every time they move, just as they have to locate new polling places. Since they typically do not pay property taxes and have children in the public schools, the immediate benefits to electing a particular candidate and shaping public policy are less obvious. They are less rooted in the community, unlike those who are established in neighborhoods and who tend to be more familiar with the candidates, the issues, and the nuts-and-bolts of voting, such as when local elections are held and where one goes to vote. In this sense, costs are lower for older voters.[8]

Beyond life-cycle effects, we suspect that Generations X and Y may have had less effective political socialization experiences than their predecessors. Academic research shows that political attitudes such as civic-mindedness and party identification are initially (and largely) acquired through family socialization. People are exposed to political ideas and sensibilities through contact with family, peers, teachers, and co-workers.[9] The impact of these ideas and sensibilities is conditioned by emotional attachments (mothers seem to be especially influential) and the duration of the contact. The family is so influential because of the emotional attachments between parent and child and the many years of close interaction. Peers become important because they are the next source of strong attachment, and this attachment is reinforced by the strong identification that pre-adults feel toward their cohort. Then come teachers and the schools, whose impact is felt through both exposure to new information and ways of thinking, as well as additional contact with peers and role models.[10]

If norms about voting and politics differ across the generations, if the transmission process was less effective for recent generations, and if generational identities are strong, it is possible that generational differences might become so substantial that the expected changes associated with aging (the life-cycle effect) may be minimal.[11] Under these conditions, generational differences might be pronounced, and changes in the political behavior and perspectives of the society could be dramatically altered over a few decades through replacement of current voters by the young ones who as of now have only a small influence.

Finally, there has been considerable research demonstrating a decline in political contacting and mobilization from the 1960s to the mid-1990s.[12] Phone calls, mail, and especially in-person visits lower the information costs associated with voting and may enhance the recipient's sense of civic duty.[13] As newcomers to voting for whom the costs of participation can be quite steep, this decline may have had a disproportionate effect on the young. Given the well-documented resurgence of personal contacting by both parties in 2000 and 2004, we might also expect that such contacting has had a disproportionate effect on younger voters in our most recent elections, although it is not at all clear how much outreach activity was targeted at young voters in these elections.[14]

Given all of this, our conversations with student reporters (and older ones) tend to be brief (and probably frustrating for them). We agree that young people don't vote but fail to provide any confirmation that what the youth of America needs to hear is a good two-hour debate on tuition regulation. In fact, we argue that the collective weight of turnout studies tell us that youth voting rates are understandable given (1) their stage in life, (2) the presumed decline in civic socialization processes, and (3) limited party and candidate mobilization efforts.

The truth, however, is that our understanding of young voters—and the potential for system-changing mobilization—needs to be constantly updated with data for the latest generation. Life-cycle effects not withstanding, all generations are not the same and society (for better or worse) evolves. Perhaps more to the point, the uptick in voting during the 2004 presidential election, which seemed to be driven by important public policy disagreements and more comprehensive grassroots outreach, might have resulted in unusually high turnout among younger voters—turnout levels that may not be sustainable in future elections. This possibility was alluded to during the 2004 campaign and was discussed afterward by both the punditry and the professoriate.

Turnout Trends among Younger Voters

Although we expect that young voters will continue to vote at lower rates than older voters, the magnitude of this difference and the trend over time are not common knowledge. In fact, it is difficult to estimate turnout by age because survey-based estimates rely on self-reported turnout and draw on small subsamples of younger respondents. Other data sources are even more problematic. Exit polls, for example, tell us what voters were thinking and how they acted at the polls but are silent on the subject of turnout. Analyses of voter files can shed light on turnout, but it typically takes months for the states to update their files with information from a given election, and even then, the files have errors and can be difficult to analyze.[15] Our solution is to rely on ANES survey data, paying particularly close attention to 2000 and 2004. Self-reported turnout tends to be inflated (as we note in Chapter 7), but there is relatively little bias in these overreports.[16]

Figure 6.1 contrasts the turnout of eighteen- to twenty-four-year-olds with that of all ages from 1980 through 2004. The dominant feature of the graph is the familiar sawtooth pattern produced by the falloff in turnout from presidential to congressional election years. But the feature of significance for our story is the lower turnout of eighteen- to twenty-four-year-olds throughout the period. Their self-reported presidential election turnout averages 53 percent while congressional midterm turnout averages 24 percent. Overall turnout runs some 22 to 35 percentage points higher, at 75 percent in presidential years and 59 percent in the off years.

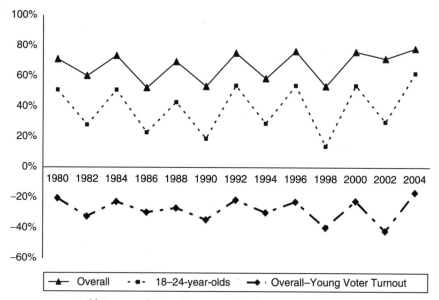

FIGURE 6.1. Self-Reported Turnout, Overall Electorate versus Young Voters (18 to 24). *Note*: Bottom line equals the difference between the overall turnout rate and the young voter rate. *Source*: ANES 1980 to 2004.

The heavy, dashed line at the bottom of the graph plots the differential between eighteen- to twenty-four-year-old turnout and overall turnout. The line shows that younger voters consistently and significantly underperform on election day. It also shows that the turnout gap between the young and the electorate as a whole is sharply different between presidential and congressional elections. In presidential elections, this difference averages 20 percentage points; in congressional election years, it averages a whopping 34 points. Younger voters are obviously more fully engaged by presidential elections, as are older Americans who respond to the intensity of the presidential campaign, but the young are more likely than their elders not to vote when the presidency is not on the line because their intrinsic interest is lower. The variance in this pattern increases in the 2002–2004 election cycle. That is, the largest young-to-overall differential is 42 points for the 2002 midterm whereas the smallest is the 17-point difference in the 2004 presidential election. The 62 percent turnout reported in the 2004 election is also the high-water mark for the eighteen- to twenty-four-year-old cohort, easily topping their 54 percent turnout in 1992.

Figure 6.1 also confirms a standing interpretation of younger citizens: they develop more political interest as they get older. If this were not happening, total turnout rates would decline over time as older citizens die off and the young become a larger share of the electorate (the eighteen- to twenty-four-year-olds of 1980 and 1984 are the forty- to fifty-year-olds of 2000 and 2004). The aggregate stability in turnout demonstrates the political maturation of each generation.

Figure 6.2 presents the data a bit differently, breaking out reported turnout by four age cohorts. Americans born after 1977 (Generation Y) are compared to their predecessors: the 1963–1977 cohort (Generation X), the 1946–1962 cohort (the Baby Boomers), and those born before 1946 (the War Generation).[17]

The data show that the Generation Y cohort votes at lower rates than its predecessors. In 2004, the difference was 15, 19, and 20 percentage points, respectively. The gap, however, may be narrowing: the upward slope for the Gen Y cohort is slightly steeper than that of Gen X and much steeper than that of the Baby Boomer or War generations. Moreover, a comparison of the turnout rates of each generation when they were at similar points in their life cycle strongly suggests that much of

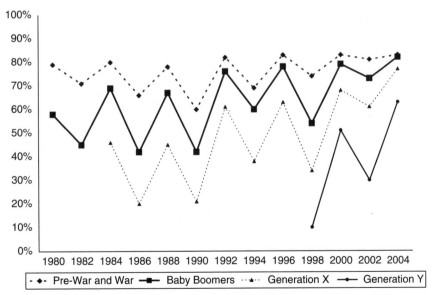

FIGURE 6.2. Self-Reported Turnout by Generation, 1980 to 2004. *Source*: ANES 1980 to 2004.

the generational turnout difference may be attributable to the life cycle. In 2004, for example, the Generation X cohort turned out at approximately the same level as the Baby Boom generation in 1996 and 2000 (and exceeded the Boomers' performance in the 1980s). In 2004, Generation Y voted at higher rates than Generation X from 1984 to 1988 and came close to the mark of the Baby Boomers in these years.[18] In fact, the data indicate that Gen Y has been, historically speaking, a relatively high turnout group.

Issues, Ideology, and Young Voter Turnout

While we believe that low rates of young voter turnout stem from weak party ties, lack of interest, and inexperience, media accounts often attribute young voting behavior to candidates and the issues they emphasize. Popular wisdom often suggests that the issues that preoccupy their elders, get them to the polls, and allow them to easily choose between candidates are mostly uninteresting to the young. The irrelevance of many old issues and conflicts for younger cohorts or the relative homogeneity of their perspectives confound the political choices they are asked to make. If the turnout of the young is low, we are often told, it is because neither the candidates nor the issues they debate are salient to young voters. Older voters may dash to the polls to choose Bush or Kerry because of their perspectives on taxes, government spending, gay marriage, or abortion, but young voters are less engaged by these issues.

This presumed generation-specific concern with issues is a consistent and persuasive story line about generational differences but one with little factual foundation. We demonstrate this on two fronts. First, we look at generational differences around liberal-conservative self-identification because—for all its well-known faults—it correlates at a respectable level with party preference, candidate choice, and a host of individual policy issues. Second, we consider the proposition that young voters suffer from disproportionate alienation toward the government, so much so that they've lost their will to vote.

Liberal and Conservative Identification

Figure 6.3 presents data from 2000 and 2004 to compare the general ideological predisposition of the generations regarding the perceived issue preferences of the candidates. Differences in the ideological orientation

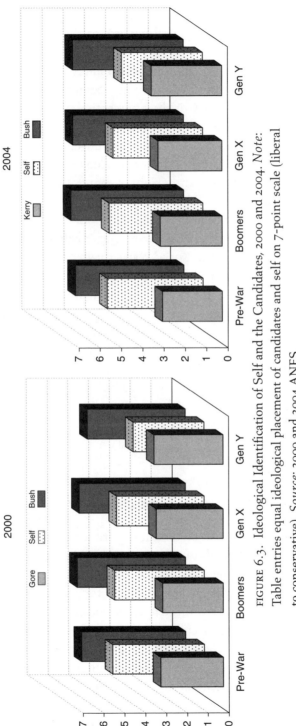

FIGURE 6.3. Ideological Identification of Self and the Candidates, 2000 and 2004. *Note:* Table entries equal ideological placement of candidates and self on 7-point scale (liberal to conservative). *Source:* 2000 and 2004 ANES.

of younger voters or a sense that they, compared to their elders, are less represented by the ideological posture of the candidates has been offered as an explanation for lower participation rates of younger voters. A quick inspection of Figure 6.3 contradicts both possibilities: the relatively low turnout rates of the young seem unlikely to reflect either a distinct ideological identity or their perception of the situation.

Ideological differences across the generations are muted. In both recent presidential elections there was no difference among the War, Baby Boomer, and Gen X cohorts in their ideological identity. All three groups saw themselves as slightly right of center. The Gen Y cohort does stand out with a more liberal predisposition, and it is a significant difference. However, their relative liberalism should not have represented a reason to abstain from voting since the Gen Y cohort in both 2000 and 2004 was closer to Gore and Kerry, respectively, than the other cohorts were to *either* candidate in either year. The War, Boomer, and (to a lesser degree) Gen X cohorts were closer to Bush than either Democrat, but none of these groups was as close to Bush as the Gen Y cohort was to Gore and Kerry. The generations are substantially alike in viewing Bush as conservative and both Democrats as liberals: each generation—in equal measure—saw a choice in the election. The Gen Y cohort—with the lowest turnout rates—not only perceived a choice but found in Gore and Kerry candidates closer to their own political conception of themselves than did any of the other cohorts, who nonetheless voted more heavily. This result makes it hard to sustain an argument about alienated younger voters.

Engagement and Attitudes toward the Parties

A second political proposition stemming from the low turnout of the young is that the millenials of Generation Y are uninterested, uncaring, and perhaps even hostile to American elections and the current party system. Table 6.1 provides some evidence for this proposition. More than one-third (36 percent) of Gen Y'ers said that they "are not very much interested" in the election. Only 22 percent of the War generation gave this response. More striking is that 55 percent of Gen Y'ers said they "don't care very much" about the congressional election. Only 35 percent of the War generation offered this response. Probing a bit further, we find that millenials are the least enamored with the current two-party system—only 28 percent would like to see it continue. But

TABLE 6.1.   Political Attitudes across Different Generations

	War Generation (Before 1946)	Baby Boomers (1946–1962)	Generation X (1963–1977)	Generation Y (1978–1993)
Interest in Election				
Not very much interested	22%	26%	31%	36%
Somewhat interested	42	50	51	49
Very much interested	35	24	18	15
Care about Congressional Elections				
Don't care very much	35	44	52	55
Care a great deal	65	57	48	45
Party System Satisfaction				
Continue the current Democratic-Republican two-party system	53	36	31	28
Conduct elections without party labels	21	27	31	42
Prefer new parties to challenge the Democrats and Republicans	26	37	38	30

Note: Table entries represent averages.
Source: ANES cumulative file, 1980–2004.

while a plurality of Gen X'ers and Baby Boomers would like to see new parties, 42 percent of Gen Y'ers preferred elections without party labels. Education also has an interesting effect on support for the party system. More than two-thirds of college graduates in all of the post-War cohorts supported the elimination of party labels on the ballot. A near majority of the college-educated Gen X and Y cohorts indicated they would support new parties in place of the Democrats and Republicans.

We are uncertain about the long-term consequences of this apparent distaste for the parties. On the one hand, the Gen Y responses are only slightly different from the Gen X responses, and the latter are relatively heavy voters. Further, the Gen X voters are substantially similar to the Boomers, and the voting rates of the Boomers are almost indistinguishable from those of the War generation—who are America's premier participators in elections. Yet many in Generations X and (especially) Y, whatever their policy preferences, may consider the current party system "broken" and unworthy of support. This could have consequences for the long-term commitment of voters to the party system, and it may limit the ability of either the Republicans or the Democrats to mobilize young voters above their current rates of participation.[19]

Generational Feelings about Government and Politics

A third proposition about the young is that there are substantial generational differences in attitudes toward government in general and the federal government in particular. Namely, the young are more cynical and jaded with respect to the federal government's ability to "deliver the goods," and they are therefore unlikely to vote heavily for Democratic candidates even though they prefer their activist policy positions. In fact, there is little in the way of a generational difference in the perceived trustworthiness and effectiveness of government. Questions about the trustworthiness of government, whether it works for the people or "big interests," and the honesty of public officials elicit relatively small differences among the cohorts (although the youngest cohort seems particularly inclined to view government as wasteful). There is, in brief, something of an American perspective on government's effectiveness and trustworthiness, and it is shaped by values that are unrelated to age.

One interesting perspective on this is apparent in Figure 6.4, which contrasts enthusiasm for greater government spending with a generalized lack of confidence in the government's ability to do things well. The spending-support measure in both years is a summary of support for government spending on welfare, poor people, social security, schools, fighting crime, and child care.[20] The numbers in the figure are an average percentage difference, calculated by subtracting the proportion who

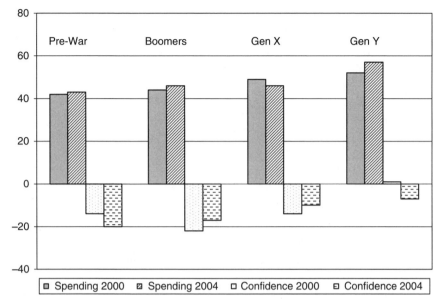

FIGURE 6.4. Confidence in Government Efficacy. *Note*: Spending measures equal the difference between the percentage who want to spend more and the percentage who want to spend less on welfare, poor people, social security, schools, fighting crime, and child care. The confidence measures equal the difference between the percentage who believe that the government can be trusted and spends money wisely and the percentage who express low trust in government and believe that it is wasteful. *Source*: 2000 and 2004 ANES.

wanted the government to spend less on a particular problem or area from the proportion who wanted the government to spend more. A positive value indicates a plurality preferring more government action. The key finding is that Americans, by a wide margin, want the government to do more about these problems. In fact, Americans of almost every political persuasion (Democrat and Republican, liberal and conservative) and within almost every demographic subgroup (regardless of race, religion or religiosity, income level, and so forth) want the government to spend more to resolve almost all the problems presented to them.

The confidence measure is a simple index of two questions: whether government can be trusted to do the right thing and whether it is wasteful. It is constructed in the same fashion—as a percentage difference index—with positive numbers representing a surplus of trust in government efficiency and negative numbers indicating the opposite. The key finding about confidence in the government is that Americans, albeit by a narrower margin, do not believe that the government can be trusted to handle problems efficiently. Again, the result is true of Democrats and Republicans, liberals and conservatives, and all racial and ethnic groups, income levels, and so on.

Age and cohort differences are small, as Figure 6.4 documents. The youngest cohorts echo the enthusiasm of their elders for more government effort to resolve problems while also not showing any particular confidence in the government's efficacy. Gen Y'ers, however, are somewhat different from the others. They are even more supportive of remedial government spending and a bit more inclined to see government as effective, illustrating again that young voters are *slightly different* in their political beliefs but never enough to support an alienation explanation for their lower levels of political involvement.

Thus, the posture of the young toward government, politics, and the parties is not dramatically different from that of the older cohorts. Their low rates of participation in politics seem to reflect more personal social concerns (long associated with youth) that make it easy to find something more rewarding than watching political news and participating in elections and campaigns. There are indications of weak support for key institutions (especially the parties), but lacking a lengthy data time series to examine these generational differences it is impossible to know if this is new and distinct or something that is simply characteristic of people in that part of the age cycle. The most reasonable conclusion is that nothing in the data constitutes evidence of restless new voters eager for change.

Party Identification

The expectation that the young are liberal Democrats is another bit of timeless received wisdom. We have all heard the chestnut that a young person who is conservative has no heart while his elder who is liberal has no brain. It captures the conventional expectation: new ideas are embraced by the young, who are forever at the cutting edge of change. In contrast, the old are stodgy in their conventions, resist technology (does anybody under thirty *not* have a cell phone?), and reject almost every new fashion or viewpoint they encounter.

Table 6.2 reports the party allegiances of the different generations. The main finding is that Gen X'ers have been decidedly more Republican than either their older or younger counterparts. Generation Y voters, on the other

TABLE 6.2. Party Identification across the Generations

	War Generation (Before 1946)	Baby Boomers (1946–1962)	Generation X (1963–1977)	Generation Y (1978–1993)
Party ID				
Strong Democratic	23%	15%	12%	10%
Weak/Lean Democratic	30	34	34	43
Independent	9	12	13	13
Weak/Lean Republican	24	27	29	25
Strong Republican	14	11	12	8
Democratic minus Republican	16	12	4	20

Note: Table entries represent averages.
Source: ANES cumulative file, 1980–2004.

hand, look a lot like the Baby Boomer and War generations, 20 points more Democratic than Republican. The caveat here is that Gen Y'ers are (1) less likely to identify as "strong" Democrats and (2) much more likely to identify as weak partisans or independents (as younger voters typically do).

Given the Democratic leanings of Generation Y, is it a foregone conclusion that they will fuel a reemergence of a Democratic majority? We explore this possibility in Table 6.3. Academic research maintains that the social and political environment during which citizens first become politically engaged can leave a strong imprint on the partisanship of new voters.[21] The distinctive partisan composition of any age cohort can certainly change over time, but initial party preferences are nonetheless a starting point—the intercept of a line yet to be determined. And as illustrated in Table 6.3, all generations do not start at the same point.

Our analysis divides the electorate into age cohorts based upon the period during which they became eligible to vote. Thus, the pre–World War II voters (at the top of the table) came of political age prior to 1946. In 2007, they were eighty-three-plus years old. Conversely, the Clinton era voters turned eighteen sometime between 1992 and 1999 and were, as

TABLE 6.3. Democratic Party Identification Advantage among Different Age Cohorts across Time

When Respondent Became Eligible to Vote	1950s	1960s	1970s	1980s	1990s	2000–2004
Pre–World War II Voters (83-plus years) Before 1946	19	19	19	19	23	30*
Post–World War II Voters (66 to 82) From 1946 and 1962	22	28	18	15	14	12
Vietnam War/Civil Rights Voters (46 to 65) From 1963 and 1979		24	25	12	11	8
Reagan Era Voters (34 to 45) From 1980 and 1991				5	9	–6
Clinton Era Voters (26 to 33) From 1992 to 1999					0	12
Today's Young Voters (18 to 24) From 1997 to 2004						27

Note: Tables entries equal the average Democratic advantage (percentage who identify or lean Democratic minus the percentage who identify or lean Republican) by each age cohort, for each decade. The age ranges in parentheses indicate how old these voters were in 2007.
*There were less than 100 respondents in this category.
Source: ANES cumulative file, 1948–2004.

of 2007, between twenty-six and thirty-three years old. We estimate the Democratic Party advantage for each group across six decades to explore the generational distinctiveness of each cohort and to examine the stability of this Democratic Party advantage over time.[22] Several important trends are evident. First, it is quite clear that each generation does not necessarily begin at the same partisan starting point. All young voters are *not* disproportionately Democratic, as illustrated by the narrow Democratic advantage among voters who became politically eligible during the Reagan era. While the pre–World War II, World War II, and Vietnam era voters all began with a considerable Democratic Party advantage (from 19 to 24 percentage points), this advantage was only 8 points among the Reagan era voters and disappeared entirely among the Clinton era voters in the 1990s. Today's eighteen- to twenty-four-year-olds exhibit a considerably higher Democratic Party advantage (27 points) than those young voters who immediately preceded them. We cannot be sure that they will maintain this lopsided support for the Democrats, but certainly they start at a point close to the New Deal and Vietnam era voters.

The contemporary U.S. party system has realigned since the 1970s, and the growing number of Republican identifiers during this period was primarily drawn from the ranks of New Deal voters and Vietnam War/ Civil Rights era voters. The Democratic Party advantage among both of these groups declined considerably over time. Reagan era voters also exhibited a comparable trend, reversing their initial Democratic advantage during the 1980s to a 6-point Republican advantage by 2004. In essence, most of the electorate became more Republican over time, but where they ended up in 2004 was, in part, a function of where they began.

The current crop of young voters exhibited a strong Democratic Party preference during the first four years of the Bush administration. Clinton era voters also moved toward the Democrats from 2000 to 2004. These data seem to suggest that voters in their late teens and twenties (Gen Y) will bring a decidedly Democratic tilt to their political preferences, but it doesn't necessarily imply a period of increasing Democratic dominance. After all, the Gen Y voters will be replacing older cohorts that *also* show a strong preference for the Democrats. It is impossible to determine how generational replacement will play out over the long haul (or to even know if young voters will become more politically active as they mature). But based on the evidence in Table 6.3, it is probably safe to say that in the short term, the relative proportions of Republicans and Democrats will not shift enormously—at least not as a result of young voters replacing old ones.

The Candidates and Voting

At this point, we know that young and Gen Y voters (1) do not turn out at high rates, (2) have partisan predispositions similar to the Baby Boomer and War generations, and (3) evince a distinct distaste for the party system and a general indifference to politics. We have said little, however, about the attitudes of young voters toward the candidates on the ballot or their actual behavior in recent elections.

Feelings toward the Candidates

Just as there are no significant generational differences explaining the marginal political interest and low turnout of the young, neither is there anything noteworthy about their assessments of recent presidential candidates. Figure 6.5 uses candidate "feeling thermometer" ratings to compare the Gen X and Gen Y cohorts with the pre-War generation and Baby Boomers (combined) in their evaluation of presidential candidates from 1980 through 2004.[23] There is considerable election-to-election oscillation, reflecting differential candidate appeal but no cohort differences that support a notion of an alienated generation. The Gen X cohort largely tracks with older voters. Consistent with their partisanship and attitudes, Gen Y'ers stand out for their significantly more positive feelings about Gore and Kerry and their more negative dispositions toward George W. Bush.

This finding is particularly clear in Figure 6.6, which contrasts the cohorts' thermometer assessments by subtracting the rating of the Democrats from the rating given to the Republicans. The movement of Generation X toward the GOP is apparent in Figure 6.6, which also documents the greater Democratic sympathies of the Gen Y cohort. Gen Y assessments of Bush and Kerry are among the most lopsided cohort-related candidate assessments observed in the past twenty-five years. Of course, there is no way to know if this will persist. A stronger regard for the Democratic candidates among the Gen X cohort in the early 1990s became a preference for Dole in 1996 and for Bush in 2000 and 2004. That noted, candidates help to shape long-term partisanship, so the assessments of the Gen Y cohort cannot make the GOP feel comfortable for the future.

A last point to be made about candidate assessments is that the intensity of each generation's feelings about the candidates is similar and uniform across the period. Figure 6.7 reports a transformation of the thermometer scores designed to measure whether sentiment is polarized.[24] Thinking of polarization as a possible way in which the generations assess political stimuli gives us some notion of whether we

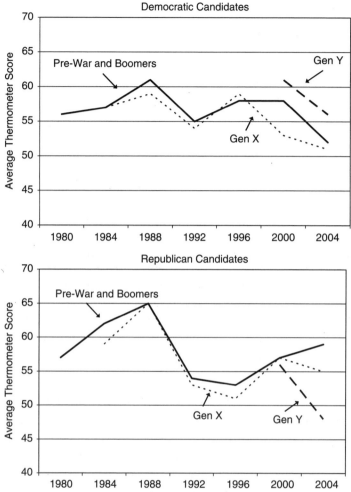

FIGURE 6.5. Candidate Evaluations across Generations. *Note*: Lines represent the average thermometer ratings given to Democratic and Republican candidates in each year for the Pre-War and Baby Boomers (combined), Gen Y, and Gen X. *Source*: ANES from selected years.

are looking at generations that share the same partisan culture or, by contrast, a division in the satisfaction that each generation feels about the party system and its elections.

Figure 6.7 documents moderately intense partisanship but provides little evidence of polarization. If Americans were indifferent toward the presidential candidates, the lines in the figure would run close to zero.

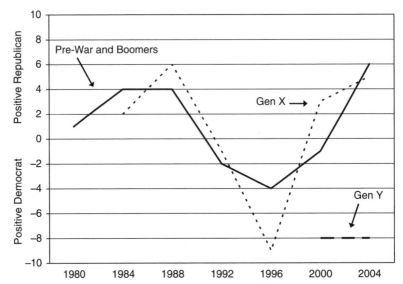

FIGURE 6.6. Partisan Bias of Candidate Evaluations by Generation. *Note*: Lines chart the mathematical difference between the average thermometer ratings of Republican and Democratic candidates for each year for the Pre-War Voters and Baby Boomers (combined), Gen X, and Gen Y. *Source*: ANES from selected years.

An enthusiastic or angry electorate would produce a line of values near 50, indicating that on average, individuals were assigning very "cold" values near zero or very "warm" values near 100 on the rating thermometers. In fact, they are running in the 20 and 25 range, suggesting that from 1980 through 2004, those with positive views of the presidential candidates gave them scores between 70 and 75 while those who had negative views rated them nearer 25 to 30. The 2004 election stands out for the intensity of Americans' feelings about George Bush. But more striking than the intensity of feelings about Bush is the similarity of all cohorts throughout the period. The cohorts even agree in their feelings about George Bush. There is little evidence of generational differences in candidate polarization over the period.

Voting Patterns

As alluded to earlier, if young voters are going to change American electoral politics, they have to act on preferences that are distinct from those still participating and those they replace. We have shown (and considered

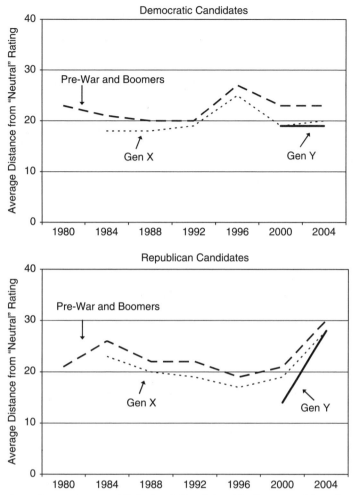

FIGURE 6.7. Generations and Polarized Candidate Evaluations. *Note*: Lines represent average candidate evaluation polarization scores for the Pre-War generation and Baby Boomers (combined), Gen Y, and Gen X. See note 24 in the chapter for a description of the polarization measure. *Source*: ANES from selected years.

at length) the lower turnout rates of young and Gen Y voters, arguing that they are not as attitudinally distinct as is often suggested. But for whom do they vote? When they have voted, have they provided distinct support for the Democrats?

Table 6.4 averages the vote of different age and generational cohorts across presidential and midterm elections for the 1980s, 1990s, and

TABLE 6.4. Democratic Voting across the Generations

	1980s	1990s	2000s	AVG.
Presidential Vote				
18- to 24-Year-Olds	41%	53%	65%	51%
War (before 1946)	43%	52%	51%	48%
Baby Boomers (1946–1962)	41%	49%	49%	46%
Generation X (1963–1977)	44%	51%	49%	48%
Generation Y (1978–1993)	—	—	66%	66%
Senate Vote				
18- to 24-Year-Olds	52%	53%	60%	54%
War (before 1946)	54%	55%	53%	54%
Baby Boomers (1946–1962)	54%	52%	52%	53%
Generation X (1963–1977)	59%	51%	49%	53%
Generation Y (1978–1993)	—	—	67%	67%
House Vote				
18- to 24-Year-Olds	62%	55%	65%	60%
War (before 1946)	57%	54%	50%	54%
Baby Boomers (1946–1962)	58%	51%	50%	54%
Generation X (1963–1977)	64%	56%	50%	56%
Generation Y (1978–1993)	—	—	71%	71%

Note: All numbers are percent Democratic
Source: ANES cumulative file, 1980–2004.

2000s. The differences in presidential voting by age are illustrative. In 2000, eighteen- to twenty-four-year-olds preferred Al Gore to George W. Bush by 34 percentage points. In 2004, they preferred John Kerry to Bush by 24 points. Among those twenty-five years of age and older, the margins favored Gore by 4 points and Bush by 2 points in 2004.[25] In general, Table 6.4 shows that the younger cohorts have voted increasingly Democratic from the 1980s to the 2000s.

The pattern of generational voting in Table 6.4 is substantially similar. Members of Generation Y began to enter the electorate in 1996, preferring Bill Clinton over Republican senator Robert Dole by 18 points.[26] In the 2000 and 2004 elections, however, they moved decidedly toward the Democrats, preferring Al Gore and John Kerry by 31 and 33 points, respectively. Baby Boomers and Gen X'ers, by contrast, became slightly more supportive of the Republican candidates from 1996 to 2004.

Congressional voting patterns are similar. In 2000, eighteen- to twenty-four-year-olds preferred Democratic Senate candidates by 36 points and House candidates by 38 points. In 2004, the pro-Democratic margins were 36 and 43 points. The prevailing political winds in 2000 and 2004 shifted to the GOP (compared to how they blew in 1992 and 1996) but the eighteen- to twenty-four-year-old group was unresponsive, finding Democrats preferable in both years.

Younger, millennial voters have established a promising but attenuated track record as a Democratic cohort. While the nation swung to the Republicans in 2000 and 2004, Gen Y'ers swung to the Democrats. The core dilemma remains, however: the Democrats have been helped by the entry of young voters with sympathetic policy preferences, but they have yet to solve the chronic problem of how to mobilize them.

Campaigns and Youth Mobilization

Can the Democrats or anyone else tap into the market of young voters? It will be a demanding task. Younger Americans care less about politics, are less attached to the parties, and are potentially more sensitive to the prevailing political wind. They might be slower to be engaged by a campaign, and easily swayed by the electional environment, regardless of their apparent partisan preferences. More to the point, they are less likely to take up more demanding participatory tasks or to be contacted by the campaigns.

The data in Table 6.5 show no substantial generational effect regarding nonvoting forms of political participation. For example, younger Americans are unlikely to attend a political meeting (6 percent), work for a candidate (3 percent), or contribute money to a party or campaign (4 percent). But very few people of any age do these things. As one

TABLE 6.5. Campaign Activities, Outreach, and Vote Decisions across
Generations

	War Generation (Before 1946)	Baby Boomers (1946– 1962)	Gen X (1963– 1977)	Gen Y (1978– 1993)	Young Voters (18–24)
Campaign Activity					
Tried to influence others	28%	31%	27%	33%	26%
Attended political meeting	8%	7%	5%	5%	6%
Worked for party/ candidate	4%	3%	2%	2%	3%
Displayed button/ bumper sticker	9%	9%	9%	12%	10%
Contributed money	12%	7%	4%	2%	4%
Discussed politics with somebody	27%	20%	24%	25%	32%
Campaign Outreach					
Contacted by parties/ campaigns	33%	25%	19%	16%	16%
by Democrats	21%	16%	12%	10%	10%
by Republicans	21%	16%	11%	8%	8%
by someone else	11%	10%	8%	7%	7%
Voting					
Decided in last two weeks before election day	18%	21%	22%	21%	21%
Voted before election day	18%	11%	13%	16%	16%
Voted absentee	16%	12%	17%	15%	15%

Note: Table entries represent averages.
Source: ANES cumulative file, 1980–2004.

moves to less demanding participatory activities, young people again look much like their senior counterparts. They are, in fact, almost equally likely to discuss politics (32 percent) or to try to influence others (26 percent). The failure to find noteworthy differences is not surprising: every cohort, even the youngest, contains a cadre of intensely interested, committed politicos. Beyond these committed partisans, though, Gen Y'ers are generally less interested and less participatory.

This broader lack of interest and participation may cause—or may be caused by—the lower rates at which younger voters are contacted by parties and candidates. Only 16 percent of younger voters report having been contacted by a party or campaign about voting compared to 28 percent for older voters. Perhaps more than anything else, this discrepancy has spawned a plethora of youth outreach programs. The data attesting to the fact that young voters are less likely to be visited, phoned, or mailed about voting are indisputable. What is less obvious is whether parties and candidates could reap an electoral benefit by addressing this gap. There are two reasons that parties and candidates are reluctant to contact voters. First, it is unclear whether young voters will actually show up even if they are contacted repeatedly. Our data, in fact, point to many reasons for the young to be particularly unlikely to vote. Second, even if they were to show up, it is far from certain how they would vote. Because they are inexperienced, independent, and less engaged, they are more likely than stronger partisans to be influenced by short-term forces that cannot be controlled by the campaign. In light of all this, a rational and strategic campaign that is looking to maximize the impact of scarce resources may be better served by investing its money and energy elsewhere. The disparate results of ostensibly nonpartisan efforts to increase youth turnout reinforce the uncertainty involved with this sort of endeavor.

Setting aside the issue of campaign outreach, we *can* say that younger voters look like older voters with respect to decision timing and the means by which they vote. Gen Y'ers are a little more likely to make up their minds late in the campaign—21 percent decided their vote in the last two weeks or on election day (compared to 20 percent for all others)—but the difference is trivial. They were also equally likely to vote before election day (16 percent, to 15 percent for everyone else), and they were significantly more likely to vote by mail (11 percent, to 2 percent for everyone else).

All told, it does not appear that younger voters are particularly indecisive, nor are they substantially more likely to vote early. Vote-by-mail differences, on the other side of the ledger, suggest that younger voters are very likely to avail themselves of technological innovations when it comes to voting. Whether this will draw additional young voters to the polls or will simply afford those committed to voting a more convenient means of casting a ballot is unclear.

Conclusion

Analyses of national survey data reinforce the conventional wisdom that turnout among young Americans is distressingly low. The data, however, call into question whether Generation Y'ers—the current cohort of eighteen- to twenty-nine-year-olds—are any less likely to vote than their immediate predecessors. Generation Y turnout rates in 2000 and 2004 make its performance comparable to that of the Baby Boomers and perhaps even a little better than that of Generation X at comparable stages of the life cycle. Future studies ought to consider whether these relatively high levels of voting among Gen Y are a result of the outreach efforts in these recent elections. If so, the youngest cohort might experience a dropoff in turnout in 2008 and beyond should 2004-level mobilization efforts not be maintained.

Beyond turnout, and contrary to the conventional wisdom, we find that young Americans are no more cynical than everyone else in the United States. Young people may laugh at the biting satire of Jon Stewart's *The Daily Show*, Stephen Colbert's *The Colbert Report*, and David Letterman's *The Late Show*, but their dominant characteristic is not bitter disappointment but rather general disinterest in government, politics, and elections – like the generations that preceded them.

This disposition and the concomitant sense that elections don't matter is part of the reason that young Americans do not identify with the political parties as much as their older counterparts. It is also why, despite favoring greater social welfare spending, Gen Y'ers are no more likely to be Democrats than Baby Boomers or those of the War generation. Rather, they are much more likely to stay at home on election day.

We are not, of course, arguing that it is impossible to engage young voters and capture a disproportionate percentage of their support. Their voting in recent elections suggests that the Democrats may be on the verge of gaining a long-term advantage with Generation Y voters. We may be witnessing the formation of the Clinton generation, in much the same way the Gen X'ers became the Reagan generation. However, there are solid reasons for young voters to be less interested in (and attentive to) politics, and courting these voters with significant resources is an expensive gamble for any party or campaign—which is why it was rarely done in the past and is not usually a central feature of current campaigns plans.

Chapter Seven

The Partisan Bias of Turnout

One truism that has guided strategists for years is that higher voter turnout favors Democrats, lower turnout favors Republicans. That's why Republicans usually spend Election Day praying for rain.

—Katharine Q. Seelye, *New York Times*, March 4, 2001

FOR MOST OF THE TWENTIETH CENTURY, QUESTIONS OF VOTER TURNOUT received great rhetorical attention but relatively small effort from political campaigns. In presidential elections, when campaigning was at its most energetic, candidates spent the bulk of their resources to influence the direction of the vote with campaign ads. Campaigns behaved as though turnout would rise to a predictable level and that the best way to win elections was to "improve" the vote share among expected voters. To be sure, ads sometimes urged viewers to vote and some fraction of those contacted on behalf of a candidate or party were subjected to little more than a "get-to-the-polls-on-election-day" message. On balance, however, campaign ads attempted to persuade voters of the superior merit of one of the candidates and get-out-the-vote (GOTV) efforts were focused on personal contacts during which a likely voter (and supporter) was urged to vote and offered assistance to get to the polls.

Everything that we know about recent campaign strategies suggests that these patterns are changing. Typically about a quarter of the electorate reported contact by a party or candidate worker through the 1970s and 1980s. Contacting hit a new high-water mark of 37 percent in 2000, and then surged again to 44 percent in 2004.[1] The 2004 election particularly stood out, as an additional 6 percent of the electorate was contacted by someone other than a party or candidate. Overall, approximately 50 percent of Americans remember an in-person or telephone contact by someone working on behalf of a political candidate in 2004.[2] Both the Democratic National Committee (with its "5104" plan) and the Republican National Committee (with its "72 Hour" plan) invested substantial resources in GOTV, canvassing, and grassroots programs in 2004. Some of the surge in GOTV activity resulted from plans that were made in response to campaign finance changes that both parties thought would limit previous ways of spending money on elections. But some of it also reflected the success of Democratic outreach programs in 1998 and 2000. Hoping for victory in 2004, the Democrats invested more in GOTV and outreach; Republicans, fearing the Democrats might be successful, poured resources and strategy into their own GOTV plans for 2004. The 6-percentage-point increase in turnout between 2000 and 2004 (from just over 55 percent of the eligible in 2000 to 61 percent in 2004) probably demonstrates the ability of voter mobilization efforts to increase participation.[3]

The possibility that such mobilization efforts will be institutionalized as we proceed into the twenty-first century remains an open question. But it raises familiar ideas about whether the Democrats will prosper with increases in turnout. Traditionally Democrats have thought so, and Republicans have feared they were correct. Democrats, consequently, like proposals that increase registration and turnout (automatic registration, same-day registration, systems to register citizens at social service agencies, "Motor Voter" initiatives, etc.); Republicans tend to be suspicious, viewing the desire for higher turnout largely as a scheme to increase the Democratic vote.

This chapter brings both familiar and new data to the question of whether turnout helps the Democrats. The data support a conclusion quite different from the common wisdom: we demonstrate that turnout does *not* have a consistent bias in favor of the Democratic Party.

Sometimes, turnout increases the Republican vote share. Turnout is often a consequence of electoral tides that are also driving candidate choice. Who is helped is a function of short-term forces (policy successes and failure, scandals, and so forth) that clearly burden (or help) one of the parties; and it is *those election-specific factors*, not turnout, that will determine the election. The key factor in determining which party benefits from turnout is, net of GOTV efforts by the parties, the size and direction of the short-term forces in the election. In a mature democracy such as the United States, feelings about the candidates and the issues in a given election influence turnout. Sometimes these feelings and issues help Democrats and at other times they help Republicans. The direction of the vote and the level of turnout are a product of these feelings and issues.

A caveat: The following data do *not* demonstrate that a vigorous GOTV effort is inconsequential. If one party mobilizes its supporters while the other does not, the former is more likely to win. That concern, after all, is what led both parties to unparalleled mobilization efforts in 2004. The 2004 election also illustrates a related fact about voter mobilization efforts: mobilization provokes countermobilization that can increase turnout without either side improving its relative position.

The Source of the Conventional Wisdom

As Table 7.1 demonstrates, Republicans are more likely to vote than Democrats. Republicans reported a turnout rate in 2004 of 85 percent, but only 76 percent of Democrats reported going to the polls.[4] This 9-point difference had a measurable impact on the partisan composition of the electorate in 2004. Democrats outnumbered Republicans by 48 to 42 percent among all voter-eligible adults, but the different turnout rates produced a voting population that was 47 percent GOP and 46 percent Democratic. Put more strikingly, a 6-point Democratic advantage among adults eroded to a 1-point disadvantage in the electorate because of the turnout differences between Democrats and Republicans.

Inaccurate reports of turnout do not change this pattern. Many who did not vote in 2004 nonetheless reported that they did. We might expect Republicans, more middle class and conventional in their beliefs, to misreport that they participated because, one might argue, of their greater

TABLE 7.1.   Party Differences in Turnout

	Election Year				
	2004			1984–1988	
	Reported Voting	Share of		Reported Voting	Validated Vote
		Pop.	Voters		
Strong Republican	94	17	22	81	74
Weak Republican	84	13	15	68	61
Lean Republican	72	12	11	67	54
Independent	50	10	6	50	39
Lean Democratic	71	17	16	57	53
Weak Democratic	73	15	13	63	54
Strong Democratic	85	16	17	76	67

Note: Table entries are percentages.
Source: ANES from selected years.

likelihood of subscribing to the conventional sense of citizen duty that motivates many to vote. But overreports of turnout do not alter the pattern. In both 1984 and 1988, the ANES checked official records to determine who did participate (1988 was the last year in which this was done). While the reported turnout rates in 1988 were lower than they were in 2004, and the validated turnout rates were lower still, the validated turnout data showed the same pattern. Republicans were more likely than Democrats to vote; a Democratic advantage of 6 percentage points among all eligible voters became a narrow 1-point advantage among actual voters.

Party identification is not the vote, of course, but the data in Table 7.1 are consistent with reported links between turnout and electoral mobilization.[5] Subsequent analyses of election results provided empirical support.[6] Popular political commentary sporadically reports stories that reinforce the notion that turnout levels influence election outcomes.[7] Commentaries that attribute the success of the GOP, especially in presidential elections, to a decline in turnout since the 1960s have created support among Democrats for proposals to increase turnout, such as same-day registration and "Motor Voter."[8]

The Facts of Turnout and Vote Share in National Elections

Despite suggestive patterns such as those in Table 7.1, a consistent Democratic advantage in high turnout races is not observed in election outcomes. As Figure 7.1 shows, turnout is unrelated to the Democratic presidential vote between 1948 and 2004. A look at specific elections also makes the point. The five elections with turnout rates above 60 percent (1952 through 1968) produced two Democratic presidents and three Republicans; the four with turnout rates below 55 percent produced Democratic wins in 1948 and 1996 but GOP victories in 1988 and 2000.

Figure 7.2, which plots House elections in the on-years (filled squares) and the off-years (empty squares), shows the same pattern. Turnout is higher in the presidential election years, but the Democratic vote for House candidates in both types of elections is unrelated to the turnout rate. In off-years, where the turnout rate averaged approximately 15 points below the turnout typical of presidential elections, the Democratic share of the congressional vote was actually slightly higher (by about

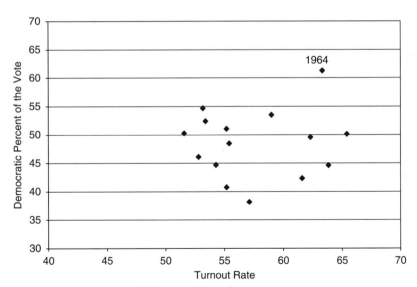

FIGURE 7.1. Turnout and the Presidential Vote, 1948 to 2004. *Source:* Statistical Abstract of the United States.

1 percent). The reason for this outcome reflects what really drives turn-out and the direction of the vote: the pro-GOP tides of some presidential elections were absent from the congressional elections, so there was a less depressing effect on the Democratic vote in the off-years.

In brief, there is no aggregate relationship between turnout and the size of the Democratic vote because there is usually no large difference between the preferences of voters and nonvoters. As a result, when turnout goes up from a previous election and some of the nonvoters from last time join the ranks of voters, there is no certain corresponding increase in the size of the Democratic vote. There is also no predictable decline in the Democratic vote when turnout goes down. Why this is so and how it works is the subject of this chapter.

Voters, Nonvoters, and Short-Term Forces

The preceding data are not novel, and the pattern is certainly familiar to most students of voting. Kernell was among the first to demonstrate that the on-year/off-year oscillation in party fortunes (described by Campbell in 1966) was less a function of turnout differences than it was a retrospective reaction to the incumbent president (a short-term

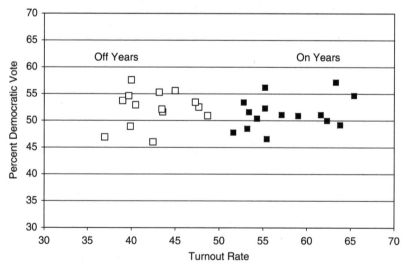

FIGURE 7.2. Turnout and the Congressional Vote, 1948 to 2004. *Source:* Statistical Abstract of the United States.

force) and perhaps the loss of coattails in the off-year contest.[9] In general, political scientists have found little to no support for the turnout bias thesis.[10] The most recent research that reports a bias in Senate elections in the 1990s finds it to vary in size and party beneficiary according to election-specific factors that included incumbency, campaign resources, and other forces.[11]

The Directional Bias of Short-Term Forces

Voting itself is rarely at issue in the United States. In rare circumstances, election-specific factors motivate turnout for the simple sake of voting. Something akin to this happened in 2002 and 2004 following the balloting irregularities of the 2000 election. There was a strong push to mobilize African Americans in Florida in 2002 and 2004 with arguments that efforts were made in 2000—and would be made again—to suppress black participation. But such appeals stand out for their rarity. Rather, policy disputes, military engagements, the hoopla of the campaign, and candidate-specific enthusiasm (one of the candidates has a hero's war record, is young and personally appealing, and so forth) motivate marginally interested citizens to vote.

The foundation for this effect rests on the well-understood distinction between "core voters" and "peripheral voters." The former are typically interested in public affairs and fairly regular participants in elections. The latter have significantly less interest in public affairs, are less involved and less informed about government and politics, and are irregular or infrequent voters.[12] The unusually appealing candidates (and the issue choices represented by them) create a surge in turnout by mobilizing the peripheral voters. The above-average susceptibility of peripheral voters to the candidate-favoring forces that increase interest in the race lead them to support the candidate favored by these forces more heavily than voters with average or high levels of involvement (the "core" electorate) who otherwise share their partisan or demographic profile.

The key facts about peripheral voters who turn out in a particular election are not their age, ethnicity, social class, or—to a substantial degree—even their partisanship. Their most meaningful quality is a marginal interest in politics, which predisposes them to respond more strongly to election-specific events than the more interested, informed, and regular participants whose active and latent political predispositions do more to moderate short-term political influences. For example, almost 95 percent of the most motivated and involved Democrats (those in the top half of the involvement index; see note 14 for a description of the index) voted for Gore and an equal percentage of the most involved Republicans voted for Bush.[13] In contrast, the defection rate of the least-involved voters (those in the lowest quartile of the involvement index) was considerably higher. Thirty-eight percent of the least-involved Democrats and 17 percent of the least-involved Republicans defected from their party's candidate. The 2000 election wasn't unusual. Republican defection among the lowest involvement quartile was high in 1992 when short-term forces favored Clinton and the Democrats. In 1980, when Reagan and the GOP benefited from short-term forces, defection was unusually high among low involvement Democrats.

Involvement, Turnout Change, and Vote Switching

Figure 7.3 demonstrates how a voter's involvement moderates the influence of short-term forces.[14] The figure plots the rate of vote switching according to an individual's level of involvement for three adjacent elections—1984 and 1988, 1996 and 2000, and 2000 and 2004. In all three instances, the magnitude of the shift is related to voter involvement. Virtually all of the difference between the pairs of elections was contributed by voters whose involvement score placed them in the bottom 50 percent of the distribution. Some attentive, involved, and partisan citizens changed their vote in response to the election environment, but it is the least attentive, involved, and partisan who contributed most of the shift in the vote share between elections.[15] If the data in Figure 7.3 hold across most elections (and there is no reason to believe they should not), we expect peripheral citizens to be more susceptible to short-term influences because they lack the accumulated preferences and reinforced habits of the more involved.

The consequence of these patterns for the directional influence of turnout is clear. The candidate who benefits from turnout will be the one favored by the electoral mood, whether the candidate is a Democrat or a Republican. The effect is strongest on the most uninvolved and marginally interested voters.[16] Social characteristics and even nominal partisanship among these individuals are less predictive of their choices than they are for core voters. Low involvement partisans tend to have

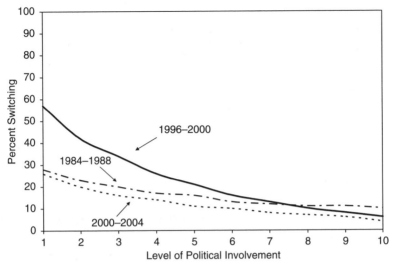

FIGURE 7.3. Vote Switching by Levels of Political Involvement. *Note*: The political involvement measure is described in note 14. *Source*: ANES from selected years.

weaker party attachments than their high involvement counterparts and, consistent with our findings in Chapter 2, they are more open to short-term forces (a particular issue, event, or candidate) that favor the opposition. The typical influence of party identification among peripheral voters is weaker, and the political guidance provided by normally important social cleavages (class, ethnicity, religion, etc.) is also more tenuous. A lack of political involvement makes them less likely to respond to political events in the same manner as their politically involved peers because they lack the political sensitivities of otherwise similar regular voters.

The net result is that nonvoters echo the preferences of voters and perhaps even exaggerate them depending on the magnitude of the factors influencing the vote. A closely divided vote among the more involved produces a roughly similar division among the less involved peripherals. Short-term forces sufficient to tilt the candidate preference of the core electorate have an even greater influence on the peripheral electorate. Consequently, not only are lopsided elections unlikely to be undone by higher turnout but they are also likely to become even more lopsided as turnout increases since the entering voters create an electorate with a larger than normal proportion of peripheral voters.[17]

Figure 7.4 demonstrates this pattern by comparing the reported vote for the winner in presidential elections from 1952 through 2004 and the percentage who preferred the winner among those who did not vote. The preferences of nonvoters were expressed prior to the election, eliminating the bandwagon effect that might be observed when candidate preference is obtained after the election.[18] The pattern is clear. Whether the election is lopsided or close, a two-party struggle, or one with a significant third-party candidate, nonvoters expressed almost the same candidate preferences as did voters—and sometimes a bit more so. There are a few cases in which the preferences of voters and nonvoters diverged. Nonvoters preferred the losers Stevenson in 1952, Carter in 1980, and Kerry in 2004.[19] But overall, nonvoters generally expressed the same candidate preference as voters. In a few cases (noted above), nonvoters were more tilted toward the loser but never by so large a margin that the election would have been changed by their participation. Over most of the elections graphed in Figure 7.4, 100 percent turnout would have produced the same winner at the same or a slightly greater margin. The

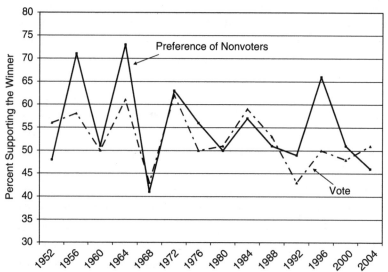

FIGURE 7.4. The Presidential Preferences of Voters and Nonvoters.
Note: The solid line represents the percentage of nonvoters who, in preelection polls, indicated that they preferred the winning candidate in each year. The dashed line is the percentage of the actual vote garnered by the winning candidate. *Source*: ANES from selected years.

runaway victories of Eisenhower and Johnson in 1956 and 1964, for example, would have been even larger with higher turnout because nonvoters preferred Ike and Johnson by a wider margin than the voters. The insurgent appeals of Wallace and Perot in 1968 and 1992 were especially strong among peripheral citizens. In both elections, 100 percent turnout would have increased the margins of George Wallace and Ross Perot, respectively (data not shown). On the other hand, the close elections of 1960 and 1976 produced narrow wins for Kennedy and Carter and a similarly even division in the preferences of nonvoters. The ANES voter validation studies corroborate the results in Figure 7.4. Nonvoters echoed the preferences of validated voters in three of the four studies—1964, 1984, and 1988—and expressed a different preference only in 1980—where a plurality indicated a preference for Carter.[20]

A Direct View: Changes from Election to Election

In ordinary language, the turnout bias thesis appears in claims such as "the Democrats lost seats because the weather kept turnout down" or "we'll win if we can increase turnout in this election." But very few analyses examine this asserted election-to-election correlation. The typical approach has been to analyze the relationship between turnout and the vote among elections where the election is the unit of analysis (Figures 7.1 and 7.2 are examples). There is nothing wrong with this way of demonstrating that a turnout bias is mostly mythological, but a comparison of turnout changes with vote changes from one election to the next for a large number of offices may be a more direct assessment of the bias thesis because confounding idiosyncrasies are dampened by the large number of offices.[21] We make such a comparison by examining whether the Democratic vote varied with changes in turnout from one election to the next *within* each of the 435 congressional districts over three decades, thereby directly examining whether *the rise or fall in the turnout rate from one election to the next causes the Democratic vote to rise or fall.*

The congressional district, organized by the three periods during which each district was constant, is our unit of observation. We calculated the turnout rate and Democratic vote for each election in the congressional district that existed for the 1972–1980 apportionment period, the period from 1982 to 1990, and from 1992 to 2000. The *turnout rate* is calculated as the total number of votes cast in the district in that election year divided by the voting-age population.[22] The three separate decades offer three distinct observatories for the relationship, essentially presenting multiple opportunities to test for a correlation between turnout and the vote. Within each decade the districts are unchanged, largely eliminating any chance that a shift in the composition of the district's population could affect the turnout-vote relationship.[23] Uncontested races were eliminated from the analysis, reducing the total number of districts for some decades.

The "Responsiveness Coefficient"

Our measure of the relationship between turnout and the vote is what we term a "responsiveness coefficient."[24] A positive value indicates that the Democratic vote during the period increased with turnout; a negative value indicates that the Democratic vote declined with turnout; a zero value indicates that the two were unrelated.

Figure 7.5 presents examples of the measure calculated for three districts selected at random: Ohio's 5th district as it existed from 1982 through 1990, Iowa's 1st for the period from 1992 through 2000, and New York's 2nd district for 1982–1990. New York 2 illustrates a pro–Democratic party bias to turnout. Iowa 1 and Ohio 5 demonstrate a pro-GOP turnout bias. The three examples display the other characteristics of the turnout and the vote pattern we expect.[25] First, it is not strong in any of the examples. Second, two of the three slopes are negative, presaging findings below. Finally, the relationship between turnout and the direction of the vote does not depend on the underlying partisanship of the district or the typical level of turnout.

The Results: No Bias

Figure 7.6 presents the distribution of the responsiveness coefficients for the districts for each decade separately. If turnout systematically favored the Democrats, the distribution would be shifted to the right of each graph (where positive responsiveness coefficients appear); if it favored the Republicans, it would be shifted to the left (indicating that the coefficients are negative for the most part); if neither party benefited from turnout, the distribution of coefficients would be centered around

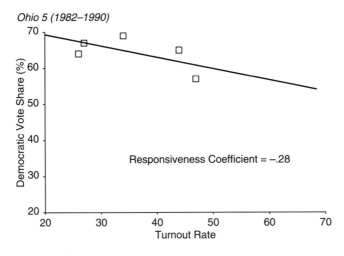

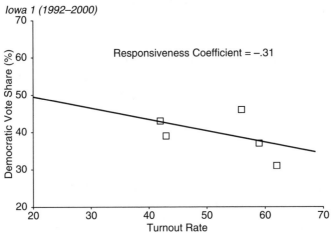

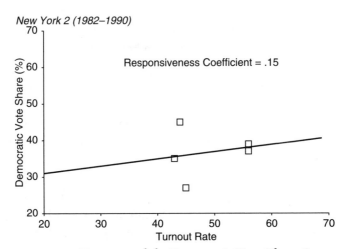

FIGURE 7.5. Turnout and the Democratic Vote: Three Cases.
Source: Congressional District Data Book.

the zero point, and it would be substantially symmetrical. We observe all three outcomes.

Turnout seems to help the Democratic vote in some districts: these are the responsiveness coefficients on the right side of the graph. Turnout seems to increase the Republican vote in other districts: there are a lot of districts with responsiveness values on the left of the graph. Most of the values cluster very close to zero, indicating that among these districts, over three decades, turnout and the Democratic vote tended not to vary together. An important fact not highlighted in the figure is that there are very few districts where the relationship ever comes close to reaching significance, and there was no case showing a district that had large and significant values across all three decades.[26] We checked to see whether the relationship between turnout and the Democratic vote varied between on- and off-year elections: it does not. We looked to see whether the party of the incumbent had an influence: it did not, although one might have expected a relationship. Average turnout rates also did not have any effect on the results in Figure 7.6.

Is Competitiveness a Factor?

The competitiveness of the district is also irrelevant, although one might have expected it to matter. It might have been the case that the generally negative coefficients of the 1972–1980 decade reflected the strength of Democratic candidates in minority communities, central cities, and rural southern districts with a tradition of low turnout but strong support for the Democrats. In such a case, influences unrelated to turnout and Democratic voting, but embedded in both, might be a source of the negative relationship in Figure 7.6.

To examine this possibility, we repeated the analysis but limited it to competitive districts.[27] The top of Table 7.2 reports the pattern for all of the cases in Figure 7.6. The bottom half reports only the competitive districts. The table also includes a control for the 1994 election, guarding against the possibility that the GOP win in 1994 distorted the results during the 1992–2000 period. Nothing changes. The data in the bottom and top parts of the table are virtually identical, establishing that district competitiveness does not account for the results. During the 1970s and 1980s turnout aided GOP candidates overall *and in the competitive districts*. During the 1990s, turnout seems to have been an asset for Democratic candidates overall and in the competitive districts. However, as the correlations indicate,

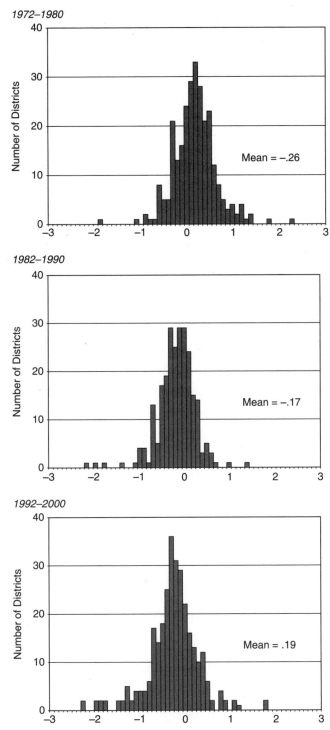

FIGURE 7.6. Responsiveness of the Democratic Vote to Turnout.
Source: Congressional District Data Book.

TABLE 7.2 The Effect of Turnout on the Democratic House Vote

	1970s	1980s	1990s	
			All Elections	Without 1994
All Districts				
Slope	−0.26	−0.17	0.19	0.09
Correlation	−0.01	−0.01	0	0
N of districts	299	247	275	288
Districts with a Democratic two-party vote between 45 and 55 percent				
Slope	−0.22	−0.16	0.22	0.17
Correlation	−0.01	−0.01	0	0
N of districts	63	29	57	57

Note: Slopes refer to the average unstandardized regression coefficients for all districts. Negative slopes correspond with turnout aiding the Republicans and positive slopes indicate that higher turnout benefited the Democrats. Source: The Statistical Abstract of the United States for various years.

the tendencies represented by the coefficients are marked by considerable dispersion. It was not possible, even in the 1990s, to expect increases in turnout to boost the Democratic vote in congressional elections.

The Change in the 1990s

We have no explanation for why turnout marginally advantaged the Republicans during the 1970s and 1980s but reversed to slightly help the Democrats in the 1990s. We might be observing the robust operation of minority-party effects of the sort proposed by Duverger and later used by DeNardo.[28] Perhaps the minority Republicans in the 1970s and 1980s and minority Democrats in the 1990s enjoyed a more easily tapped reservoir of support.[29] Alternatively, and more likely, the shift in the sign of the coefficients may capture the dominance of the presidential elections by the Democrats during the 1990s compared to GOP success during the 1970s and 1980s. Coattail effects, while weak, have always been apparent in American elections. Presidential elections, always associated with strong short-term forces and higher turnout, benefit their congressional candidates by virtue of the directional forces associated with the surge of the presidential election. Clinton's wins in 1992 and 1996 boosted the Democratic congressional vote slightly in both years. Gore's *losing majority percentage* in 2000 also helped Democratic congressional candidates in that year because it exceeded Clinton's *winning pluralities* in 1992 and 1996, albeit not enough to give the Democrats control in 2000. In any case, the 1990s notwithstanding, it is clear that turnout does not consistently aid the Democrats.

Turnout Usually Will Not Matter

Turnout seems very nonpartisan. It is hard to maintain the turnout bias argument in the face of the data we have examined. It seems clear that turnout does not always aid Democratic congressional candidates, just as it appears unrelated to the vote for Democratic presidential candidates. The relationship is negative overall for congressional elections over the last three decades, with turnout, on average, boosting the GOP congressional vote during the 1972–1980 and 1982–1990 periods, and slightly helping the Democrats during the 1990s.

The evidence against a turnout bias is also consistent. At the level of survey data there is no indication that the preferences of nonvoters would have reversed many—or any—elections for which we have reliable evidence. Most of the data indicate that nonvoters, had they gone to the polls, would have reinforced the decision of the voters. To the extent that there is a consistent difference, nonvoters seem likely to exaggerate the choices of the active electorate by virtue of their greater responsiveness to short-term forces. Election returns—whether looked at longitudinally by election district, in the aggregate, or as a pooled cross-sectional time series—do not show a turnout bias. We have no reason to believe that what we observed in presidential and congressional elections would not also be found in senatorial, gubernatorial, and state legislative elections. We are confident that turnout variation—in the range within which it normally varies in the United States—does not affect the Democratic vote as popular wisdom presents it.

Chapter Eight

Campaign Effects in the Twenty-First Century

From every corner of the media empire, the explanations came fast and furiously: The Democrats were clueless on moral values. John Kerry was a lousy candidate. A northerner can't win any more. The Bush team was better at manipulating the press. No one trusts the Democrats on national security. The gay marriage issue badly hurt the party. The Democrats need to move right, or left, or south, or undergo a personality transplant, or change the Constitution so Bill Clinton can run again.

—Howard Kurtz, *Washington Post*, November 8, 2004

BY EMPHASIZING THE STABLE PSYCHOLOGICAL PREDISPOSITIONS OF voters, rather than the strategic maneuvers of candidates, we appear to question seriously the idea that campaigns determine presidential election results in the United States. However, we think that campaigns do matter, even though many voters behave predictably. Past behavior and models that predict presidential elections, ignoring a campaign, can and do get it wrong (as most predictions of the 2000 election did). We believe that these models are useful because they help to explain—to the candidates, pundits, and voters—the context in which an election will be contested. They tell us what to expect in the absence of a presidential campaign. They are the starting points for campaigns and for the analysis of the campaign's effect.

The balance that we suggest contrasts sharply with some common views of presidential campaigns, which are frequently characterized by three myths. First, the conventional view, especially in news reports during the election season, is that the winner of the election is, by definition, the one who campaigned or is campaigning better. This perspective is acknowledged and lampooned by Howard Kurtz's quotation above—and we share his skepticism. We do not think that pundits and journalists completely discount the importance of context when assessing presidential elections; rather, we think they tend to focus disproportionately on the news of the day and often ignore the bigger picture for a host of professional reasons.

Second, practitioners and the news media present voters as easily manipulated by subtle shifts in campaign strategy. For example, postmortem accounts of the 2000 presidential campaign focused considerable attention on the Gore campaign's strategy to pound Bush on social security late in that election season, and many argued that Gore's resurgence in the polls was driven by this canny maneuver. Perhaps even more memorably, in 1988 voters were supposedly turned against Michael Dukakis by the Republican advertisements that primed racial stereotypes and fears concerning crime.

Third, pundits and the media clearly believe that the kinds of campaign phenomena that affect voters are many and various. In 2004, we were treated to fascinating ruminations on influential films (*Fahrenheit 9/11* and *The Manchurian Candidate*), the videotape released by Osama bin Laden, Bill Clinton's autobiography, the takeover of a Russian school by Chechnyan rebels, and the candidates' physical appearances (Kerry's supposed use of Botox and tanning gel). According to the news media, each of these events swung voter preferences back and forth between candidates.

From our perspective, these myths are caricatures. Rather, we maintain that presidential campaigns are important to elections because they (1) produce small but important persuasive effects, (2) help to activate partisan preferences, and (3) mobilize voters to the polls. Even so, we readily acknowledge that campaigns influence one voter at a time, their effects cumulate day by day, and they typically move only a small percentage of the total vote. This chapter considers our long-standing fascination with presidential campaigns and details what we think we know about their impact on voters and elections. We offer original analyses by examining across-time data on voter attitudes toward the campaign; campaign contacting and resource allocation; and participation and preference dynamics. The argument throughout is that presidential campaigns matter because they alert voters to issues and conditions while simultaneously providing information about the candidates.

Renewed Scholarly Interest in Campaign Effects

The news media focus an enormous amount of time and attention on presidential election campaigns. Moreover, the principal developments in communications technology since 1990—the rise of the 24/7 cable news networks and the Internet—have only served to heighten the preoccupation of reporters, officials, and partisans with what Republican media consultant Stuart Stevens so eloquently referred to as "the big enchilada." Beyond serving as the most visible instrument by which Americans select the occupant of the most powerful office in the world, presidential campaigns offer strategy, drama, intrigue, and occasionally comedy. Political and news media elites treat them as if the fate of the world hangs on their every twist and turn.

But the prevailing view of public opinion in general, and citizen knowledge and interest in particular, suggests that few will hear and even fewer will *listen* to the messages and issue appeals of the campaign. Indeed, until recently, the preponderance of evidence was that there was little empirical reason to cling to the belief that campaigns have a strong, independent impact on American elections. We believe that the most current research somewhat undermines the classic academic wisdom and actually provides considerable support for the popular conception that campaigns are influential. This is not to say that we believe campaigns have powerful and persuasive effects on mass electorates. Rather, we believe campaigns reach wide audiences and are important conduits of information that activates many partisans, persuades some party identifiers, and shapes the candidate preferences of independents.

The preponderance of evidence from contemporary studies of campaigns and voting is critical to our argument. There is neither a single event nor a unique date that one could pinpoint as signaling the beginning of the new era of campaign studies. By 1990, however, it is clear that objective, professional developments were pushing academics to refocus their energies on campaign effects. The reasons for this interest are twofold. First, political scientists began to argue that the psychological processes used by voters to deal with campaign information provided by candidates and the news media are not as simple as listening and retention.[1] This means that just looking at gross measures of campaign "input" and subsequent voting "outputs" can be seriously misleading. More subtle campaign effects, such as what voters think is important and the criteria they rely on for evaluations, are now what we study. More broadly, we also suspect that voters use campaign information to reach reasonable decisions even if they fail to remember or even know the specifics of policy proposals or candidate records.[2]

Second, the interest of political scientists in the campaign effects debate was piqued by the greater availability of data in the 1990s. More and better data have, in turn, led to more precise and compelling estimates of campaign effects on voters. This may sound like an "insider's" complaint, but the issue of data is critical. Since the advent of mass campaigns in the 1820s, empirical studies have been hampered because campaigns do not keep thorough records, jealously guard their secrets for success if they win, disappear from the face of the earth if they lose, and always have an interest in shading their versions of what happened to protect themselves.[3] Although these tendencies still exist, campaigns have been forced by federal election law to keep records since 1974. Moreover, they have been more willing systematically to transcribe and share resource allocation information since 1988. Scholars, on the other hand, not only have become interested in these data but have been more aggressive in approaching campaigns and securing data-sharing agreements.

On the formal end of the spectrum, there are campaign resource clearinghouses such as the Federal Election Commission (FEC) and the Campaign Media Analysis Group (CMAG), which compile and code expenditure information for all federal (and some state) elections. There are similar entities that compile public opinion and polling information, such as the Roper Center, the Inter-university Consortium for Political and Social Research (ICPSR), and Web sites such as pollingreport.com. Although Roper and ICPSR are by no means new, they have expanded their holdings considerably over the past two decades and made them available to a wider academic community. There are also the presidential libraries, especially the Eisenhower, Kennedy, Johnson, Nixon, Carter, Reagan, Bush, and Clinton libraries, which offer internal documents, memos, and even polls from past presidential campaigns. On the informal end of the spectrum, campaigns and individual scholars have struck agreements that have allowed for the academic use of campaign data after election day.[4] Political pollsters have also used their campaign data to write more formal analyses of broad electoral phenomena.[5]

Contemporary Campaign Effects Research

A great deal of recent research attempts to answer the question of whether campaigns matter, but nowhere to our knowledge have these studies been synthesized and used to construct a "political science" conventional wisdom on campaigns. In what follows, we briefly review studies of overall campaign effects and then offer an extensive and detailed look at the impact of specific candidate and campaign activities. A summary of the results is presented in Table 8.1. The upshot is that electioneering tends to mobilize rather than persuade and typically produces small but discernible effects.

TABLE 8.1. Estimates of Campaign Effects

Aggregate Effects

Berelson et al. (1954)	Presidential	+5%–8% change in margin.
Markus (1988)	Presidential	+2% change in margin.
Finkel (1993)	Presidential	+2% change in margin.
Bartels (1993b)	Presidential	+0%–2% change in margin.
Campbell (2000)	Presidential	+2% change in margin.
Holbrook (1996)	Presidential	+10% change in margin.

Presidential Forecast Models

Campbell (2004)	Presidential	+/−2% average deviation from prediction.
Abramowitz (2004)	Presidential	+/−2% average deviation from prediction.

(*continued*)

TABLE 8.1. *(continued)*

Norpoth (2004)	Presidential	+/−4% average deviation from prediction.
Wlezien and Erikson (2004)	Presidential	+/−2% average deviation from prediction.
Lewis-Beck and Tien (2004)	Presidential	+/−3% average deviation from prediction.
Holbrook (2004)	Presidential	+/−6% average deviation from prediction.
Lockerbie (2004)	Presidential	+/−6% average deviation from prediction.

Television Advertising

Gerber (1998)	Senate	Incumbent spending advantage increases support by 6%.
Shaw (1999b, 2006)	Presidential	+1%−+3 change in margin.
Goldstein and Freedman (2002a, 2002b)	Presidential	Significant change in turnout.

Negative v. Positive TV Ads

Ansolabehere and Iyengar (1995)	Governor/ Senate/ Mayoral/ Presidential	+3% increase in turnout after seeing advocacy ad. −3% decrease in turnout after seeing negative ad.
Lau et al. (1999)	Meta-	
Finkel and Geer (1998)	Presidential	No effect on turnout.
Lau and Pomper (2004)	Senate	No effect on turnout.
Freedman and Goldstein (1999)	Presidential	Negative ads stimulate turnout.
Wattenberg and Brians (1999)		Negative ads stimulate turnout.
Clinton and Lapinski (2004)	Presidential	Negative ads stimulate turnout.
Geer and Lau (2006)	Presidential	Negative ads stimulate short-term turnout. Negative ads stimulate turnout.

TABLE 8.1.   *(continued)*

Radio Advertising

Overby and Barth (2003)	Statewide	Significant effect on political information.
Geer and Geer (2003)		Attack ads are more memorable than advocacy ads.
Panagopoulos and Green (2006)	Mayoral	+1%–+6% increase in turnout per 90 GRPs.
McCleneghan (1987)	Mayoral	+10% change in margin. Significant effect on margin.

Direct Mail

Miller, Bositis, and Baer (1981)	Primary	+19% increase in turnout.
Gerber and Green (APSR, 2000)	City council	+1% increase in turnout.

Telephone Calls

Adams and Smith (1980)	City council	+9% increase in turnout.
Miller, Bositis, and Baer (1981)	Primary	+15% increase in turnout.
Gerber and Green (APSR, 2000)	City council	−5% decrease in turnout.

Door-to-Door Contacting

Miller, Bositis, and Baer (1981)	Primary	+21% increase in turnout.
Gerber and Green (APSR, 2000)	City council	+9% increase in turnout.

Debates

Holbrook (1996)	Presidential	+3% change in margin.
Shaw (1999)	Presidential	+2% change in margin.
Hillygus and Jackman (2001)	Presidential	+1% change in margin.
Johnston, Jamieson, and Hagen (2004)	Presidential	+2% change in margin.

Nominating Conventions

Campbell (2000)	Presidential	+7% change in margin.
Holbrook (1996)	Presidential	+4% change in margin.

(continued)

TABLE 8.1. *(continued)*

Shaw (1999)	Presidential	+7% change in margin.
Hillygus and Jackman (2001)	Presidential	+8% change in margin.
Johnston, Hagen, and Jamieson (2004)	Presidential	+7% change in margin.

Candidate Appearances

Shaw (1999, 2007)	Presidential	+0 – +2 change in margin.
Holbrook and McClurg (2005)	Presidential	Conditional effects on partisan composition.
Holbrook (2002)	Presidential	Significant change in margin.

Note: Campbell (2004), Abramowitz (2004), Norpoth (2004), Wlezien and Erikson (2004), Lewis-Beck and Tien (2004), Holbrook (2004), and Lockerbie (2004) are all found in PS: Political Science and Politics, *October 2004.*

Estimations of Overall Campaign Effects

Since the 1990s, the preponderance of campaign analyses has produced conservative estimates of overall effects. In fact, much of the recent research has concentrated on a narrower but still important question: the relative effects of "activation" (getting partisans to back their party's candidate) and "persuasion" (convincing independent voters to support a particular candidate).[6] The bulk of this research uses survey data—either from the ANES or from exit polls—to argue that while persuasion is minimal in presidential elections, the efforts of parties and candidates are nonetheless critical to activating partisan predispositions.[7] A few very recent studies, however, based on massive numbers of survey respondents, such as the Annenberg "rolling cross section" and the Knowledge Networks "web-enabled panel study" (in which the same individuals are interviewed multiple times over the election year) have been more successful at detecting the persuasive effects of campaigns.[8]

Some studies look at shifts in the presidential vote during the campaign by aggregating results from all publicly available national polls.[9] By and large, these analyses show that there is significant volatility in preelection survey estimations of the vote but that the vote tends to converge on a predictable point on or around election day. Presidential campaign "effects" are thus predictable.

In addition to studies of preference shifts, some have suggested that presidential election campaign effects can be understood as the difference between political science presidential election forecasting models and the actual vote.[10] Using seven prominent presidential forecasting models, we calculate that the mean error of these forecasts between 1992 and 2004 is between 1.5 and 5.6 points.[11] The predictive accuracy of these models can, of course, be seen as additional validation of the activation perspective.

Estimations of Specific Campaign Effects

Analyses of specific types of campaign activities have further sharpened our understanding of *how*—and how much—campaigns influence voters. This trend toward disaggregating the specific manifestations of presidential campaigning has been matched by a tendency toward more innovative data and research designs. Consider the following aspects of electioneering that have received substantive empirical treatment over the past ten years.

Get-Out-the-Vote and Other Mobilization Activities

Political scientists often champion the need for parties and groups to contact voters and encourage them to vote. Not only do we typically find that these sorts of activities have an effect, but some have even argued that decreased turnout from the 1960s through the 1980s coincided with a reduction in GOTV and mobilization activities by a variety of interest groups.[12] How much turnout decline and what might have caused any decline is a common subject for debate,[13] but there is good evidence that GOTV work by parties, candidates, and interested groups increases turnout. Political scientists and the national parties have independently conducted "field experiments" in which voters are randomly assigned to "treatment" groups, which get some sort of campaign contacting, or "control" groups, which receive no contacting. Most show that door-to-door contacting significantly increases the likelihood that someone will cast a ballot (see Table 8.1). Direct mail can also increase turnout, though not as substantially as an in-person visit. Personalized, high-quality phone calls can also mobilize partisans, but automated phone calls ("robo-calls") are completely ineffective. Results across a wide range of experimental conditions and settings indicate that the quality of contacting is the most important factor affecting the impact on turn-out—quality trumps the type of contact and even the message.[14]

Persuasive Phones, Direct Mail, and E-mail

Once again, the most notable works on the partisan vote effects of campaign contacting have been the field experiments, especially those conducted by Alan Gerber and Donald Green.[15] During the 1998 elections in Oregon, Gerber and Green randomly selected voters from statewide voter lists, assigning them to control and treatment groups. The treatment groups received either (1) campaign mail from a candidate but no phone calls, (2) campaign phone calls but no direct mail, or (3) direct mail and phone calls. The control group received no campaign contacts. The authors took pains to ensure that their mail and phone calls were as realistic as possible, using genuine campaign consultants to design the materials. Controlling for a host of factors, Gerber and Green found that direct mail increased the candidate's vote share 10 percent beyond what would otherwise be expected but that phone calls actually had a negative impact on aggregate vote share. They also tested the effects of face-to-face contacting, which they found had a highly significant and positive impact on vote share.

Television Advertising

The renewed interest in campaign effects has been most evident in television advertising. Initially, studies found that televised political ads elicited minimal effects; but a number of these also pointed out that campaigns do not expect these ads to persuade a large percentage of voters.[16] Still, even these narrow, targeted effects were difficult to uncover through traditional, observational approaches. In the late 1980s and early 1990s, however, experimental studies confronted the minimal effects thesis by demonstrating that campaign ads significantly correlate with changes in candidate appraisals as well as expressions of interest in turning out to vote.[17]

The controversial experimental findings prompted a slew of challenges. Several, for example, took issue with the particular finding that negative advertising decreases turnout; in fact, these studies maintain that negative campaigns actually tend to be coincident with relatively higher turnout.[18] Most definitively, though, a comprehensive examination of all available evidence from U.S. Senate campaigns makes a strong case that negative ads neither mobilize nor demobilize.[19]

Candidate Appearances

Several studies have updated the classic work on the effects of candidate appearances on the preferences of local voters.[20] Collectively, these studies have found minimal effects, but the patterns uncovered and some of the attendant analyses are worth noting. For example, a study of the pattern and impact of Jimmy Carter's travel in the 1976 election argues that although the impact on the vote is not substantial, this is understandable because appearances are motivated by multiple factors, some of which are unconcerned with improving the candidate's trial ballot standing.[21] A similar study concentrates on the pattern and effect of presidential candidate appearances from 1988 to 1996 and estimates that three extra visits to a state are worth approximately one point in the polls.[22] That study also finds that major party candidates' travel patterns are heavily influenced by one another, making it difficult to visit a locale without the other side "retaliating."[23]

There is also a handful of empirical analyses of the effects of candidate appearances in the presidential primaries. These tend to find that personal contact with the candidate can do more than mobilize; it can actually persuade people to support a candidate. One study argued that New Hampshire primary voters who had met a particular candidate were significantly more likely to support the candidate, even after controlling for the fact that one is more likely to meet a candidate for whom one is predisposed to vote.[24]

Campaign Events

Several political science projects demonstrate that conventions are the proverbial 800-pound gorillas of campaign events.[25] Many of these same projects also find that presidential debates stand out.[26] So while debates may only be 400-pound gorillas, both debates and conventions clearly influence voters' preferences.

The impact of other events is less obvious. The consensus appears to be that campaign event effects—beyond conventions and debates—are inconsistent and contextually dependent.[7] Four smaller (but nonetheless important) arguments can be gleaned from the recent literature. First, gaffes or mistakes do tend to decrease support for a candidate.[27] Second, scandals do not consistently decrease support for a candidate.[28] Third, the articulation of campaign messages (or policy initiatives) tends to be uncorrelated with shifts in support for a candidate.[29] Fourth and finally, the influence of campaign events on voters' preferences can be evanescent. Some campaign event effects persist, some event effects are durable over a week or so, and some effects even grow over time.

News Media Effects

Numerous studies show that media exposure, while not influencing candidate preferences per se, influences a range of other political attitudes and impressions[30] that might in turn shape candidate preference.[31] Collectively, these analyses suggest that we should not be obsessed with vote choice when considering campaign effects and that news media coverage matters because it affects impressions of candidates and issues that, in turn, influence vote choice. More fundamentally, though, a plethora of recent studies has failed to find that the mainstream news media's election campaign coverage has an ideological slant. Perhaps the most impressive study canvasses dozens of analyses and concludes that there is no consistent demonstration of partisan bias in news coverage.[32] Instead, coverage tends to favor winners and punish losers.[33]

This is not to say, however, that bias *never* exists. Most notably, several studies of the 1992 presidential election show a significant anti-Bush tone to coverage.[34] More specifically, they show that economic coverage was far more negative than the objective condition of the economy and that this was the primary frame used to portray Bush and his administration.[35] It is also the case that Bush received unfavorable coverage even when he was ahead in the polls (up until late June of 1992), so it is difficult to blame the horse race for the tone of media coverage. Clinton, on the other side of the ledger, received positive coverage but only after he took the lead in the presidential preference polls just before the Democratic Convention.

Nineteen ninety-two appears to have been an aberrant case, though. No partisan slant was discernible in 1996, at least not after controlling for Clinton's large and persistent advantage over Dole in the horse race. Furthermore, internal studies of broadcast and print media conducted by the Bush campaigns indicate that coverage of the 2000 and 2004 races were mixed, essentially following the polls. All of these suggest news media coverage is influenced by professional biases,[36] and these tend to produce favorable coverage for front-runners and unfavorable coverage for underdogs. These biases, however, have not been connected to support shifts among voters.

Candidate and Campaign Approaches

In addition to these advances in the study of specific manifestations of the presidential campaign, there have been changes in the way we view both candidates and voters and how they interact. These new conceptualizations, in turn, have affected our view of what campaigns are about.

One intriguing conceptual possibility advanced in the past decade's studies of presidential elections is that candidates selectively (but predictably) emphasize certain issues.[37] This concept posits that candidates use election campaigns to convince voters that their issues are more important than the opposition's issues. Campaigns do not compete for the median voter along some summary left-right issue dimension; rather, they fight to set the agenda, knowing that Democratic and Republican candidates have different credibilities on different issues. Democrats, for instance, want to make elections about health care and the environment while Republicans want to make them about taxes and defense. This comports with common sense, but it is quite different from the way political scientists have traditionally conceived of electoral competition and (consequently) campaigns.

A related perspective suggests that presidential campaigns are about candidates' traits and voters' emotions. That is, campaigns are trying to develop a brand identity for their candidate. Campaigns do this by emphasizing some simple set of traits—strong leadership, empathy, or knowledge and experience—in paid advertising and speeches. An effective campaign convinces voters that its candidate possesses some desirable traits and thereby establishes an emotional bond.[38] This perspective sees the success of candidates such as Ronald Reagan, Bill Clinton, and George W. Bush as a function of their "likeability."

Voters and Campaigns: Attitudes and Behavior, 1952–2004

With a few notable exceptions,[39] the literature on campaigns ignores the availability of survey data measuring attitudes toward—and exposure to—presidential campaigns. We believe these data give us an important perspective on campaign influence.

The ANES data in Table 8.2 show whether people follow or participate in the presidential campaign. For simplicity's sake, and because the

TABLE 8.2. Does Anyone Follow the Campaign?

	1972	1976	1980	1984	1988	1992	1996	2000	2004
Care who wins the presidential election									
Care a good deal	60%	57%	56%	65%	61%	75%	78%	76%	85%
Don't care	40	43	44	35	39	25	22	24	15
How close will presidential race be									
Close race	32%	69%	70%	48%	70%	79%	53%	85%	81%
Will win by quite a bit	56	14	14	46	25	17	46	14	18
How often are you interested in politics									
Most of the time	36%	38%	26%	26%	22%	26%	27%	20%	26%
Some of the time	36	31	35	36	37	41	37	36	41
Only now and then	16	18	23	23	25	21	25	29	23
Hardly at all	11	12	15	14	15	11	13	16	10
Monitoring the campaign									
Watched on TV	88%	89%	86%	86%	—	89%	74%	82%	86%
Listened to radio	43%	45%	47%	45%	31%	37%	38%	38%	51%

Read newspapers	57%	73%	71%	77%	64%	65%	55%	56%	67%
Read magazine articles	33%	48%	35%	35%	25%	23%	32%	—	28%
Campaign participation									
Tried to influence how others vote	32%	37%	36%	32%	29%	37%	28%	34%	48%
Attended a political meeting	9%	6%	8%	8%	7%	8%	5%	5%	7%
Worked for a candidate or party	5%	4%	4%	4%	3%	3%	2%	3%	3%
Wore a button or put a bumper sticker on a car	14%	8%	7%	9%	9%	11%	10%	10%	21%
Contributed money to a candidate or campaign	10%	16%	8%	8%	9%	7%	8%	9%	13%
Cases	2,699	2,857	1,567	2,251	2,036	2,478	1,714	1,807	1,212

Source: 1972–2004 ANES.

questions that animate the time series stabilize beginning in 1972, we focus on the time period between 1972 and 2004. Initially, we find that the vast majority of Americans claim to care about who wins the White House. The percentage of Americans saying that they "care who wins" the election is not only high (68 percent, on average) but has been rising (85 percent in 2004, and 78 percent over the last four presidential elections). In fact, there is an 18-percentage-point increase in the proportion of people who say they care a good deal about the election from the 1970s and 1980s to the 1990s and 2000s.

Do competitive presidential elections increase interest in the campaign (and perhaps boost its effects)? In the 2000 election, we see high percentages of people who cared about the outcome and correctly judged the race to be close, but the percentage saying they cared was actually higher in 1996 even though far fewer people saw that race as competitive. In 1980, 70 percent saw a close race but only 56 percent cared about the election.

Overall attentiveness to presidential campaigns is quite high, with a striking increase in 2004. Across the thirty-two years of the time series, Table 8.2 shows that, on average, 85 percent of respondents say that they follow the campaign on television, 65 percent say they follow it in the newspapers, 41 percent on radio, and 29 percent in the news magazines. These numbers suggest the American presidential campaigns do not fall on deaf ears.

But what about more active forms of campaign engagement? Predictably, more demanding campaign activities see significantly lower rates of participation. The percentage of Americans who reported attending a political meeting or working for a candidate or party never reached double digits between 1972 and 2004. Similarly, the percentage wearing a button or displaying a bumper sticker rises above 14 percent only in 2004 (21 percent). Levels of participation rise significantly, however, when it comes to talking about the campaign: on average, 33 percent of Americans report trying to influence how someone else voted in the election. In 2004, 48 percent reported such an effort. Again, it is interesting to note the increase in many forms of political activity between the 2000 and 2004 races (attempting to influence others, wearing a button, and contributing money trend upward). Whatever the potential deleterious consequences of alleged polarization in recent elections (see Chapter 3), one possible salutary effect is increased political participation.

If we know that citizens profess to be interested in campaigns and that political activity levels are up, can we also say that Americans are responsive to the modern campaign where it counts most, at the ballot box? Across the ANES time series, there appears to be significant variation in how committed voters are to major party candidates over an election year. Forty-six percent of the voters in the 2000 election stated that they decided on their candidate after the conventions (Table 8.3). Similarly, in 1992, 47 percent decided during the fall. In contrast, only three of ten voters were undecided by the end of the conventions in 2004. The percentage of voters who stated that they "knew all along" who they would vote for appears to coincide with blowout elections (1972, 1984, and 1996) *except for 2004*. In this way, 2004 looks like a typical successful reelection bid—as opposed to losing efforts in 1980 and

TABLE 8.3.   Voter Preference Dynamics

	1972	1976	1980	1984	1988	1992	1996	2000	2004
Timing of Decision									
Knew all along	33%	20%	20%	30%	15%	19%	28%	12%	33%
When candidate announced	11	14	20	22	17	21	23	32	22
During conventions	18	21	18	18	29	14	13	10	14
Post-convention	15	22	15	17	22	22	17	23	15
Last 2 weeks of campaign	17	17	17	10	12	17	12	18	13
Election day	9	7	9	4	5	8	7	5	2
Undecided									
Voting, but no candidate preference	6%	2%	13%	6%	7%	13%	8%	7%	5%
Cases	2,699	2,857	1,567	2,251	2,036	2,478	1,714	1,807	1,212

Source: 1972–2004 ANES.

1992—except for the margin. But while the range in reported decision timing here is significant, even a relatively certain electorate seems open to a campaign.

The percentage of voters claiming to be undecided in September and October ANES interviews also backs the claim that voters are open to presidential campaigning. The high percentage (13 percent) occurs in 1992 and 1980—which coincides with the independent challenges of Ross Perot and John Anderson, respectively—while the low (2 percent) occurs in 1976—which provided a standard two-party contest. Once again, voters seem to have been less open in 2004, as only 5 percent said they were undecided, a result that is consistent with the polarization and candidate attitude findings in Chapter 3. The main point, however, is that a high percentage of Americans say they are interested in and actively following the presidential race while a small but significant percentage have not committed to a candidate as the fall campaign unfolds.

As suggested above, aggregate preference volatility differed greatly in the 2000 and 2004 presidential elections. Some of the ebbs and flows presented in Figures 8.1 and 8.2 also appear to correspond to prominent events in the campaign, such as the announcement of vice-presidential nominees, national conventions, and candidate debates. In 2000, Republican candidate George W. Bush held a double-digit lead over Democrat Al Gore heading into the Democratic National Convention. Within a week, Gore erased Bush's lead and held a 5-point advantage of his own. Bush then surged ahead during the debate period of early October but saw Gore catch up and pass him again the day before the election. Conversely, in 2004 the race hardly moved from mid-March until election day. Bush held a small lead until the Democratic National Convention, when Kerry's announcement that North Carolina senator John Edwards would be his running mate and the nomination festivities propelled him to an equally small lead in the polls. Bush regained the lead in polls conducted after the GOP convention. The race narrowed again with the October debates.

Taken together, the 2000 and 2004 presidential election polling data suggest that campaigns might have influenced people. In 2000, voter preferences flipped. In 2004, we cannot rule out this possibility even though it is not apparent in aggregate preference shifts. But the case for campaign effects would be bolstered if we could establish that the campaigns are, in fact, pervasive and that not everyone receives equal input from both sides. The next section tackles this task.

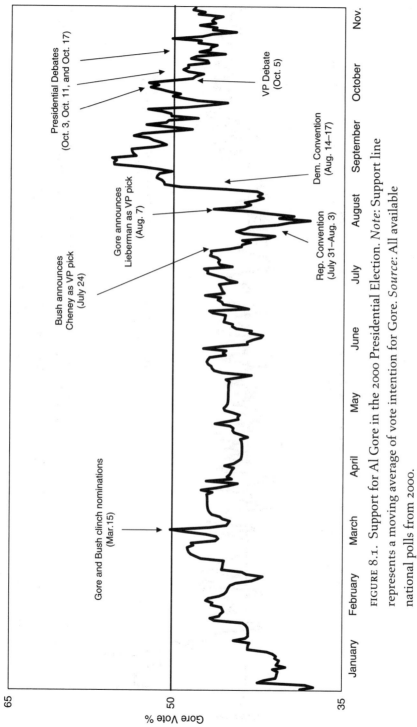

FIGURE 8.1. Support for Al Gore in the 2000 Presidential Election. *Note*: Support line represents a moving average of vote intention for Gore. *Source*: All available national polls from 2000.

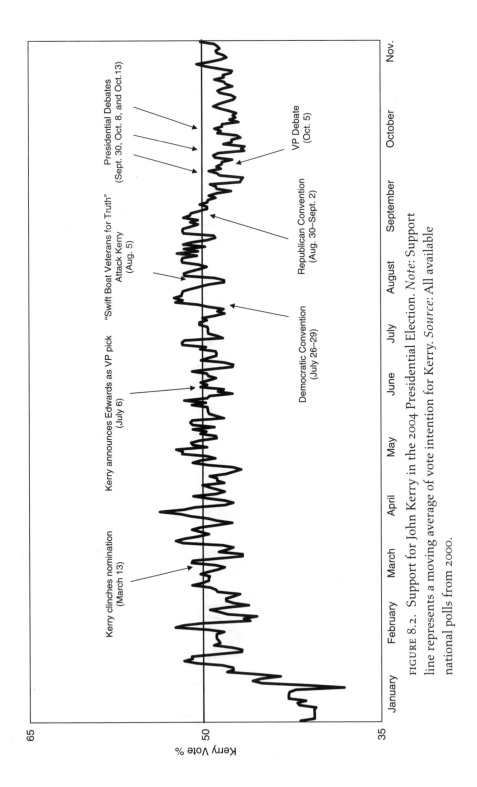

FIGURE 8.2. Support for John Kerry in the 2004 Presidential Election. *Note:* Support line represents a moving average of vote intention for Kerry. *Source:* All available national polls from 2000.

Kerry Vote %

65

50

35

January February March April May June July August September October Nov.

Kerry clinches nomination
(March 13)

Kerry announces Edwards as VP pick
(July 6)

"Swift Boat Veterans for Truth"
Attack Kerry
(Aug. 5)

Democratic Convention
(July 26–29)

Republican Convention
(Aug. 30–Sept. 2)

Presidential Debates
(Sept. 30, Oct. 8, and Oct.13)

VP Debate
(Oct. 5)

Campaign Activity in 2000 and 2004

While Americans *say* they follow the campaign, we have thus far presented no evidence proving that they are actually exposed to partisan electioneering. Table 8.4 considers campaign effects by gauging whether people recall being contacted by the campaigns. Put another way, if people participate at higher levels in a given election, can we link this to more energetic party outreach efforts? The data offer strong support for this common story line. There is, for instance, some evidence that registration contacting increased in 2000 (there was no comparable question in 2004). More impressively, the percentage of Americans who report being contacted by one or both sides rose in 2004. In fact, the percentage reporting a contact rose not only compared to 2000 (up from 37 percent to 44 percent) but also compared to the series average (29 percent).[40] These findings speak to significant rates of contacting—direct mail, phone calls, and face-to-face contacts—and a connection between such contacting and participation. This outreach by campaigns to voters was not random. Partisans were significantly more likely to be targeted than independents. Moreover, if one examines the data from 1988 to 2004, contacting and turnout rates were slightly higher in battleground states than in non-battleground states, allowing us to entertain the notion that phone, mail, and door-to-door campaigning works.[41]

But what about the most visible forms of campaigning: television advertising and candidate appearances? Are candidates and parties working hard to reach voters with TV ads and visits from the campaign and its surrogates? Are these resources allocated strategically such that some voters are much more likely to receive this campaign information? And, more narrowly, is there any partisan advantage to this outreach or do the campaigns mimic each other's resource allocations such that targeted voters get equal doses from both sides?

The first and most obvious point to make is that the volume of campaign ads in contemporary American elections is significant. Initial estimates were that close to $2 billion worth of political ads were purchased for the 2006 midterm elections (FEC Web site). In the presidential general election campaigns of 2000 and 2004, slightly less money was spent, but the average voter got a large dose of thirty-second spots. But the second point that must be made is that these numbers conceal enormous variation in TV ad exposure. Voters in a battleground state saw (on average) over one hundred political ads in each of these elections.[42]

TABLE 8.4. Campaign Contacting

	1972	1976	1980	1984	1988	1992	1996	2000	2004
Campaign Mobilization (overall)									
Contacted by either major party	29%	29%	24%	24%	24%	20%	28%	37%	44%
By Republicans	15%	16%	14%	13%	13%	11%	19%	26%	28%
By Democrats	20%	19%	14%	15%	14%	14%	15%	23%	31%
Contacted by other	—	—	10%	8%	8%	10%	11%	11%	18%
Turnout	73%	71%	71%	74%	70%	75%	77%	76%	78%
Campaign Mobilization (Battleground States)									
Contacted by either major party	26%	26%	26%	29%	29%	20%	28%	43%	60%
By Republicans	14%	15%	16%	17%	16%	12%	20%	33%	46%
By Democrats	19%	16%	14%	17%	18%	13%	16%	27%	42%
Contacted by other	—	—	9%	9%	10%	10%	12%	12%	22%
Turnout	72%	74%	68%	77%	73%	74%	75%	77%	82%
Cases	2,699	2,857	1,567	2,251	2,036	2,478	1,714	1,807	1,212

Note: Battleground states are classified according to Shaw (2006) for 1988–2004. For 1972–1984, we rely on newspaper accounts, candidate and consultant biographies, and preelection polls. Source: 1972–2004 ANES.

Figures 8.3A and 8.3B show this variation by reporting gross ratings points (GRPs or points) of television advertising by designated market areas (DMAs or media markets) for the 2000 and 2004 presidential election campaigns.[43]

Even a cursory glance at the data makes clear that presidential campaigns target battleground states and voters while virtually ignoring those in safe states. Therefore, as with phone, mail, and door-to-door activities, TV ads and candidate appearances are not equitably allocated across voters. We do not have a lot of evidence for what consequences this variation might have on the electorate. For the campaigns, it is a sensible way to spend money. It may, however, have consequences for voters that are less optimal. We know, for example, that campaign activity raises interest and turnout. If areas deemed less competitive by the campaigns receive less attention, this negligence may create a self-fulfilling prophecy. It may diminish participation and have other negative consequences for representation. A recent analysis showed that the absence of a vigorous campaign in the safe states may be especially consequential for the poor, further depressing their turnout rates and attention from campaigns.[44]

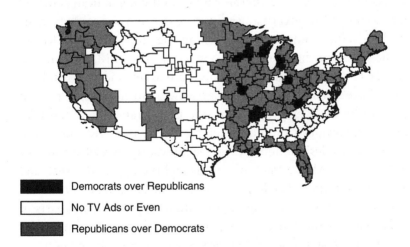

FIGURE 8.3A. 2000 Presidential Television Advertising Differentials. *Note:* Calculations are based on total Republican minus total Democratic Gross Rating Points (August 24, 2000, to November 7, 2000). *Source:* Shaw (2006).

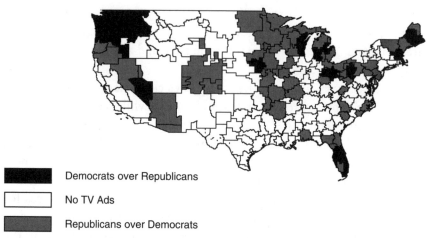

Democrats over Republicans

No TV Ads

Republicans over Democrats

FIGURE 8.3B. 2004 Presidential Television Advertising Differentials. *Note*: Calculations are based on total Republican minus total Democratic Gross Rating Points (September 4, 2004, to November 1, 2004). *Source*: Shaw (2006).

Also, it is worth emphasizing that these differentials tend to persist across elections because the factors that cause campaigns to make allocation decisions are long term and stable, although striking differences do occur. In 2000, the Bush campaign and the Republican National Committee enjoyed an advertising advantage in a number of media markets. In Florida, for example, the Republican edge topped 1,000 GRPs in each of the state's media markets. This was also true in Maine. Only in a few Great Lakes, Arkansas and Tennessee markets did Gore and the Democrats have an edge. In 2004, the spread was much closer. Television ad purchases by the Kerry campaign, the Democratic Party, and left-leaning interest groups (commonly referred to by their IRS nonprofit, tax-exempt status designation, "527s") significantly exceeded those of the Republicans in Maine, parts of Florida and the upper Midwest, and the state of Washington. The Republicans held an advantage in Arizona, Colorado, most of the markets along the Mississippi River, and parts of Florida. Perhaps the most interesting point is that despite the similarities in statewide GRPs, significant differences existed market by market.

The story of market-by-market volume and variation is much the same with respect to personal appearances by the presidential and vice-presidential candidates. Voters in a battleground market could expect to see at least one candidate in their locale every week. Figures 8.4A and 8.4B show candidate appearance differentials for the 2000 and

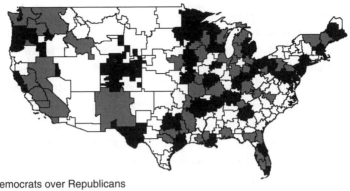

Democrats over Republicans

No Appearances or Even

Republicans over Democrats

FIGURE 8.4A. 2000 Presidential Candidate Appearance Differentials. *Note*: Calculations are based on number of Bush/Cheney appearances minus the number of Gore/Lieberman appearances from August 24, 2000, to November 7, 2000. *Source*: Shaw (2006).

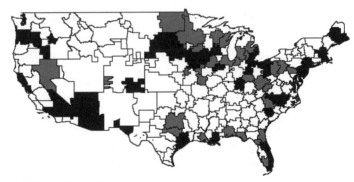

Democrats over Republicans

No Appearances or Even

Republicans over Democrats

FIGURE 8.4B. 2004 Presidential Candidate Appearance Differentials. *Note*: Calculations are based on number of Bush/Cheney appearances minus the number of Kerry/Edwards appearances from September 3, 2004, to November 1, 2004. *Source*: Shaw (2006).

2004 presidential election campaigns.[45] As expected, the total number of Republican and Democratic candidate appearances were often equal across media markets. Still, discrepancies exist. In 2000, George W. Bush and Dick Cheney had the edge in the Pacific coast states and in parts of Michigan and Pennsylvania, while Al Gore and Joe Lieberman had the edge in Wisconsin, Iowa, Minnesota, and parts of Florida. Part of the Gore-Lieberman edge in eastern Iowa and western Wisconsin reflects the postconvention riverboat trip that allowed them to hold events on the Mississippi River. Postelection analyses show significant increases in Democratic turnout in precisely these counties—a testimony to voter responsiveness to campaigns.[46]

In 2004, John Kerry and John Edwards held an advantage in the Pacific coast states, the Atlantic coast of Florida, and in parts of Iowa and Wisconsin while Bush and Cheney held the advantage in parts of Michigan and Pennsylvania as well as in the Florida Panhandle. Once again, the partisan edge in visits to northern Florida coincided with significant increases in Republican turnout in precisely these counties.

None of this, of course, constitutes a causal analysis of campaign effects. It does, however, strongly suggest that American campaigns (1) are pervasive, (2) are disproportionately concentrated in battleground media markets, and (3) do not necessarily cancel each other out. Put another way, certain voters are bombarded with TV ads, candidate appearances, mail, phone calls, and door-to-door visits, and sometimes one campaign reaches its voters more often.

Conclusion

What can we now say about how campaigns influence voters and elections? Let us return to the summary of recent empirical research. Based on Table 8.1, we can average the effects estimated by important studies of campaigns across a variety of categories. For example, the top two sections show the overall effects of campaigns. Averaging across all of the "aggregate effects" studies suggests a presidential campaign effect of 4 percentage points; this drops to 3 if you omit the high-end estimate from Holbrook (1996). Similarly, the average deviation from presidential forecast models across elections from 1992 to 2004 is 3 points.

The remainder of Table 8.1 provides estimates of the effects associated with specific categories of campaign activities. The television advertising and radio studies show that these campaign tactics can have a significant influence on candidate support. Direct mail and telephone analyses, including the recent field experiments of Gerber and Green, show mixed effects. The direct mail studies show minimal effects on turnout, as do the Yale phone studies. Two other phone call analyses, however, find significant turnout effects.

Empirical analyses of candidate appearances, debates, conventions, and door-to-door contacting consistently show a significant impact on voter behavior. Candidate appearances, interestingly, appear to influence voters, but some research strongly suggests these effects are conditioned by partisanship.[47] There is comparatively little subtlety to presidential debate and convention effects. Averaging across four studies, the margin between the candidates moves by approximately 2 points after a presidential debate. But this effect is dwarfed by the convention bump, which averages 7 points across five analyses. The persuasive impact of door-to-door campaigning has thus far been difficult to ascertain. But all available studies suggest a statistically significant effect on turnout.

Given this impressive array of research, do we know enough to substantively improve upon the prevailing current perspective on campaigns offered by the U.S. news media? We would answer "yes." More specifically, let us respond directly to the "myths" offered at the outset of this chapter. First, the collective weight of evidence from Table 8.1, along with that from the rest of the chapter, indicates that presidential campaigns have an effect on voter participation rates, candidate preferences, and aggregate election outcomes. This effect, however, is rarely decisive and is almost always conditional. The main campaign effect is the activation of partisans; the persuasion of undecided voters is a lesser order effect, both with respect to its magnitude and its net impact on election results. That is, more people are activated and mobilized than persuaded, and it is more common to win an election by disproportionately activating and mobilizing your supporters than by persuading undecided voters.[48]

Second, voters are not easily manipulated. Most political events do not affect voters' preferences. Moreover, the data clearly show that high-quality, personalized contacting is more effective than mass, one-size-fits-all campaigning. Taken broadly, this observation suggests that one-on-one visits, micro-targeted mail and phone calls, and contact by locally known persons are superior to automated outreach, undifferentiated mail and phone calls, and contact by paid professionals, respectively. There is also the more controversial argument that broadcast television might be less effective than lower cost alternatives, especially in non-presidential contests where there is no need to reach beyond a local or state audience

Third, the popular belief that many and various campaign phenomena can affect voters is only partially true. Different sorts of occurrences, events, and types of outreach *can* matter to individual voters. Most campaign phenomena are irrelevant to voters' candidate preferences, however, and those that do matter, while diverse, tend to be the "big" events of the fall campaign (conventions, debates, and the like).

The upshot of all this is that voters do not bounce around like ping-pong balls in response to the most recent campaign gambits. Instead, campaigns are critical for American democracy because they prime partisan commitments and provide valuable information about issues and conditions and candidates. Political context can be partially shaped by the campaign, but this potential is limited in national elections when both sides bring considerable money and expertise to the fight. Reporters and pundits thus "over-interpret" shifts in the polls—many of which are either predictable or temporary—and thereby cloud perceptions about what matters. This is not only misleading analysis; it could be substantively meddlesome. This "over-interpretation" could contribute to a candidate's momentum with effusive praise about his campaign strategy. Even more perniciously, such a perspective could create a false sense of why a candidate wins an election, making accountability problematic. Our proposed antidote is to temper our reaction to the ups and downs of the campaign with greater emphasis on political context.

Chapter Nine

Hard Facts and Conventional Wisdom as We Look to the Future

Fed by polls...commentators often implied—as they have in past elections—that we are a nation of flakes who don't know from one day to the next whom to vote for. But we're not....In 1996, the char-ismatic candidate, widely described as a masterful politician, got just less than 50 percent of the vote. On Tuesday, the stiff, changeable, uncertain Democrat got just less than 50 percent of the vote.

—Robert G. Kaiser, *Washington Post*, November 12, 2000

THE FOUNDATION OF MUCH OF WHAT WE KNOW ABOUT AMERICAN voters stems from the research conducted during the 1950s with the advent of large-scale, academic public opinion surveys. The important role that families and peer groups play in shaping our party attachments, the enduring loyalty that party members show for their own parties, and the influence these party attachments have on political choices continue to be as true today as they were almost sixty years ago. As we write this book during the late summer of 2007, it is sometimes hard to reconcile the durability of these hard facts with the enormous social, political, and technological transformations that mark the past sixty years. When Angus Campbell and his colleagues were writing *The American Voter* in the late 1950s, citizens got their political news from newspapers and radios (and from families, friends, and co-workers). There were no network or cable news broadcasts; there were no presidential debates; TV advertising by presidential candidates was rare; and there were no bloggers. The information revolution that defines the last half century has changed a good many things about how we conduct elections in the United States, but it has not changed the essential nature of how voters make choices in American politics.

We are *not* arguing that change has not occurred or that the influences on future elections will be identical to what we observed in the past. The proliferation of political commentary—on cable television, talk radio, Web sites, and blogs, and in magazines and newspapers—has reshaped the information environment for Americans. Much of it has an "all skepticism and criticism, all of the time" quality, and we suspect that our contemporary cynicism toward politics, politicians, political parties, government, and the press reflects this evolving media environment. In addition, the nation has struggled through unpopular wars, economic recessions, divisive policy debates, and political scandals. These events have battered candidates of both parties, and we have witnessed what seems to be a permanent shift in the loyalties of some groups of voters. But the habits and mind-sets of American voters have not changed greatly. The parties provide most of the political guidance to citizens who are attentive to politics and governance only when it seems necessary. American voters are not on any kind of political "war-footing," but you might forgive a contrary impression from someone who has spent a lot of time attending to commentators, reporters, bloggers, and the like.

That is where this book enters. Our major purpose in writing it was to balance the cacophony of political commentary that sees change and tumult in every corner of the political system with a historical perspective of electoral politics based on generally accepted facts about American voters. Some of what we offer is received wisdom in political science while many of our arguments (often building on the work of others) offer new insights. In all cases, however, we bring years of data to bear on the questions that we study. Many of the popular myths addressed in these pages are misleading portrayals of how American voters behave and how American electoral democracy works. To the extent that public discussion, whether it is promoted by reporters or pundits, repeats the same inaccurate stories over and over again, mischaracterizations and half-truths become intractable parts of the political landscape, often to our collective detriment.

Many of the conventional wisdoms offered to the public as fact lack empirical foundations and create false perceptions of our fellow citizens. The idea that people who live in Red states are fundamentally at odds with those who reside in Blue (or Purple) states promotes negative stereotypes and false rivalries about values that we largely share. Voters in Red states and those in Blue states may have developed increasingly suspect feelings for one another, but this animus stems from popular depictions often unsupported by facts. As we demonstrate in Chapter 3, voters hold a broad and moderate consensus on most political matters that supersedes geography and party labels. That we are becoming ever more contemptuous of our political opposition is a contemporary fact, stemming from real accounts of elite disagreement and from exaggerated portrayals of voters and their differences. Ongoing coverage of party polarization coincides with charges and countercharges that our leaders and representatives are playing "politics" with most, even the most critical, issues on the public agenda. This negative view of contemporary government erodes the public's faith in its institutions.

In spite of these low levels of public trust, the government continues to conduct its business but not without costs. Many good men and women who might have aspired to elected office choose private sector careers over public service; many good citizens who, in past generations, would have looked to statehouses and Washington for their role models, look elsewhere. Politicians are regular fodder for comedians and late-night talk show hosts, and while many of their jokes are undeniably funny, there is little practical upside to perpetuating an overly pessimistic view of our democracy.

This divisive imagery spills into other facets of our electoral politics. Take, for example, the myth of turnout bias assessed in Chapter 7. The belief that Democrats benefit from higher turnout is so pervasive that legislators almost always take partisan sides on questions of registration and voting procedures. The net effect of the myth is endless controversy over often sensible initiatives to increase participation, which in turn feeds growing public laments about how indifferent and alienated Americans are from the democratic process. Repeated often enough and long enough, the lament becomes part of the common political culture, to no good end. In the absence of this myth, and with the knowledge that both parties can (and do) benefit by increased turnout, Republican and Democratic legislators, faced with proposals to change registration and voting laws, would not need to consider their own partisan interests against those of their opponents, as they *really are one and the same*. Rather, partisan lawmakers could consider each proposal on its merits, balancing the risks (voter fraud) and benefits (enhanced turnout) without ever having to worry that they are handing the keys to victory to their political rivals.

In another example, if the reporting and commentary offered a more faithful rendering of swing voting, gross depictions of mothers, fathers, racial minority groups, and various sports fans might fade into the background of our political discourse. Yes, politics may seem to be more fun when swing voters are described in terms of caricatures, but these caricatures do not necessarily serve the interests of the larger public. They create images of popular anger and indecisiveness that usually does not exist, and they often legitimate unflattering portraits that exacerbate stereotypes—to no beneficial purpose. The related mythology associated with young voters is equally troublesome. Young voters as a group participate at lower rates than their older counterparts but not because this generation (or any generation) is particularly flawed. Rather, like every generation before them, they simply are going through the life cycle that yields mature and participating citizens.

The media's arguably disproportionate focus on the day-to-day strategies employed by political campaigns also distorts our collective understanding of elections. "Play-by-play" commentary dominates election stories, suggesting a contest in which the strongest players and best coaches always win. Furthermore, the overwhelming attention paid to whether candidates are good campaigners negates an appropriate understanding of the extent to which elections are periodic public debates about what represents the country's important problems and how they ought to be solved. Campaign tactics play a role in politics, but they are not what elections are about.

Conventional Wisdom about the Primaries

Political scientists know a good deal more about the dynamics of general elections than about what shapes decisions in primaries, so this book is more useful for assessing what will become more prominent after the nominations. The reason for the difference is, quite simply, the irrelevance of party identification in primaries. Party identification accounted for more than 80 percent of the vote in the last two presidential elections, with the residual almost equally spread between independents (whose vote we can't predict because they lack any party preference) and defectors. But since there is no party basis by which voters can sort candidates within a primary, candidate choices reflect many different considerations: the perceived issue posture of the candidates, judgments about the personal and "presidential" qualities of the candidate, and feelings about which candidates seem more electable. These factors, however, are consistently less accurate in predicting the primary vote than they are in predicting general election outcomes.[1] Nonetheless, we know at least two things about primaries that ought to be kept in mind by any and all interested observers: (1) the news media are hugely important for the nomination contests, and (2) these contests are not always dominated by extremist ideologues.

The Special Role of Attentive Elites in Primaries

Candidate selection in the primary process is heavily shaped by the assessments of attentive elites (media, public intellectuals, and mavens of many types) who handicap candidates at the start and periodically pronounce who is ahead, who is moving up, and who is moving down. They offer their opinions about the general election, too, of course, but their influence is less because only two candidates are involved and because individual partisan ties temper their persuasiveness. During the primaries, when most voters have yet to really engage with the campaign, the fortunes of candidates are shaped disproportionately by commentators whose judgments about candidate viability influence everything from attention in the press to campaign contributors who provide the money that is the lifeblood of all campaigns.[2] Candidates who are deemed unlikely to succeed are rarely able to raise the money needed to fund the ads, make the visits, and hire the staff that makes them newsworthy. Even first-tier candidates can be undone by a failure to meet the expectations of the attentive elites in the media and the political establishment. A candidate whose fund-raising fails to meet anticipated levels (which are often announced by the candidates as well as elite observers) is judged to be losing the race by the only measure that elite observers can use early in the primary cycle. If money can't be raised, a judgment of insufficient support is rendered, usually depressing subsequent fund-raising. The cycle often drives the candidates from the first tier to an early exit, and quickly.

Turnout and Ideologues in Primaries

Since the Republican and Democratic parties began their structural and procedural overhauls in the early 1970s, primary elections have become the main way by which parties nominate their candidates. Roughly 80 percent of the state parties rely on primary elections to determine their statewide nominees and presidential nominating convention delegations. While caucuses and conventions still have their place in the system, primaries are the dominant means by which a candidate secures the party's blessing for the general election. Much has been written about the biases in the primary process. The argument is straightforward: because primaries garner less media attention than general elections (with the possible exception of the New Hampshire primary) and fall early in the election season, Americans are less interested than they are during the general election and thus only the most politically involved voters show up at the polls. The most attentive also happen to be the most ideologically committed and are disproportionately likely to be motivated by a single issue and to vote for "extreme" candidates. This dynamic, critics argue, produces excessively conservative or liberal candidates who are out of step with the general public.

The low turnout rate for primaries makes this scenario plausible. Much anecdotal evidence backing these claims comes from the presidential selection process in which candidates like George McGovern, Ronald Reagan, and Michael Dukakis triumphed over more moderate, "electable" challengers. Perhaps even more to the point is the surprising levels of support for failed "extreme" candidates like Jesse Jackson, Pat Robertson, and Pat Buchanan. Furthermore, corroborative anecdotal evidence that more extreme candidates are advantaged by turnout biases in primaries can be found in a myriad of Senate, House, gubernatorial, and local races (a fact that is often used to explain the ideological polarization of legislative bodies, no matter how moderate the officeholder's voters). The tendency, it is worth pointing out, seems more pronounced in closed primaries than in open or blanket primaries.[3]

Studies of state and presidential nominating conventions also weigh on the side of the argument that primaries produce issue and ideologically extreme electorates. Delegates to these conventions have opinions and attitudes that are highly skewed to the right (in the case of the Republicans) and to the left (in the case of the Democrats) of the general electorate. This is, we hasten to add, apparently in marked contrast to the scattered studies we have on conventions held in the 1950s and 1960s.[4]

The twist is that systematic evidence of bias has been difficult to come by. Survey data show that primary voters are demographically and (to a lesser extent) attitudinally distinct from other party followers. The data also show, however, that their positions on most important policy issues are similar to those of party followers. Thus, in spite of the lower turnout in primaries than in general elections, there is relatively weak evidence to support the common notion that primary electorates are unrepresentative.[5] Primary voters are different from nonvoters in about the same ways that general election voters differ from those who do not turn out in November. When an arguably appropriate comparison is made between primary voters and political party followers, few important differences emerge. Primary voters are slightly older, better educated, more affluent, better integrated into their communities, less black or Latino, but their positions on key policy issues are little different from those of party followers. On empirical grounds, then, it is difficult to sustain the argument made by some critics of party reforms that primary electorates are less representative of the party than those people who chose party nominees several decades ago. They may be less representative of the party organization per se, but the organization is only one component of the party.

Also, there is some evidence that electability trumps whatever ideological motivation the primary electorate may harbor. In 1992, the number one reason Democratic primary voters gave for supporting Clinton was the belief that he had the best chance to defeat Bush. A similar logic was at play in the 1996 GOP primaries, in which Republican voters rallied around Dole as Buchanan's candidacy became more serious. Electability seems to be a more pivotal decision criteria in recent elections, and it may very well continue to shape voter choices in future election cycles.

How biased primary elections might be when all these considerations are in play is unknown. A priori, it seems reasonable to suspect that the more conservative (or liberal) of two equally viable candidates is advantaged among the more ideologically committed primary electorate. However, while there is some evidence for this in congressional primary elections, it has not been observed in recent presidential primary elec-torates.[6] Presidential primary voters from both parties have generally been quite representative of party identifiers who did not participate in their primary. We do not know whether this effect is general. We do not, for example, have good data demonstrating what the bias might be like in lower level primaries (for governor, state legislatures, or even for the House or Senate). It is possible that the nomination bias is less a feature of the primary electorate than it is a feature of ideological party elites and a conventional wisdom of commentators and observers who feed shared images of a candidate's standing with key constituencies within the party's electorate.

A Look to the Future: The General Election

The factors that should influence the 2008 general election outcome are more easily predicted (albeit perhaps not with exactitude). Party identi-fication will be the preeminent influence on the vote, and given what we know about the partisan composition of the electorate and the expected vote, the Democratic nominee enters the election with an advantage. We expect, ceteris paribus, for the Democrat to receive about 53 percent of the two-party vote. Of course, everything will not be equal, and so the actual vote could be closer or larger for the Democrat. The Republican will win only by generating defections among Democratic identifiers, but Democratic defection has been declining recently. About 16 percent of Democrats defected in 2000, but only about 12 percent did so in 2004. Democratic defection in the 2006 congressional election was only about 10 percent, following Democratic defection rates of 23 percent in 2002 and 27 percent in 1998. Independents have also voted more heavily for the Democrats recently, and entering new voters have a much more Democratic and liberal tilt than the older electorate, as we documented in Chapter 6.

The unpopularity of the military stalemate in Iraq and a weariness that often burdens the party of a two-term presidency are adding to an election environment in which the short-term forces should encourage Republican defection, Democratic loyalty, and a Democratic tilt among the unaffiliated (8 to 10 percent of the likely electorate). If current polls are any indication, it should be easy for Democrats to emphasize social spending issues that typically advantage them and foreign policy failures by the Republican incumbents, further enhancing the Democratic advantage.[7] If the 2008 elections were being held in late 2007, we would label it a "Good Democratic Year." Then again, as we know from many prior elections, things can change. The war in Iraq was not the top concern of voters in 2004 (about 16 percent mentioned it as the most important problem facing the country). The most important concern of Americans in 2004 was terrorism (37 percent mentioned it), and Bush bested a simple party vote among this larger group by a wider margin than he lost ground among those concerned with the Iraq war. More than a few commentators and strategists attributed this outcome to the president's ability to define terrorism as the underlying issue that deserved foremost consideration by Americans.[8] In 2004, concerns over terrorism trumped Iraq and social welfare issues.[9] If the Republican candidate is similarly able to reset the terms of the election in 2008, Republicans may be able to neutralize current indications of GOP defections.

We don't think that turnout is going to be a factor. Both parties have refined GOTV plans of the sort that produced a high-turnout election in 2004. We expect all of that machinery to be geared up again in 2008. There is some evidence that Democratic groups—particularly the unions—generated higher turnout rates in 2006 than they managed in the 2002 or 2004 elections.[10] On balance, however, we expect both parties and their candidates to mount significant GOTV efforts in 2008, which will yield relatively high overall turnout but with no advantage to either side.

Key Demographics for 2008?

Campaign strategists have always thought about elections in terms of voter groups that will support their candidates, groups that will support the opposition, voters they might lose, and voters they might wedge from the other candidates.[11] The surge in campaign strategy and tactics built around geodemographic targeting virtually ensures that campaigns in the primaries and the general election will identify "key groups" for their winning coalition.[12] This allows campaigns to maximize the use of resources—from money to the candidate's time—because it permits campaigns to direct appeals to the most receptive voters.[13]

New firms have emerged to market targeting techniques, and existing firms have also developed this service.[14] The results of their work may become part of the conventional wisdom about the election because of the relationships that reporters have with the principals and consultants in the firms that do it. The consultants typically have long-established links with the parties and candidates; reporters know about these ties, and it is not unusual for consultants to tell reporters what they are doing and what they think represent "keys" to the election. The consultants may tell the reporter a lot or a little, but enough usually gets out for the voter group to be characterized; and if it has the kind of "sizzle" that works well in printed stories and news shows, it often becomes part of the story of the election. This material doesn't just appear in politics-heavy venues such as the *Washington Post, New York Times,* and *Los Angeles Times.* Content-hungry cable TV news shows make these consultants regular guests (we have all seen them repeatedly). References to their work in news stories and guest appearances on TV shows constitute valuable opportunities for the consultants to promote future business, so they are often eager to participate.

Exactly what groups will be touted is hard to know right now, but the increasing use of geodemographic targeting and the corresponding ability of campaigns to "narrow-cast" their efforts virtually assures that campaigns will segment the electorate and craft messages for the medium (cable TV shows, direct mail, particular kinds of radio programs or stations, and so forth) that is most likely to reach members of the group. So, if we do not have the 2008 equivalent to "NASCAR dads" and "soccer moms" before us at the moment, we should expect some to show up. They may be important parts of a winning coalition strategy. They may also be little more than the focus of conventional chatter for this election cycle.

When all is said and done, most voting in the 2008 presidential election will be determined by the party identification of voters—individually or as they are defined by their social group characteristics—and by the short-term forces at play during the campaign. It seems virtually assured that a woman or an African American will top the Democratic Party ticket for the first time in history. There is also a strong chance that a political maverick/war hero will lead the GOP. All of this points to a lively election season where faithful partisans may be tested on many new fronts. Certain factions of both parties may defect (or stay home). Yet we strongly expect, with the certainty of history on our side, that most voters will support their party's nominee by the time election day rolls around.

The Normal Vote and Presidential
Votes in 2000 and 2004

T HE FOLLOWING DATA PROVIDE A BREAKDOWN OF THE 2000 AND 2004
presidential votes of demographic groups that are standard parts of
most presidential analysis by the media and academics. Most of the figures in the table report results for whites only since, as the last part of the
table indicates, African Americans and Latinos, but especially the former,
strongly prefer the Democratic Party and only a small fraction ever vote for
a Republican candidate regardless of their income, age, or gender. Among
whites, on the other hand, differences related to social class, religiosity,
marital status, and so forth are almost always an influence on the vote.

The data largely confirm the general understanding of how different
Americans responded to Bush in 2000 and 2004. However, there are also
some differences between the years. Bush's success in both years, but
especially in 2004, heavily depended on high levels of support among the
most religiously oriented voters. Their vote for Bush exceeded a simple
party vote by 10 or more percentage points (compare the reported vote in
the first two columns of data with the Bush vote expected by virtue of the
party identification of these individuals as reported in the last column).
Overall, Bush's support had a "middle America" flavor. Married whites
were more likely than those who were unmarried to vote for him, and the
level of support exceeded a simple party vote. The gender gap was there in

both years and of similar magnitudes. Interestingly, in 2000 and 2004—as has been true so often—the gender gap in the vote exceeded the gender gaps dictated by party identification because Bush's vote among men exceeded their party vote by a greater margin than it did among women.

APPENDIX TABLE 2.1.   Presidential Voting in 2000 and 2004

Demographic Categories and Party Coalition Segmentation	Reported Vote for Bush in		Expected Bush Vote from Partisanship
	2004	2000	
White respondents only			
Less than high school	47	49	46
High school	61	56	50
High school plus	63	60	53
College degree	61	55	55
Post-college degree	44	51	50
Up to $25,000	49	46	45
$25,000 to $50,000	50	61	51
$50,000 to $80,000*	66	55	54
Over $80,000*	62	61	53
Male	61	60	52
Female	55	52	48
Age is 18–29	41	56	48
30–45	67	64	55
46–60	61	51	53
61 and above	56	53	48
Married	62	59	54
Previously married	52	46	46
Never married	47	52	48
Attend religious services weekly	68	65	57
Once or twice a month	68	57	55
A few times a year	50	48	47
Never	47	47	47

APPENDIX TABLE 2.1. *(continued)*

Demographic Categories and Party Coalition Segmentation	Reported Vote for Bush in		Expected Bush Vote from Partisanship
	2004	2000	
Bible is the actual word of God	72	68	55
Bible is not God's word	58	57	53
Bible is the work of men	35	28	40
Religion is important in R's life	62	60	53
Not so important	45	41	47
All respondents			
Blacks	10	9	14
Hispanics	33	37	43
Jews	18	9	28
Catholic-downscale	36	59	50
Catholic-upscale	58	54	49
Protestant-downscale	62	50	52
Protestant-upscale	70	63	59
Secular	52	45	47
Union household	43	43	45
Religious Catholic	50	57	50
Religious Protestant	76	71	60
Others	57	43	47
Total	52	50	46

*Income for the third quartile ends and the fourth quartile begins at $75,000 for the 2000 data.

Note: Data in the top portion of the table are calculated for white respondents only, since the demographic differences presented here have little known effect on the partisanship or votes of non-whites. The last segmentation, at the bottom of the table, includes respondents of all races.

Source: Expected Bush vote is based on authors' calculations. Reported vote is from the 2000 and 2004 ANES.

Causes of Polarization: Issues versus Affect

THE DEPENDENT VARIABLES IN ALL FOUR ORDINARY LEAST SQUARES regressions are measures of polarized views pertaining to the political parties. We calculate individual-level polarization by subtracting the thermometer score of one's opposing party from the score she gives her own party. Larger scores equate to greater polarization. The dependent variables range from 0 to 100.

The independent variables were constructed using questions from the 2000 and 2004 ANES. Social Welfare Attitudes is an additive scale that includes questions pertaining to the desirable level of services versus spending, whether the government should guarantee jobs, and whether the government should provide health insurance. Racial Attitudes (in 2004) is also an additive scale combining four questions regarding whether blacks should try to make it on their own, whether history has made it difficult for blacks to succeed, whether blacks have gotten less than they deserve, and whether blacks should try harder. As all of these questions were not available in earlier years, the 2000 racial attitude measure only includes whether blacks have gotten less than they deserve. The Abortion measure is a single item that pertains to how accessible abortions should be and is the same in both years. The Gay Marriage variable is a single item that gauges support for or opposition to gay marriage. As the gay marriage question was not asked in earlier years, we use a question about whether laws should protect gays from discrimination (Gay Laws) in 2000. All of the issue variables are scaled from 0 to 1 and from most liberal to most conservative.

To measure affective orientations toward the parties, we construct additive measures for Democratic groups (environmentalists, feminists, unions, blacks, and Hispanics) and Republican groups (Christian fundamentalists, military, big business, and southerners) combining individual thermometer ratings. We rescale both of these variables so that they run from 0 to 1, cold to warm. Ideally we would have liked to include both composite measures (feelings toward Republicans and feelings toward Democrats) in our analysis simultaneously, but as these two measures are highly correlated for Republicans (.485), we chose to avoid problems stemming from multicollinearity and use the single liberal and conservative thermometer ratings to assess out-group animosity. The conservative and liberal thermometer ratings are strongly correlated with the corresponding partisan group measures but are virtually uncorrelated with opposing group measures. Given this, our specification satisfies our theoretical concerns without posing any statistical problems that might bias our findings.

Finally, we collapse the ANES 7-point party identification variable into pure independents, leaners, weak identifiers, and strong partisans and rescale this variable (0–1), leaners to strong identifiers.

APPENDIX TABLE 3.1. Predicting Polarized Views toward the Parties, 2000 and 2004

	2000		2004	
	Democrats	Republicans	Democrats	Republicans
Approve/Disap- prove Iraq War	—	—	−32.5* (6.2)	18.3* (5.3)
Social Welfare Attitudes	−19.7* (8.9)	−7.9 (9.4)	−18.3* (6.2)	5.5 (5.3)
Racial Attitudes	−2.3 (5.1)	2.9 (5.4)	4.8 (5.7)	10.3 (6.7)
Abortion	−15.5* (5.0)	9.5* (4.8)	3.1 (4.2)	−2.3 (3.4)
Gay Laws/Gay Marriage	0.9 (4.2)	3.3 (3.8)	1.9 (2.9)	5.9 (3.4)
Partisan Strength	28.3* (6.4)	31.5* (6.2)	40.9* (4.8)	34.6* (4.9)
Feelings toward Democratic Groups	34.7* (11.6)	—	16.3* (7.8)	—
Feelings toward Conservatives	−27.9* (9.6)	—	−37.8* (7.5)	—
Feelings toward Republican Groups		25.4* (12.1)	—	36.8* (4.9)
Feelings toward Liberals		−34.2* (8.0)	—	−30.1* (9.1)
Constant	13.2	5.3	24.85*	−27.4*
R Square	0.20	0.30	0.36	0.39
N =	283	216	354	354

Estimating Swing Voting

APPENDIX 4.1.   Probit Regression Models Predicting Swing Voting Behavior

	All Respondents		Self-Reported Voters	
	(dF/dx)	S.E.	(dF/dx)	S.E.
New Deal Groups				
Westerner	0.1062***	0.0190	0.0389***	0.0128
Union	0.0291**	0.0078	0.0030***	0.0016
College grad	0.1571***	0.0274	0.0277***	0.0102
African American	0.0069	0.0034	0.0002**	0.0002
Top income third	−0.0022***	0.0006	−0.0001***	0.0000
Catholic	−0.0015***	0.0004	−0.0001***	0.0000
Male	−0.0006	0.0004	−0.0001*	0.0000
Senior	0.0006	0.0007	0.0000	0.0000
White southerner	0.0002	0.0006	0.0000	0.0000
Jewish	0.0007	0.0014	0.0000	0.0000
Latino	−0.0013***	0.0003	−0.0001***	0.0000

(*continued*)

APPENDIX TABLE 4.1. *(continued)*

	All Respondents		Self-Reported Voters	
	(dF/dx)	S.E.	(dF/dx)	S.E.
Cross-Pressured Groups				
Waitress mom	0.0812	0.0759	0.0118*	0.0308
Suburban	−0.0078***	0.0016	−0.0005***	0.0003
Rural	−0.0050**	0.0011	−0.0002***	0.0001
Some college	0.0027**	0.0015	0.0001*	0.0001
Under 30	−0.0009*	0.0004	0.0000	0.0000
Office park dad	−0.0002	0.0006	0.0000	0.0000
Soccer mom	0.0007	0.0033	0.0000	0.0001
Middle income third	−0.0017***	0.0005	−0.0001***	0.0000
Political Information Groups				
Independent	0.4957***	0.0313	0.5267	0.0486
Politically informed	0.0129***	0.0026	0.0003***	0.0002
Interactive Effects				
Independent*informed	−0.0140***	0.0028	−0.0003***	0.0002
Latino*informed	0.0126**	0.0032	0.0003***	0.0002
Suburban*informed	0.0085***	0.0019	0.0002***	0.0001
Waitress mom* informed	−0.0080	0.0029	−0.0003	0.0003
Rural*informed	0.0074***	0.0018	0.0002***	0.0001
Union*informed	0.0067***	0.0016	−0.0002***	0.0001
Westerner*informed	−0.0042***	0.0010	−0.0001***	0.0001
Top income third* informed	0.0035***	0.0011	0.0001*	0.0000
Some college*informed	−0.0033***	0.0012	−0.0001	0.0001
Catholic*informed	0.0033***	0.0010	0.0001***	0.0001
Middle income third*informed	0.0025***	0.0009	0.0001*	0.0000
African American* informed	−0.0022*	0.0010	−0.0000	0.0000

APPENDIX TABLE 4.1.   *(continued)*

	All Respondents		Self-Reported Voters	
	(dF/dx)	S.E.	(dF/dx)	S.E.
White southerner* informed	−0.0021*	0.0010	−0.0000	0.0000
Under 30*informed	0.0018*	0.0009	0.0000	0.0000
Senior*informed	0.0017	0.0091	0.0000	0.0000
Office park dad*informed	0.0012	0.0013	0.0000	0.0000
Male*informed	0.0002	0.0006	0.0000	0.0000
Jewish*informed	−0.0003	0.0021	0.0000	0.0001
Soccer mom*informed	−0.0018	0.0034	−0.0001	0.0001
College grad*informed	−0.0078***	0.0018	−0.0002***	0.0001
Total Cases	11,829		7,376	
Log Likelihood	−1,505.06		−642.12	
LR Chi-Square (31)	3,872.51***		2,543.05***	
Pseudo R2	0.563		0.664	

Note: Probit estimation techniques are used to predict whether a respondent is a swing voter (did not vote for the same party candidate in the 1996, 2000, and 2004 elections). All independent variables are scored from 0 to 1. The coefficients (dF/dx) can be interpreted as the marginal change in the probability a respondent is a swing voter associated with the given independent variable. Total effects associated with the variable take into account both the direct and interactive effects. A similar model was estimated on the 1972 to 1976 panel survey.
*significant at .05
**significant at .01
***significant at .001
Source: ANES 2000 to 2004 panel survey.

Measuring Issue Salience
over Time

APPENDIX TABLE 5.1 REPORTS THE FINDINGS FROM FOUR SEPARATE regressions: men and women during Period I (1988 to 1996) and men and women during Period 2 (1996 to 2004). The analysis uses ordinary least squares regression to assess the relative importance of issues and demographic characteristics with regard to male and female party identification. The ANES 7-point party identification measure is used as the dependent variable and is scaled from Strong Democrat (at the low end) to Strong Republican (at the high end). The explanatory variables include three cultural issues (abortion, gay rights, and the proper role of women), a measure of social welfare beliefs, a question pertaining to the government's responsibility to help minorities, opinion on defense spending, and various demographic factors that traditionally correspond with party identification. All of the attitude measures are made up of identical questions from the five selected years, thus any differences across time cannot be interpreted as a function of the measures themselves; furthermore, all of the measures are scaled from 0 to 1—most liberal to most conservative. Our objective is to measure relative changes in issues salience over these two time periods. To accomplish this, we model party identification using interaction terms that multiply the values of the explanatory factors by a time variable. The time variable in Period I is coded 0 for 1988 and increases by one for each subsequent election year. This same method is used for Period 2 with 1996 as the baseline 0 value. The top half of the regression table estimates the effects of issue attitudes and demographic traits in the baseline year when the time variable equals 0. As each factor is scaled from 0 to 1, the coefficients in the top half of the table reflect the increase or decrease in Republican identification moving from the lowest to the highest point on the measure, controlling for all other factors. Coefficients reported in the bottom half of Appendix Table 5.1 calculate the extent to which each explanatory factor has grown or diminished in relative importance since the baseline year. One can estimate the change in the coefficient for each independent variable over time by adding or subtracting the value of the interaction term coefficient for each subsequent presidential election year. To the extent that cultural values are driving partisan change among women, the over-time coefficients in the bottom half of the table for abortion, gay rights, and women's role should be statistically significant.

APPENDIX TABLE 5.1. Issue Salience to Party Identification over Time, 1988 to 2004

	1988 to 1996		1996 to 2004	
	Men	Women	Men	Women
Abortion Attitudes	0.39*	0.69**	.78**	1.02**
	(.22)	(.24)	(.23)	(.25)
Laws to Protect Gays	0.48*	0.26	.52**	.99**
	(.18)	(.23)	(.18)	(.21)
The Proper Role of Women	0.41	−0.26	.15	.69*
	(.26)	(.31)	(.29)	(.31)
Social Welfare Attitudes	4.05**	2.87**	4.46**	3.22**
	(.40)	(.48)	(.42)	(.45)
Racial Attitudes	−0.54*	0.5	.82*	.28
	(.32)	(.36)	(.33)	(.33)
Defense Spending	1.78**	1.76**	.99**	.73*
	(.30)	(.34)	(.33)	(.38)
Live in the South	−0.49**	−0.7**	−.10	.05
	(.15)	(.19)	(.15)	(.17)
Time (1988 to 1996)	−0.8**	−0.94**	.13	.24
	(.28)	(.29)	(.33)	(.32)

APPENDIX TABLE 5.1. *(continued)*

	1988 to 1996		1996 to 2004	
	Men	Women	Men	Women
Over Time Effects				
Abortion * time	0.14	0.11	−.08	.05
	(.18)	(.19)	(.20)	(.21)
Gay Rights * time	0.01	0.42*	−.01	−.07
	(.14)	(.17)	(.17)	(.21)
Women's Role * time	−0.05	0.48*	.39	−.12
	(.21)	(.23)	(.28)	(.30)
Social Welfare * time	0.29	0.39	−.48	.05
	(.31)	(.35)	(.35)	(.41)
Racial Attitudes * time	0.56*	−0.17	−.31	.17
	(.26)	(.28)	(.28)	(.27)
Defense Spending * time	−0.26	−0.55*	.82**	.41
	(.21)	(.26)	(.23)	(.26)
South * time	0.2	0.33*	.11	.06
	(.12)	(.14)	(.13)	(.15)
Constant	−0.06	1.21**	−1.52**	−.90*
	(.35)	(.40)	(.38)	(.38)
Adjusted R2	0.32	0.27	.35	.29

Note: Table entries represent unstandardized regression coefficients; standard errors are in parentheses. Party identification is the dependent variable scaled 0 to 6, Strong Democrat to Strong Republican. All independent variables (main effects) are scaled from 0 to 1. Models include controls for income, education, and age (note shown).

*$p < .05$

**$p < .01$

Source: Pooled ANES from selected years. Sample is restricted to white respondents only.

Notes

Chapter One

1. Lewis-Beck and Rice 1992.
2. Petrocik 2004.
3. See, for example, Gosnell and Merriam 1924; Gosnell 1927; and de Sola Pool, Abelson, and Popkin 1965.
4. When the Literary Digest poll erroneously forecast a Republican landslide in the presidential election of 1936 while Gallup predicted a win for Franklin Roosevelt based on a much smaller random sample, the conflict was resolved in favor of social science. This resolution became more definitive in 1945, when Gallup's surveys accurately predicted the stunning triumph of the Labor Party in the British national elections.
5. See Lazarsfeld, Berelson, and Gaudet 1948; and Berelson, Lazarsfeld, and McPhee 1954.
6. Campbell et al. 1960; Key 1961, 1966.
7. See Patterson 1993.

Chapter Two

1. These data are also from the 2000 ANES.
2. Pew Research Center polls from October 2000 and November 2006.
3. The literature that makes this assertion is voluminous. Representative examples include King 1997; Fiorina 1977a; Wattenberg 1990; Herrnson 2000; and Burden and Kimball 2002.

4. See Fiorina and Rivers 1989 and, more generally, Jacobson 2004.

5. Mayhew 1974 is the seminal piece on this topic.

6. This measure is based on the open-ended questions that asked respondents what they liked or disliked about the parties. Figure 2.2 reports the percentage who responded with positive comments and negative comments.

7. See Wattenberg 1990.

8. Maggiotto and Piereson 1977.

9. See Hetherington 2001 for more data on this.

10. Nie, Verba, and Petrocik 1979.

11. Bartels 2000 and Hetherington 2001 have good data for voters. Comparable evidence about the parties in government is found in Aldrich 1995; Miller and Overby 2007; and Cox and McCubbins 1993, 2003.

12. Noteworthy party organization data are in Cotter et al. 1984 and Kolodny 1998.

13. See Aberbach and Rockman 2000 and Aldrich 1995.

14. de Sola Pool et al. 1965 describe early voter targeting schemes first developed for the Kennedy campaign in 1960. A 2007 *Washington Post* article details the modern incarnation of this methodology and highlights one of its foremost practitioners (Alex Gage).

15. Green, Palmquist, and Schickler 2002 are identified with the social identity interpretation. Party identification as a summary statement of issue preferences is associated with Fiorina 1977b and Erikson, MacKuen, and Stimson 2002.

16. There has also been an ongoing debate about how generalizeable any conceptualization of party identification is outside of the political context of the United States. For example, it is common to argue that party identification is equivalent to the vote, especially in other nations. Budge, Crewe, and Farlie 1976 have an early and comprehensive overview of these issues.

17. This does not foreclose the possibility of some or even many people changing their party loyalties. We know this happens during periods of realignment. It also happens on a more individual and idiosyncratic basis in response to issues and events that are particularly meaningful for an individual even when the existing party alignments are stable. These types of changes, however, are generally modest and often short term, frequently involving variability in the intensity of a person's attachment to a party.

18. The "probe" is a follow-up question to those who assert they are independents or have no preference or prefer another party; they are then asked: "Do you think of yourself as closer to the Republican Party or to the Democratic Party?" Those who indicated they are closer to the Republicans or Democrats are typically described as "Leaning Republicans" and "Leaning Democrats."

19. See Keith et al. 1992.

20. Those who identified themselves as Democrats and Republicans in the question are sorted into two groups: (1) those who strongly "think" of

themselves as Democrats or Republicans and (2) those who not so strongly "think" of themselves as Democrats or Republicans.

21. In the interest of minimizing the size of the table, every presidential election is not individually reported. The pattern in the table is identical to what would be observed if they were presented for every year. The years are grouped because they represent meaningful political eras.

22. This *closet partisanship* is well known if not always acknowledged. Petrocik 1974 was the first to identify these features of *closet partisanship*, a term coined by Keith et al. 1992, which produced a systematic analysis of what they described as the "myth" of the independent voter.

23. The "thermometers" are rating scale questions that ask respondents to express their warmth (positive feeling) on a 0 to 100 scale, with 0 representing an extremely negative feeling and 100 an extremely positive feeling.

24. See Petrocik 1974.

25. The regression slope for the elections in the top panel averaged about 14.5; it was 16.9 for the elections in the bottom panel (and approached 18 for the 2004 election).

26. The difference between this percentage and 100 percent is the share of the electorate who are independents (varying from 10 to 15 percent)—not party voters by definition—and the fraction who defect to a candidate of the opposing party (a Democratic identifier who voted for the Republican candidate, for example).

27. See the symposium in the March 2001 issue of *PS*, which offers various accounts for the failure of almost all standard models to predict Bush's victory.

28. See Petrocik 1989 for a full discussion of the data set and the analysis that produced the results in Table 2.3. Note that "balanced" is understood to mean an election environment in which neither candidate is significantly advantaged by the issues or personal judgments about the qualities of the candidates.

29. Converse 1969, 1976.

30. The calculation is quite simple. Consider the following example of a district with 1 Strong Democrat, 3 Weak Democrats, 2 leaning Republicans, and 4 Strong Republicans. The expected Democratic vote is equal to $(1^*.87) + (3^*.70) + (2^*.56) + (4^*.15) = .413/10$—or 41.3 percent Democratic (and, with rounding, 59 percent Republican).

31. The use of a priori estimates based on party identification may lead to underestimations. The underestimation may be large if an issue is leading voters to report a party identification that is changed or changing by virtue of an issue or candidate evaluation. Judgments about the relative importance of an issue or candidate will be erroneous in direct proportion to the magnitude of the change as a consequence of these issues and candidate assessments. However, in any given election, changes in partisanship are not large. Moreover, if

the intent is not to compare effects or test a model but to determine whether the vote or vote intention of some group differs from what might have been expected, a party identification–based expected vote is a conservative test for whether something is going on. A difference that shows up when the test is biased against finding a difference is one that is almost certainly worthy of attention.

32. A regression model that controls for partisanship can answer a part of this question. It can indicate whether partisanship alone explains the vote of the group. It cannot indicate whether the group's intended vote is different from its typical vote, which of course is what observers want to know before the election and what analysts need to know afterward.

33. Simultaneously increasing electoral security *and* the number of seats is difficult, but the right balance assures victory for the majority party's most marginal candidates and produces the largest possible majority. Some number of majority party incumbents will face a stiff challenge, but most of them will enjoy easy wins. See Kousser 1996 and Cain 1985 for more on this. Incumbents in well-designed districts may still face primary election challenges that make them subsequently vulnerable to a general election defeat. See Stone and Maisel 1999.

34. Cox and Katz 1996.

35. Jacobson and Kernell 1981.

36. The party identity of a seat is equivalent to the party of the incumbent seeking reelection or the previous holder of the seat.

37. This survey is a proprietary campaign survey. The firm that provided the data does not want the campaign identified to protect the interests of the candidates.

38. A more detailed analysis appears in Petrocik 2007.

39. Ladd 1999, page 7. Putnam's social capital argument, in both his 1995 article and his 2000 book, asserted that a decline in associational group activity in the United States was a principal cause of an overall decline in political activity and citizen involvement. The thrust of Ladd's analysis was to show that associational activity had not declined and could not, therefore, be a source for the citizenship ills asserted by Putnam. As Ladd's anecdote tried to demonstrate, evidence often fails to trump a common wisdom.

40. We recognize that the Putnam-Ladd disagreement has partisans. We are not taking sides in that debate. We mention it only to illustrate Ladd's interesting parallel between what the data document and the social conventions that many embrace.

41. However, the proliferation of new communication technologies and the development of new targeting methodologies have also permitted more "narrow-casting" by campaigns of every type. We have a comment on this in the conclusion.

42. It is worth a quick observation that the rise of conservative/Republican and liberal/Democratic sympathizing news outlets on TV and the Internet may get us back to a party-supporting information environment. The 2000 and (especially) 2004 elections might be early examples.

Chapter Three

1. American Political Science Association 1950.

2. While the report called for more "responsible" parties, it did caution against polarized parties with such rigid adherence to party principles that they could preclude compromise and interparty cooperation.

3. Poole and Rosenthal 1997, 2001; Jacobson 2000; Fleischer and Bond 2004.

4. Rhode 1991; Stonecash, Brewer, and Mariani 2003.

5. Bartels 2000.

6. Layman and Carsey 2002a, 2202b.

7. Frank 2004.

8. Abramowitz and Saunders 2005.

9. For example, see Fiorina, Abrams, and Pope 2005; and Jacobson 2007.

10. Abramowitz and Saunders 1998; Hetherington 2001; Layman and Carsey 2002a and 2002b; Zaller 1992.

11. Layman and Carsey 2002a, 2002b; Hetherington 2001; Abramowitz and Saunders 2005; Brewer 2005.

12. Petrocik 1981a, 1987a.

13. Layman and Carsey 2002a, 2002b; Hetherington 2001.

14. 2004 ANES.

15. Downs 1957; Hinich and Munger 1994; but see Rabinowitz and Macdonald 1989.

16. Nie, Verba, and Petrocik 1979.

17. Layman and Carsey 20002b; Abramowitz and Saunders 2005; Brewer 2005.

18. Also see Hetherington 2001.

19. We choose to restrict our polarization analysis to this time period for several reasons. First, question wording consistency over this period enhances the reliability of our trends. Second, the presidential election in 1976 is often noted as an outlier in the ANES time series as Gerald Ford had not been elected and the Nixon pardon had a short-term influence on party sentiments. Finally, the Reagan revolution is often noted as an important turning point in American national politics where the southern realignment toward the Republican Party began to take hold in a substantial way.

20. As we noted earlier, thermometer ratings are commonly used in the social sciences to gauge positive or negative feelings toward individuals and

groups. A "0" score reflects cold feelings toward a particular person or group while "100" indicates very warm feelings.

21. Assuming that answers to these questions are normally distributed, the bars represent the opinions held by approximately 68 percent of Republicans and Democrats.

22. A description of our measures and the results of our statistical analyses are found in the Appendix Table 3.1.

23. Campbell et al. 1960; Green et al. 2002.

24. The Democratic constituent groups (for purposes of this analysis) include feminists, environmentalists, unions, blacks, and Hispanics. The Republican constituent groups include Christian fundamentalists, big business, the military, and southerners. We add individual thermometer ratings for the groups within each category to create a summary score of relative warmth (or coldness) toward groups currently associated with the Democratic and Republican parties.

Chapter Four

1. In an October 3, 2004, article for the *New York Times*, William Safire traces the lineage of the term: "Lexicographer Barrett tracks this description of an undecided voter to an Oct. 11, 1958, observation in *The New York Times*: 'The Republican problem in western Pennsylvania and West Virginia is to capture Democratic and swing voters to add to the usual Republican minorities.' Checking the *Times* archives reveals the author—my old Op-Ed colleague, the columnist Russell Baker—whose observation remains pertinent today....While splashing about in the archives, I found an earlier use of swing voter, equally apt. *The Washington Post* reported in 1956 that the G.O.P. candidate running for re-election as vice president said in Ohio that he was trying to 'appeal to swing voters, whom we must have to win not only the presidency, which I am sure we will win, but also to elect congressmen and senators.' To do that, Richard Nixon was certain 'it is essential to have a type of campaign persuasive to independents and Democrats.' "

2. Berelson et al. 1954; Lazarsfeld et al. 1948.

3. Campbell et al. 1960.

4. Behaving rationally is defined as seeking to realize one's preference, which is (in this case) winning the election.

5. See Downs 1957.

6. Shea and Burton 2003. This definition was articulated in *The Hotline*, a daily political newsletter and staple for Beltway politicos: "The relative volatility of the electorate is known as the 'swing factor'—a statistical measure used in order to determine where and with which sub-group the race is unpredictable. From that, the term 'swing voters' was coined" (December 10, 1999).

7. Susan Page and Jill Lawrence, "Year before the Election, Many are Undecided," *USA Today*, October 30, 2003.

8. National Public Radio, March 17, 2004.

9. An entire Web site was dedicated to "information for the undecided (no preaching to the choir)," http://www.undecided.com/election.html.

10. Bowers 2004; Molyneaux 2005; Panagakis 1989.

11. The argument that undecided voters break for the challenger should not be confused with our claims in Chapter 7 that nonvoters commonly have the same candidate preferences as voters.

12. Gallup examined the social and political profiles of undecided voters before making their allocation.

13. See Campbell, Gurin, and Miller 1954.

14. Converse 1962; Daudt 1961; Zaller 2003.

15. Hillygus and Jackman 2003.

16. Despite our individual-level conception of swing voting, consultants and practitioners consider it an aggregate-level phenomenon. This is not to suggest that swing voting is not driven by individuals voting for different parties' candidates over some number of elections, since it clearly is. But for campaign professionals, such variance is interesting only if it affects the aggregate distribution of preferences; movement that cancels itself out is considered trivial. Because of this, and because it is difficult to accurately estimate an individual's voting record over a series of elections, professional swing voting analyses have tended to focus on aggregate-level results from states, counties, or precincts. See Shea and Burton 2003.

17. The 1996 and 1968 presidential votes are based on the respondents' recollections of how they voted.

18. There was also a panel study conducted between 1956 and 1960. We do not analyze those data because they lack critical variables.

19. Kaufmann and Petrocik 1999.

20. Those with a household income in the middle third of the country's overall distribution are defined as "middle class." "Soccer moms" are defined as suburban, thirty- to fifty-four-year-old, stay-at-home moms with children living at home and a household income in the top two-thirds of the overall distribution. "Waitress moms" are thirty- to fifty-four-year-old females working outside the home with children living at home and a household income in the bottom one-third of the overall distribution. "Office park dads" are defined as suburban, thirty- to fifty-four-year-old males, married, working outside the home, with children living at home and a household income in the top two-thirds of the overall distribution.

21. It is possible that the specific appeals of a candidate can induce someone whose underlying party vote probability is 0.9 to vote the other way. We believe this to be quite rare, however. In addition, as a practical matter, such

behavior would shift our estimate of the underlying vote probability closer to 0.5 (as our swing voter definition is empirically derived) and could result in a reclassification of their status.

22. "Two of three party votes" include those who twice voted a party line but abstained in the other election.

23. In part, the 1972 to 1976 panel study was chosen because we thought it would provide a high estimate of swing voting. As noted in Chapter 2, this period was marked by unusually strong short-term forces that resulted in above-normal rates of partisan defection. The benefit of studying this period is that our standard analytic techniques work best when we are not constrained by limited variance and few cases.

24. Specifically, we estimated probit models with interaction terms for attitudes and social group characteristics. A description of our analysis and the results from our 1996–2004 models are presented in Appendix Table 4.1.

25. We draw this conclusion because, as a group, office park dads do not meet the criteria for swing voting. Informed dads swing less and uninformed dads swing more, which suggests that levels of engagement predict swing voting more than simply being classified as an "office park dad."

26. As stated earlier, swing voters from the 1972–1976 and 2000–2004 panel studies broke decisively for the *winning* presidential candidate in each election.

27. The tendency of undecideds to vote for the incumbent is slightly overstated with the inclusion of the 1956 and 1948 elections, in which these voters broke for Eisenhower and Truman, respectively.

28. Shea and Burton 2003.

29. See Nagourney 2003.

30. Edsall and Grimaldi 2004.

31. Micro-targeting is a process by which a campaign identifies which voters will receive particular messages. Rather than pay a company to contact every registered voter in the state and ask about issues and candidates in the upcoming election, a survey of approximately 5,500 voters is conducted and analyzed with the intent of classifying the electorate into different groups. These groups are constructed on the basis of their distinct issue agendas and positions; the campaign tailors its phone, direct mail, and door-to-door contacting so that individual voters receive messages with the greatest probability of favorably influencing their vote choice. Micro-targeting is thus less expensive than traditional voter identification methods and may be more effective.

Chapter Five

1. Tumulty and Novak 2003 provide a detailed account of the widespread media coverage of security moms. Greenberg 2004 offers a detailed repudiation of the security mom myth.

2. The specific measure of the difference has varied, but the simplest method is used here. We subtract the percentage of men who identify with the Democratic Party from the percentage of women who do. We include those who lean toward one party with the weak and strong party identifiers per Chapter 2. The same basic methodology (percentage of women who vote Democrat—percentage of men who vote Democrat) is used to estimate the vote gap.

3. Until 1964, women's partisanship and voting tilted more to the GOP than did men's. The topic did not attract much attention until women became more Democratic than men.

4. See Whirls 1986.

5. Francovic 1982; Shapiro and Mahajan 1986; Gilens 1988; Wilcox, Jelen, and Leege 1993; Conover and Sapiro 1993.

6. Chaney, Alvarez, and Nagler 1998; Kaufmann and Petrocik 1999; Kaufmann 2002.

7. Erie and Rein 1988; May and Stephenson 1994.

8. Chaney et al. 1998; Kaufmann and Petrocik 1999; Mattei 2000; Schlesinger and Heldman 2001; Kaufmann 2002; Kaufmann 2004.

9. Smeal 1984; Abzug and Kelber 1984; Conover 1988.

10. Klein 1984; Mansbridge 1985; Cook and Wilcox 1991; Seltzer, Newman, and Leighton 1997.

11. Whirls 1986.

12. Whirls 1986; Kaufmann and Petrocik 1999; Norrander 1999; Box-Steffensmeier, de Boef, and Lin 2004.

13. Kaufmann 2002; Box-Steffensmeier et al. 2004.

14. Shapiro and Majahan 1986; Plutzer and Zipp 1996; Norrander 1999; Sapiro and Conover 1997; Chaney et al. 1998; Kaufmann and Petrocik 1999; Mattei 2000; Schlesinger and Heldman; 2001; Eagly et al. 2004.

15. See Gilens 1988; Chaney et al. 1998; Kaufmann and Petrocik 1999; Kaufmann 2002; Welch and Hibbing 1992; Clarke et al. 2004.

16. In addition to the attitude and salience explanations described so far, some recent studies use time series analysis to test the effects of macro-economic conditions, macro-ideology, and international relations crises on the gender gap. Box-Steffensmeier et al. 2004 find that small changes in political climate and movements in the macro-economy contribute to gender gap fluctuations. Clarke et al. 2004, in their analysis of gender differences in presidential approval, bolster prior work on the gender gap regarding the variable economic basis of male-female differences but find inconsistent support for the thesis that men are more susceptible to the rally effect pertaining to wars and other foreign policy interventions.

17. Shapiro and Majahan 1986; Chaney, Alvarez, and Nagler 1998; Kaufmann and Petrocik 1999; Schlesinger and Heldman 2001.

18. Chaney et al. 1998.

19. See Kaufmann and Petrocik 1999 and Wilcox and Norrander 2002 for data pertaining to gender differences in attitudes regarding laws to protect gays and lesbians, and gays in the military. While the gender gap on these issues is quite substantial, the gender gap pertaining to questions of gay marriage is not. According to the 2004 ANES, 34 percent of men and 35 percent of women supported gays' and lesbians' rights to marry.

20. Chaney et al. 1998; Kaufmann 2002; Wilcox and Norrander 2002.

21. Conover and Sapiro 1993; Nincic and Nincic 2002.

22. Kaufmann 2002; Fiorina et al. 2005.

23. Layman and Carsey 2002a, 2002b; Brewer 2005.

24. Hunter 1991; Jelen 1997; Kellstedt et al. 1996; Kohut et al. 2000; Layman 1997, 2001; Petrocik, 1998, 2007; Abramowitz 1997.

25. This time division corresponds to the shifts in the partisanship of women who moved toward the Democratic Party from 1988 to 1996 and then reversed course in later years. See Appendix for further explanation.

26. A description of our statistical analysis and findings is in Appendix Table 5.1.

27. We use a fairly blunt measure of motherhood to illustrate this point, but as has been noted by Carroll (1999), there is little rigor generally in popular depictions of such constituencies. Security moms, soccer moms, NASCAR dads, and others are not social scientific categories; they are storytelling aids.

28. See Miller 1991.

29. The gender gap in the South is not constant across states; according to state exit poll data collected by Edison Media Research and Mitofsky International, there is considerable variance across the eleven southern states, ranging from an 8-point margin in favor of the Democrats in Virginia, to a 7-point margin for the Republicans in Mississippi. The gender gap in the remaining states fluctuates in a +/– 3 point range around 0. According to the national exit poll data, the white gender gap in the South was 4.2, while the gender gap in the non-South was 7.6 percentage points, with women favoring the Democrats.

30. Kaufmann 2006; Petrocik 2007.

31. We come to this conclusion by examining the partial correlations between war attitudes and vote choice controlling for party identification, income, education, and age.

32. Kaufmann 2006.

33. We identify evangelical Christians based on how respondents answer the question as to whether they are born again. The notion of adult conversion is central to the doctrine of evangelical Christian denominations and, in the absence of a more detailed set of religious behavior and belief questions, born-again status is a reliable measure of evangelicalism (Layman 2001). This analysis uses the Edison/Mitofsky national exit poll instead of ANES data because the exit poll includes a much larger number of respondents and thus permits

an examination of southern and non-southern voters by gender and religion simultaneously without encountering subgroup samples so small that they provide unreliable results.

Chapter Six

1. There is an extensive literature on this. Representative data and arguments tied to assessments of whether young voters shape political transformations appear in Nie et al. 1979; Petrocik 1981a; and Sears and Valentino 1997.

2. Examples are Campbell et al. 1960; Nie et al. 1979; Andersen 1979; Petrocik 1981a; Norpoth 1987; and Petrocik and Brown 1998.

3. Lubell 1952 offers a classic early recognition of this effect.

4. This is not always the case, however—and especially not in places such as California, Texas, Florida, or New York.

5. Although the generational demarcation points used here are widely accepted in market research, some scholars disagree. For example, see Howe and Strauss 2000. We use the popular nomenclature but generally prefer specific dates when analyzing "young" voters or cohorts.

6. See Miller and Shanks 1996 for more on generational effects and low overall participation rates.

7. Verba and Nie 1972; Wolfinger and Rosenstone 1980; Rosenstone and Hansen 1993; Teixeira, 1992; Verba, Schlozman, and Brady 1995.

8. Verba and Nie 1972; Rosenstone and Hansen 1993.

9. Niemi and Jennings 1991.

10. Initial research into Generations X and Y offered pessimistic conclusions based on high school civics curricula. In the 1970s and 1980s, empirical evaluations determined that social studies courses were mostly inconsequential in terms of political identities and preferences such as partisanship and ideology. However, recent studies by, among others, Niemi and Junn 1998 and Gimpel, Lay, and Schuknecht 2003 confirm earlier findings by Almond and Verba 1963 and Jennings and Niemi 1968 that participatory curricula—and classroom discussion of topical issues in particular—shape participation norms and the civic identity of adolescents. The question is whether ambitious projects such as *Kids' Voting USA* or more ad hoc attempts to promote political engagement are enough to offset the decline in effectiveness among other socializing agents.

11. Andolina et al. 2002.

12. Examples are Rosenstone and Hansen 1993 and Verba et al. 1995.

13. Gerber and Green 2000.

14. Partisan outreach, as we demonstrate later in this chapter, appears to have emphasized older citizens. Some nonpartisan grassroots outreach targeted the young, including bus tours and celebrity-oriented efforts through MTV. (These grassroots efforts should not be confused with expensive television

advertising campaigns aimed at young voters, such as MTV's "Rock the Vote," "Choose or Lose," and P. Diddy's "Vote or Die.") Overall, however, we really have no empirical sense of the extensiveness of young voter contacting. See Nagourney 2004; Hillygus and Shields 2007; and Chapter 8 for more detail.

15. The voter file for Texas, for example, has 9 million records and age is not usually included as a variable in the standard state file (although date of registration is).

16. The work of Presser 1990 and Silver and his colleagues 1986 indicates that using self-reported turnout inflates the significance of certain voting correlates (e.g., income, education, partisanship). There is little evidence, though, that younger people "overreport" at rates distinct from other age cohorts.

17. As mentioned earlier, it is impossible to construct age ranges that satisfy generational scholars since there is no consensus on when generations begin and end. What we do here is move backward in fourteen-year increments. This roughly matches the generational boundaries while ensuring sufficient and comparable subsamples from the ANES. Slight shifts in the year boundaries do not significantly affect the results presented here.

18. Admittedly, these numbers might be a function of political context. For example, the high turnout of Gen Y in 2004 might be attributable to higher turnout across the board.

19. See Miller and Shanks 1996.

20. These questions were selected because they were asked of respondents in both years. The pattern described here is observed whether we examined more, other, or fewer items in any given year.

21. Campbell et al. 1960; Beck 1974; Converse 1976; Andersen 1979; Petrocik 1981a; Sears and Valentino 1997.

22. We calculate the Democratic Party advantage by subtracting the percentage of Republican identifiers (including leaners) from the percentage of Democratic identifiers (including leaners.)

23. The "feeling thermometer," for those who are unfamiliar with the measure, is a self-anchoring scale with values that vary from 0 to 100. It is used in the ANES studies to measure summary assessments of groups, individuals, and organizations. The term reflects the image of a thermometer that was on a card handed to respondents as a prop to aid them in responding to questions that asked them to rate things on a 100-point scale. Respondents are asked to assign lower numbers—numbers less than 50—to people, groups, or organizations toward which they have negative feelings and use numbers greater than 50 to express positive feelings toward individuals, groups, or organizations. The specific question form is this: "I'd like to get your feelings toward some of our political leaders and other people who are in the news these days. I'll read the name of a person and I'd like you to rate that person using something we call

the feeling thermometer. Ratings between 50 degrees and 100 degrees mean that you feel favorable and warm toward the person. Ratings between 0 degrees and 50 degrees mean that you don't feel favorable toward the person and that you don't care too much for that person. You would rate the person at the 50 degree mark if you don't feel particularly warm or cold toward the person. If we come to a person whose name you don't recognize, you don't need to rate that person. Just tell me and we'll move on to the next one."

24. The polarization scores equal the absolute value of the overall thermometer rating minus 50. This creates a 0 to 50 polarization scale, from low to high, with the larger numbers indicating a stronger feeling toward the party.

25. According to the 2000 ANES, Gore commanded a 6-point advantage over Bush. In 2004, the ANES pegged Bush's margin at 1 point.

26. This estimate is based on election eve polling data. ANES data do not provide a sufficient number of Gen Y respondents for 1996.

Chapter Seven

1. These estimates, like most of the data in the book, come from the National Election Surveys from those years. The lowest number reporting a party contact is 11 percent in 1952. Reported contacts fell to a recent low of 20 percent in 1992 and then rebounded to 29 percent in 1996. Campaign contacting has, it would seem, continued to increase.

2. Some reported contacts from parties, candidates, and other organizations, which explains why the total is less than the sum of candidate/party contacting (45) and group contacting (18) percentages.

3. The estimate is based on Michael McDonald's calculations. The complete set of figures can be found at http://elections.gmu.edu/voter_turnout.htm. The turnout rate among eligible voters is considerably higher than the number that is most commonly reported, which is the percentage based on age-eligible voters. The voter-eligible turnout rate is the more valid estimate. See McDonald and Popkin 2001.

4. These percentages are based on categorizing strong, weak, and leaning partisans into Democrats and Republicans, respectively. The logic behind this presentation is developed in Chapter 2. The above table reports a more detailed breakdown.

5. Campbell 1966.

6. Recent examples include Tucker and Vedlitz 1986; Nagel 1988; Avery 1989; Radcliff 1994; Pacek and Radcliff 1995; and—more tentatively—Nagel and McNulty 1996.

7. Duncan 1991; Freedman 1996.

8. Edsall 1984; Burnham 1987; Piven and Cloward 1988.

9. Kernell 1977.

10. The literature here is very extensive. A representative part of it is Rosenstone and Wolfinger 1978; Wolfinger and Rosenstone 1980; Highton and Wolfinger 2001; Crewe 1981; Erikson 1995a, 1995b; DeNardo 1980; Petrocik 1981b, 1987b; Petrocik and Shaw 1992; Teixeira 1987, 1992; Calvert and Gilchrist 1991; Gant and Lyons 1993; and Beck and Hershey 2001.

11. Notably, the bias, even when it was observed, was almost never large enough to change the outcome of the election, even with 100 percent turnout. See Citrin, Schickler, and Sides 2003.

12. The foundation for his analysis appears in Campbell 1966 and McPhee and Ferguson 1962. Subsequent analyses demonstrated that many voters could not be easily categorized into these polar groups. Sigelman and Jewell 1986, for example, found that it was not unusual for individuals to turn out for a low salience primary or state election but then abstain in a presidential contest—not something that the core-periphery distinction would expect to observe. But although the pattern of participation and abstention did not satisfy the relatively stringent scale thresholds used by Sigelman and Jewell to test for the existence of core and peripheral voters, the scalability coefficients were high enough to demonstrate that a fraction of the subjects in their study could be characterized as core voters with the remainder reasonably categorized as peripherals who sometimes vote but often do not—and in no particularly predictable way.

13. Specifically, there was a .90 correlation between party identification and the vote among those in the top 50 percent in political involvement in the 2000 ANES.

14. The political involvement measure in the figure is an additive index based on strength of partisanship, strength of liberal conservative identification, general interest in politics, and the absolute value of the difference between the respondent's thermometer scores for the Democrats and the Republicans. The items were standardized, arithmetically summed, and divided into deciles.

15. This relationship is familiar to academics; it repeats patterns identified forty years ago by McPhee and Ferguson 1962.

16. We do not present data here on the impact of increased interest on the vote swing, but we have examined that effect, and it shows that turnout and the vote swing move in tandem. For example, a moderate short-term force election (such as represented by the 1984–1988 pair) that boosts the involvement of highly involved citizens one decile (from 8 to 9 in Figure 7.3) has a predicted 4-percentage-point effect on their turnout rate and less than a 1-point effect on their vote. In contrast, a one-decile rise in the involvement of a less involved citizen (from 2 to 3 in the figure) increases their turnout probability 7 percentage points and their likelihood of switching their vote 4 percentage points. A strong short-term force such as is represented by 1996–2000 produces much larger changes.

17. Petrocik 1987b.

18. Their voter status is determined by their postelection interview.

19. This may be an artifact of the time at which the respondents were interviewed. There is some evidence, widely promoted at the time of the election, that undecided voters shifted strongly toward Reagan in the last weeks of the campaign. The ANES survey of 1980 did not pick up this shift well because over half of the interviews were done before October 1, 1980. See Petrocik 1987b.

20. However, the preference for Carter declined as the date of interview was closer to the election. Respondents interviewed in September gave Carter a 10-point plurality; those interviewed in October gave Carter a 5-point plurality. The differences are not statistically significant because of the small size of the subgroups. But the movement toward Reagan (which is consistent with a standard wisdom that the election tilted to Reagan in the last days of the campaign) at least suggests that Reagan might have been the preferred candidate of the nonvoters. Only an election eve poll that validated turnout could test this admittedly speculative assertion. But, at a minimum, the 1980 ANES validation study seems to indicate that the apparent significant difference between the candidate preferences of voters and nonvoters in that year might not have existed.

21. We take this approach in Figure 7.6. A look at the Democratic vote among congressional districts provides a useful viewpoint because it looks at the vote of Democrats, which is the typical number of interest. Also, the large number of congressional districts over such a long time period reduces the chance of a peculiar election or two muddling the overall pattern.

22. In most cases, this total exceeds the sum of the Democratic and Republican vote for Congress. The difference reflects the presence of non–major party candidates and roll-off.

23. In the few instances in which districts did change, they were eliminated from the analysis.

24. The responsiveness coefficient is nothing more than the unstandardized regression coefficient, which we calculated for the dependence of the Democratic vote on turnout within the district if that district had at least four contested elections during the decade. No other measure is required for this analysis because the question is simply whether there is an observable relationship between the share of the vote won by Democratic candidates and the turnout rate.

25. This was a serendipitous finding for the three cases. The examples were not selected to illustrate the major point of this chapter. That they occurred in cases that were selected haphazardly is an indication of how unrelated turnout and vote are in American elections.

26. The average value for the coefficients across the three decades is −.08. The coefficient has negative values (defined as a value equal to or less than −.05)

in 53 percent of the districts, a value near zero (between −.05 and .05) in 9 percent of the districts, and positive (greater than .05) in 38 percent of the cases.

27. Competitiveness is defined as a winner's margin of no more than 55 percent.

28. DeNardo argues, as Duverger 1954 did before him, that because identification with the minority party requires a greater level of commitment than politically peripheral citizens usually muster, the majority party is likely to be overrepresented among peripheral voters. Consequently, as short-term forces associated with an election increase the turnout rate, the proportion of peripheral voters in the electorate increases—simultaneously increasing the defection rate among majority party identifiers. In his analysis, therefore, the majority party has the most to lose from an increase in turnout because it has more identifiers at risk of being influenced by the short-term forces that, in any given election, must have at least an even chance of being on the side of the minority party—making turnout a "joke on the Democrats." See DeNardo 1980.

29. The southern realignment to the GOP, however, does not play a role in the results. It is hard to see why they would except as speculation. In any case, a look by region did not alter the pattern.

Chapter Eight

1. Lodge, McGraw, and Stroh, 1989; Lodge and Stroh 1993; Lodge, Steenbergen, and Brau 1995; Zaller 1992.

2. Lupia and McCubbins 1998; Page and Shapiro 1992; Popkin 1991.

3. An illustrative example is the numerous evasions in Kathleen Hall Jamieson's edited volume on the 2004 campaign. Sometimes the people who know will simply refuse to respond. Consider Joe Lockhart's answer to a question from Jamieson about the Kerry campaign. When Jamieson insisted on a specific rather than an approximate answer, Lockhart replied that he had "no intention of answering that question." See Jamieson 2006.

4. Shaw 1999a, 1999b, and Freedman and Goldstein 1999b, for example, have published studies based on data acquired this way.

5. See, for example, Greenberg 1995.

6. Some refer to "mobilization" and "activation" synonymously. For present purposes, we believe that mobilization is convincing voters to cast ballots. The proper measure of mobilization is therefore turnout rather than vote choice.

7. Endersby and Petrocik 2001; Finkel 1993; Iyengar and Petrocik 2000.

8. Johnston, Hagen, and Jamieson 2004; Hillygus and Shields 2007.

9. Gelman and King 1993; Erikson and Wlezien 2001.

10. Bartels 1993a.

11. We include models from Abramowitz, Campbell, Holbrook, Lewis-Beck and Tien, Lockerbie, Norpoth, and Wlezien and Erikson. All presented their

historical forecasts as well as their predictions for the 2004 presidential election at the annual meeting of the American Political Science Association, Washington, DC, September 2004.

12. Rosenstone and Hansen 1993; Verba et al. 1995.

13. See McDonald and Popkin 2001.

14. For an overview, see Gerber and Green 2004.

15. Gerber and Green 2000, 2001.

16. West 1983.

17. Ansolabehere and Iyengar 1995.

18. Brians and Wattenberg 1996; Finkel and Geer 1998; Geer 2006.

19. Lau and Pomper 2004.

20. Kelley 1983.

21. Bartels 1985.

22. Shaw 1999b.

23. Two current projects are recreating candidate travel from presidential elections going back to 1948. The availability of more reliable data on candidate schedules and public opinion from the libraries of presidential candidates may allow us to calculate precise estimates of appearance effects.

24. Vavreck, Spiliotes, and Fowler 2002.

25. Holbrook 1994, 1996; Stimson 2004.

26. See Holbrook 1996. This contention is backed by specific studies of campaign events by Campbell, Cherry, and Wink 1992; Geer 1988; Lanoue 1991; and Shelley and Hwang 1991.

27. Shaw 1999a; Johnston et al. 2004.

28. Shaw 1999a; but see Fackler and Lin 1995.

29. Shaw 1999a.

30. Goldstein and Freedman 2002b; Brians and Wattenberg 1996.

31. Iyengar and Kinder 1987.

32. D'Alessio and Allen 2000.

33. Some recent studies (e.g., Groseclose and Milyo 2005) dispute the notion that news media coverage is not biased. From what we can tell, the main difference appears to be in analyzing all political coverage versus campaign coverage only.

34. See, for instance, Sabato 1993; Kerbel 1995; and Lichter and Noyes 1995.

35. Hetherington 1999; Lichter and Noyes 1995.

36. See Robinson and Sheehan 1983; and Sigal 1973.

37. Budge and Farlie 1983; Petrocik 1996.

38. Brader 2006; Hayes 2005.

39. Campbell 2000; Wlezien and Erikson 2002.

40. There is, of course, reason to view the absolute magnitude of self-reported contacting with skepticism—surely many are contacted but fail to recall the contact. But there is little reason to suspect this overreporting isn't constant over time. Thus, relative movement in the measure should be valid.

41. We do not have consistent presidential campaign battleground lists prior to 1988, although reasonably complete lists do exist for 1976.

42. Shaw 2006.

43. These figures represent total gross rating points of presidential election advertising. GRPs represent the number of times the average person sees an advertisement in a given market. For example, if a campaign purchases 1,200 GRPs, then the average person in that market will see the ad twelve times. The time frame covers the fall campaign—August 20 through election day.

44. Gimpel, Kaufmann, and Pearson-Merkowitz 2007.

45. Candidate appearances encompass both presidential and vice-presidential appearances within a media market. Only public appearances are counted (not private or closed fund-raising appearances). A candidate can be credited with only one appearance on a given day even if he or she makes multiple appearances. The time frame covers the fall campaign—August 20 to election day.

46. King and Morehouse 2004.

47. Holbrook and McClurg 2005.

48. This fits with two recent books on the subject of contemporary American campaigning: Fournier, Sosnick, and Dowd's *Applebee's America* (2006) and Halperin and Harris's *How to Win* (2006).

Chapter Nine

1. Bartels 1988; Cohen, Karol, and Zaller 2008; Steger 2007.

2. Money has always been important. It has taken different forms over the history of the nation. Patronage workers were a publicly funded campaign resource in the era of patronage politics. The staff of many officeholders provide similar resources today, but most modern campaigns collect money and spend it directly to purchase the services needed to campaign.

3. Kaufmann et al. 2003.

4. A persuasive example is Costantini's 1963 article on the 1960 California delegation.

5. Geer 1989; Norrander 1989.

6. Burden 2001; Brady and Fiorina 2000.

7. See Petrocik 1996; and Petrocik, Benoit, and Hansen 2003–2004.

8. See Jamieson 2006.

9. Petrocik 2006.

10. This is based on our calculations of the contribution of union households to the electorate in those elections. These estimates are not precise.

11. Again, see de Sola Pool, Abelson, and Popkin 1965, for a variation on this that was put to work for the 1960 election by the Democrats.

12. See the *Washington Post* story on geo-demographic targeting at WashingtonPost.com (2007).

13. A recent account that occasionally provides a glimpse of how the campaigns think about some of these matters is found in Jamieson 2006.

14. The firms use moderately sophisticated techniques to segment survey data into demographically defined groups that appear responsive to issues messages. These segmentation techniques can also be used to identify types of voters for get-out-the-vote efforts.

Bibliography

Aberbach, Joel D., and Bert A. Rockman. 2000. *In the Web of Politics: Three Decades of the U.S Federal Executive*. Washington, DC: Brookings Institution Press.

Abramowitz, Alan I. 2004. When Good Forecasts Go Bad: The Time-for-Change Model and the 2004 Presidential Election. *PS: Political Science and Politics* (October): 745–761.

———. 1997. The Cultural Divide in American Politics: Moral Issues and Presidential Voting. In Barbara Norrander and Clyde Wilcox (Eds.), *Understanding Public Opinion*. Washington, DC: CQ Press.

Abramowitz, Alan I., and Kyle L. Saunders. 2005. Why Can't We All Just Get Along? The Reality of a Polarized America. *The Forum* 2, article 1. http://www.bepress.com/forum.

———. 1998. Ideological Realignment in the U.S. Electorate. *Journal of Politics* 60: 634–652.

Abzug, Bella, and Mim Kelber. 1984. *Gender Gap*. Boston: Houghton Mifflin.

Adams, William C., and Dennis J. Smith. 1980. Effects of Telephone Canvassing on Turnout and Preferences: A Field Experiment. *Public Opinion Quarterly* 44: 389–395.

Aldrich, John H. 1995. *Why Parties? The Origin and Transformation of Political Parties in America*. Chicago: University of Chicago Press.

Almond, Gabriel A., and Sidney Verba. 1963. *The Civic Culture*. Princeton, NJ: Princeton University Press.

American Political Science Association. 1950. *Toward a More Responsible Two-Party System: A Report of the Committee on Political Parties and of the American Political Science Association*. New York: Rinehart.

Andersen, Kristi. 1979. *The Creation of a Democratic Majority, 1928–1936.* Chicago: University of Chicago Press.

Andolina, M. W., K. Jenkins, S. Keeter, and C. Zufkin. 2002. Searching for the Meaning of Youth Civic Engagement: Notes from the Field. *Applied Developmental Science* 6: 189–195.

Ansolabehere, Stephen D., and Shanto Iyengar. 1995. *Going Negative: How Attack Ads Shrink and Polarize the Electorate.* New York: Free Press.

Avery, M. 1989. *The Demobilization of American Voters.* New York: Greenwood.

Axelrod, Robert. 1986. Presidential Election Coalitions in 1984. *American Political Science Review* 80(4): 281–284.

Barrett, Liz Cox. 2004. "Security Moms" Are Everywhere! *Columbia Journalism Review,* September 22. http://www.cjr.org/politics/security moms are everywhere.

Bartels, Larry M. 2000. Partisanship and Voting Behavior. *American Journal of Political Science* 44(1): 35–50.

———. 1993a. Messages Received: The Political Impact of Media Exposure. *American Political Science Review* 87(1): 267–285.

———. 1993b. Electioneering in the United States. In David Butler and Austin Ranney (Eds.), *Electioneering: A Comparative Study of Continuity and Change,* pp. 244–277. Oxford, UK: Clarendon Press.

———. 1988. *Presidential Primaries and the Dynamics of Public Choice.* Princeton, NJ: Princeton University Press.

———. 1985. Resource Allocation in a Presidential Campaign. *Journal of Politics* 47: 928–936.

Beck, Paul Allen. 1974. A Socialization Theory of Realignment. In Richard G. Niemi (Ed.), *The Politics of Future Citizens.* San Francisco: Jossey-Bass.

Beck, Paul Allen, and Marjorie Randon Hershey. 2001. *Party Politics in America.* New York: Addison Wesley Longman.

Berelson, Bernard R., Paul F. Lazarsfeld, and William N. McPhee. 1954. *Voting: A Study of Opinion Formation in a Presidential Campaign.* Chicago: University of Chicago Press.

Blumenthal, Mark. 2004. Do Undecided Voters Break for the Challenger? http://www.mysterypollster.com/main/2004/09/do_undecided_vo.html.

Bond, John R., and R. Fleischer. 2000. *Polarized Politics: Congress and the President in a Partisan Era.* Washington, DC: CQ Press.

Bowers, Chris. 2004. Incumbent Rule Research Update. http://www.mydd.com/story/2004/9/3/22294/96534.

Box-Steffensmeier, Janet M., Suzanna de Boef, and Tse-Min Lin. 2004. The Dynamics of the Partisan Gender Gap. *American Political Science Review* 98(3): 515–525.

Boyd, R. 1985. Electoral Change in the United States and Great Britain. *British Journal of Political Science* 15: 517–528.

Brader, Ted. 2006. *Campaigning for Hearts and Minds*. Chicago: University of Chicago Press.

Brady, David W., and Morris Fiorina. 2000. Congress in the Era of the Permanent Campaign. In Norman J. Ornstein and Thomas E. Mann (Eds.), *The Permanent Campaign and Its Future*. Washington, DC: AEI and Brookings Institution Press.

Braumoeller, Bear. 2004. Hypothesis Testing and Multiplicative Interaction Terms. *International Organization* 58 (Fall): 807–820.

Brewer, Mark D. 2005. The Rise of Partisanship and the Expansion of Partisan Conflict within the American Electorate. *Political Research Quarterly* 58: 210–230.

Brians, Craig L., and Martin P. Wattenberg. 1996. Campaign Issue Knowledge and Salience: Comparing Reception from TV Commercials, TV News, and Newspapers. *American Journal of Political Science* 40: 172–193.

Budge, Ian, Ivor Crewe, and Dennis Farlie. 1976. *Party Identification and Beyond*. New York: Wiley.

Budge, Ian, and Dennis Farlie. 1983. Party Competition—Selective Emphasis or Direct Confrontation? An Alternative View with Data. In Hans Daalder and Peter Mair (Eds.), *West European Party Systems: Continuity and Change*. London: Sage Publications.

Burden, Barry. 2001. The Polarizing Effects of Congressional Primaries. In Peter F. Galderisi, Michael Lyons, and Marni Ezra (Eds.), *Congress Primaries in the Politics of Representation*. Lanham, MD: Rowman and Littlefield.

Burden, Barry C., and David C. Kimball. 2002. *Why Americans Split Their Tickets: Campaigns, Competition, and Divided Government*. Ann Arbor: University of Michigan Press.

Burnham, Walter Dean. 1987. The Turnout Problem. In A. James Reichley (Ed.), *Elections American Style*. Washington, DC: Brookings Institution Press.

Burnham, Walter Dean. 1970. *Critical Elections and the Mainsprings of American Politics*. New York: Norton.

Cain, Bruce E. 1985. Assessing the Partisan Effects of Redistricting. *American Political Science Review* 79(2): 320–333.

Cain, Bruce, John Ferejohn, and Morris Fiorina. 1987. *The Personal Vote*. Cambridge, MA: Harvard University Press.

Cain, Bruce E., and Ken McCue. 1985. The Efficacy of Voter Registration Drives. *Journal of Politics* 47(4): 1221–1230.

Calvert, J., and J. Gilchrist. 1991. The Social and Issue Dimensions of Voting and Nonvoting in the United States. Paper presented at the 1991 Annual Meeting of the American Political Science Association, Washington, DC.

Campbell, Angus. 1966. Surge and Decline. In Angus Campbell, Phillip E. Converse, Warren E. Miller, and Donald E. Stokes (Eds.), *Elections and the Political Order*. New York: Wiley.

Campbell, Angus, Philip E. Converse, Warren E. Miller, and Donald E. Stokes. 1960. *The American Voter*. Chicago: University of Chicago Press.

Campbell, Angus, Gerald Gurin, and Warren Miller. 1954. *The Voter Decides*. Evanston, IL: Peterson.

Campbell, James E. 2004. Forecasting the Presidential Vote in 2004: Placing Preference Polls in Context. *PS: Political Science and Politics* (October): 763–767.

———. 2000. *The American Campaign*. College Station: Texas A&M Press.

Campbell, James E., Lynne Cherry, and Kenneth Wink. 1992. The Convention Bump. *American Politics Quarterly* 20: 287–307.

Carroll, Susan. 1999. The Disempowerment of the Gender Gap: Soccer Moms and the 1996 Election. *PS: Political Science and Politics* 32(2): 7–11.

Chaney, Carole K., R. Michael Alvarez, and Jonathan Nagler. 1998. Explaining the Gender Gap in the U.S. Presidential Elections, 1980–1992. *Political Research Quarterly* 51(2): 311–340.

Citrin, Jack, Eric Shickler, and John Sides. 2003. What if Everyone Voted? Simulating the Impact of Increased Turnout in Senate Elections. *American Journal of Political Science* 47: 75–90.

Clarke, Harold D., Marianne C. Stewart, Mike Ault, and Euel Elliot. 2004. Men, Women and the Dynamics of Presidential Approval. *British Journal of Political Science* 35: 31–51.

Clinton, Joshua, and John Lapinski. 2004. An Experimental Study of Political Advertising Effects in the 2000 Presidential Election. *Journal of Politics* 66(1): 67–96.

Cohen, Marty, David Karol, and John Zaller. 2008. *Beating Reform: Political Parties and Presidential Nominations before and after Reform*. Chicago: University of Chicago Press.

Conover, Pamela Johnston. 1988. Feminists and the Gender Gap. *Journal of Politics* 50: 985–1010.

Conover, Pamela Johnston, and Virginia Sapiro. 1993. Gender, Feminist Consciousness and War. *American Journal of Political Science* 37(4): 1079–1099.

Converse, Philip E. 1976. *The Dynamics of Party Support: Cohort-Analyzing Party Identification*. Beverly Hills, CA: Sage.

———. 1969. Of Time and Partisan Stability. *Comparative Political Studies* 2: 139–171.

———. 1966. The Concept of a Normal Vote. In Angus Campbell, Philip E. Converse, Warren E. Miller, and Donald E. Stokes (Eds.), *Elections and the Political Order*. New York: Wiley.

———. 1964. The Nature of Belief Systems in Mass Publics. In David E. Apter (Ed.), *Ideology and Discontent*, pp. 206–261. New York: Free Press.

————. 1962. Information Flow and the Stability of Partisan Attitudes. *Public Opinion Quarterly* 26: 578–599.

Cook, Elizabeth Adell, and Clyde Wilcox. 1991. Feminism and the Gender Gap—a Second Look. *Journal of Politics* 53: 1111–1122.

Costantini, Edmund. 1963. Intraparty Attitude Conflict: Democratic Party Leadership in California. *Western Political Quarterly* 16 (December): 956–972.

Cotter, Cornelius P., James L. Gibson, John F. Bibby, and Robert J. Huckshorn. 1984. *Party Organizations in American Politics*. Pittsburgh: University of Pittsburgh Press.

Cox, Gary W., and Jonathan Katz, 1996. Why Did the Incumbency Advantage in U.S. House Elections Grow? *American Journal of Political Science* 40(2): 478–497.

Cox, Gary W., and Mathew D. McCubbins. 2003. *Legislative Leviathan Revisited*. Cambridge, UK: Cambridge University Press.

————. 1993. *Legislative Leviathan*. Berkeley: University of California Press.

Crewe, Ivor. 1981. Electoral Participation. In David Butler, Howard R. Penniman, and Austin Ranney (Eds.), *Democracy at the Polls: A Comparative Study of Competitive National Elections*. Washington, DC: American Enterprise Institute.

Dahl, Robert A. 1961. *Who Governs? Democracy and Power in an American City*. New Haven, CT: Yale University Press.

D'Alessio, D., and M. Allen. 2000. Media Bias in Presidential Elections: A Meta-Analysis. *Journal of Communication* 90(3): 133–156.

Daudt, Hans. 1961. *Floating Voters and the Floating Vote: A Critical Analysis of American and English Election Studies*. Leiden: H. E. Stenfert Kroese.

DeNardo, James. 1980. Turnout and the Vote: The Joke's on the Democrats. *American Political Science Review* 74(2): 406–420.

de Sola Pool, Ithiel, Robert P. Abelson, and Samuel Popkin. 1965. *Candidates, Issues, and Strategies: A Computer Simulation of the 1960 and 1964 Elections*. Cambridge: MIT Press.

Desposato, Scott W., and John R. Petrocik. 2001. The Variable Incumbent Advantage: New Voters, Redistricting, and the Personal Vote. *American Journal of Political Science* 47: 33–45.

Dionne, E. J., Jr. 2004. What Kind of Hater Are You? *Washington Post*, March 15, A19.

Dobbs, Michael. 2001. Investment in Freedom Is Flush with Peril. *Washington Post*, January 25, A1.

Dobson, Douglas, and Douglas St. Angelo. 1975. Party Identification and the Floating Vote: Some Dynamics. *American Political Science Review* 69(2): 481–490.

Downs, Anthony. 1957. *An Economic Theory of Democracy*. New York: Harper and Row.

Duncan, Dayton. 1991. *Grass Roots: One Year in the Life of the New Hampshire Presidential Primary*. New York: Penguin.

Duverger, Maurice. 1954. *Political Parties*. London: University Paperbacks.

Eagly, Alice H., Amanda B. Dickman, Mary C. Johannesen-Schmidt, and Anne M. Koenig. 2004. Gender Gaps in Sociopolitical Attitudes: A Social Psychological Analysis. *Journal of Personality and Social Psychology* 87(6): 796–816.

Edsall, Thomas Byrne. 1984. *The New Politics of Inequality*. New York: Norton.

Edsall, Thomas, and Mark Grimaldi. 2004. GOP Made Better Use of Its Millions. *Washington Post*, December 28, A-1.

Eldersveld, Samuel J. 1949. Influence of Metropolitan Party Pluralities on Presidential Elections. *American Political Science Review* 49: 1189–1206.

Endersby, James W., and John R. Petrocik. 2001. Campaign Spending Influence on Turnout: Mobilization versus Agenda-Setting. Presented at the annual meeting of the Southwestern Social Science Association, Fort Worth, TX, March 16–18.

Erie, Steven P., and Martin Rein. 1988. Women and the Welfare State. In Carol M. Mueller (Ed.), *The Politics of the Gender Gap: The Social Construction of Political Influence*, pp. 173–191. Newbury Park, CA: Sage.

Erikson, Robert S. 1995a. State Turnout and Presidential Voting: A Closer Look. *American Politics Quarterly* 23 (October): 387–396.

———. 1995b. Pooling and Statistical Control: A Rejoinder to Radcliff. *American Politics Quarterly* 23 (October): 404–408.

Erikson, Robert S., Thomas D. Lancaster, and David W. Romero. 1989. Group Components of the Presidential Vote, 1952–1984. *Journal of Politics* 51(2): 337–346.

Erikson, Robert S., Michael B. MacKuen, and James A. Stimson. 2002. *The Macro Polity*. New York: Cambridge University Press.

Erikson, Robert S., and Christopher Wlezien. 2001. After the Election: Our Forecast in Retrospect. *American Politics Research* 29: 320–328.

Fackler, Tim, and Tse-min Lin. 1995. Political Corruption and Presidential Elections, 1929–1992. *Journal of Politics* 57(4): 971–993.

Finkel, Steven. 1993. Reexamining the "Minimal Effects" Model in Recent Presidential Campaigns. *Journal of Politics* 55: 1–21.

Finkel, Steven, and John G. Geer. 1998. A Spot Check: Casting Doubt on the Demobilizing Effect of Attack Advertising. *American Journal of Political Science* 42: 573–595.

Fiorina, Morris P. 1981. *Retrospective Voting in American Elections*. New Haven, CT: Yale University Press.

———. 1977a. *Congress: Keystone of the Washington Establishment*. New Haven, CT: Yale University Press.

————. 1977b. An Outline for a Model of Party Choice. *American Journal of Political Science* 21 (August): 601–626.

Fiorina, Morris P., Samuel J. Abrams, and Jeremy C. Pope. 2005. *Culture War? The Myth of a Polarized America,* 2nd ed. New York: Pearson Longman.

Fiorina, Morris P., and Douglas Rivers. 1989. Constituency Service, Reputation, and the Incumbency Advantage. In Morris P. Fiorina and David Rhode (Eds.), *Home Style and Washington Work.* Ann Arbor: University of Michigan Press.

Fleisher, R., and John R. Bond. 2004. The Shrinking Middle in the U.S. Congress. *British Journal of Political Science* 34: 429–451.

Fournier, Ron, Douglas Sosnick, and Matthew Dowd. 2006. *Applebee's America.* New York: Simon and Schuster.

Frank, Thomas. 2004. *What's the Matter with Kansas? How Conservatives Won the Heart of America.* New York: Metropolitan.

Frankovic, Kathleen. 1982. Sex and Politics—New Alignments, Old Issues. *PS: Political Science and Politics* 15: 439–448.

Freedman, Paul, and Kenneth M. Goldstein. 1999. Measuring Media Exposure and the Effects of Negative Campaign Ads. *American Journal of Political Science* 43: 1189–1208.

Freedman, Samuel G. 1996. *The Inheritance: How Three Families and America Moved from Roosevelt to Reagan and Beyond.* New York: Simon and Schuster.

Gant, M., and W. Lyons. 1993. Democratic Theory, Nonvoting, and Public Policy: The 1972–1988 Presidential Elections. *American Politics Quarterly* 21: 185–204.

Geer, John G. 2006. *In Defense of Negativity.* Chicago: University of Chicago Press.

————. 1989. *Nominating Presidents: An Evaluation of Voters and Primaries.* New York: Greenwood Press.

————. 1988. The Effects of Presidential Debates on the Electorate's Preferences for Candidates. *American Politics Quarterly* 16: 486–501.

Geer, John G., and James H. Geer. 2003. Remembering Attack Ads: An Experimental Investigation of Radio. *Political Behavior* 25: 69–95.

Geer, John G., and Richard R. Lau. 2006. Filling in the Blanks: A New Method for Estimating Campaign Effects. *British Journal of Political Science* 2: 269–290.

Gelman, Andrew, and Gary King. 1993. Why Are American Presidential Election Polls So Variable When Votes Are So Predictable? *British Journal of Political Science* 23: 409–451.

Gerber, Alan S. 2004. *Get Out the Vote.* Washington, DC: Brookings Institution Press.

————. 2001. Do Phone Calls Increase Voter Turnout? A Field Experiment. *Public Opinion Quarterly* 65: 75–85.

————. 1998. Estimating the Effect of Campaign Spending on Senate Election Outcomes Using Instrumental Variables. *American Political Science Review* 92(2): 401–411.

Gerber, Alan S., and Donald P. Green. 2000. The Effects of Canvassing, Telephone Calls, and Direct Mail on Voter Turnout: A Field Experiment. *American Political Science Review* 94: 653–663.

Gilens, Martin. 1988. Gender and Support for Reagan: A Comprehensive Model of Presidential Approval. *American Journal of Political Science* 32: 19–49.

Gimpel, James G., Joshua J. Dyck, and Daron R. Shaw. 2007. Election-Year Stimuli and the Timing of Voter Registration. *Party Politics* 13(3): 347–370.

Gimpel, James G., Karen Kaufmann, and Shanna Pearson-Merkowitz. 2007. Battleground States versus Blackout States: The Behavioral Implications of Modern Presidential Campaigns. *Journal of Politics* 69(3): 786–797.

Gimpel James G., J. Celeste Lay, and Jason E. Schuknecht. 2003. *Cultivating Democracy: Civic Environments and Political Socialization in America.* Washington DC: Brookings Institution Press.

Goldstein, Kenneth, and Paul Freedman. 2002a. Campaign Advertising and Voter Turnout: New Evidence for a Stimulation Effect. *Journal of Politics* 64(3): 721–740.

————. 2002b. Lessons Learned: Campaign Advertising in the 2000 Elections. *Political Communication* 19: 5–28.

Gosnell, Harold F. 1937. *Machine Politics: Chicago Style.* Chicago: University of Chicago Press.

————. 1927. *Getting Out the Vote: An Experiment in the Stimulation of Voting.* Chicago: University of Chicago Press.

Gosnell, Harold F., and Charles E. Merriam. 1924. *Non-Voting: Causes and Methods of Control.* Chicago: University of Chicago Press.

Green, Donald P., Bradley Palmquist, and Eric Schickler. 2002. *Partisan Hearts and Minds: Political Parties and the Social Identity of Voters.* New Haven, CT: Yale University Press.

Greenberg, Anna. 2004. Breaking down the Security Mom Myth. http://www.greenbergresearch.com/index.php?ID=1240.

Greenberg, Stanley B. 1995. *Middle Class Dreams: The Politics and Power of the New American Majority.* New York: Times Books.

Groseclose, Timothy, and Jeffrey Milyo. 2005. A Measure of Media Bias. *Quarterly Journal of Economics* 120(4): 1191–1237.

Halperin, Mark, and John F. Harris. 2006. *How to Win.* New York: Random House.

Harman, Danna. 1999. Carville: This Game Is Over, and I Am Outta Here. *Jerusalem Post,* May 20.

Hayes, Daniel. 2005. Candidate Qualities through a Partisan Lens: A Theory of Trait Ownership. *American Journal of Political Science* 49(4): 908–923.

Herrnson, Paul S. 2000. *Congressional Elections: Campaigning at Home and in Washington*, 3rd ed. Washington, DC: CQ Press.

Hetherington, Marc J. 2001. Resurgent Mass Partisanship: The Role of Elite Polarization. *American Political Science Review* 95: 619–631.

———. 1999. The Effect of Political Trust on the Presidential Vote, 1968–96. *American Political Science Review* 93: 311–326.

Highton, Benjamin, and Raymond E. Wolfinger. 2001. The Political Implications of High Turnout. *British Journal of Political Science* 31: 179–192.

Hillygus, D. Sunshine, and Simon Jackman. 2003. Voter Decision-Making in Election 2000: Campaign Effects, Partisan Activation, and the Clinton Legacy. *American Journal of Political Science* 47(4): 583–596.

Hillygus, D. Sunshine, and Todd Shields. 2007. *The Persuadable Voter: Strategic Candidates and Wedge Issues in Political Campaigns*. Princeton, NJ: Princeton University Press.

Hinich, Melvin J., and Michael C. Munger. 1994. *Ideology and the Theory of Political Choice*. Ann Arbor: University of Michigan Press.

Holbrook, Thomas M. 2002. Did the Whistle-Stop Campaign Matter? *PS: Political Science and Politics* 35(1): 59–66.

———. 1996. *Do Campaigns Matter?* Thousand Oaks, CA: Sage.

———. 1994. Campaigns, National Campaigns, and U.S. Presidential Elections. *American Journal of Political Science* 38: 973–998.

Holbrook, Thomas M., and Scott D. McClurg. 2005. Presidential Campaigns and the Mobilization of Core Supporters. *American Journal of Political Science* 49(4): 689–703.

Holley, David. 2003. Voters Doubt Fairness of Georgian Election. *Los Angeles Times*, November 3.

The Hotline. December 10, 1999. http://nationaljournal.com/about/hotline/.

Howe, Neil, and William Strauss. 2000. *Millenials Rising: The Next Great Generation*. New York: Vintage Press.

Hunter, James Davison. 1991. *Culture Wars: The Struggle to Define America*. New York: Basic Books.

Iyengar, Shanto, and Donald R. Kinder. 1987. *News that Matters*. Chicago: University of Chicago Press.

Iyengar, Shanto, Mark D. Peters, and Donald R. Kinder. 1982. Experimental Demonstrations of the "Not-So-Minimal" Consequences of Television News Programs. *American Political Science Review* 76(4): 848–858.

Iyengar, Shanto, and John R. Petrocik. 2000. "Basic Rule" Voting: Impact of Campaigns on Party- and Approval-Based Voting. In J. A. Thurber, C. J. Nelson, and D. A. Diulio (Eds.), *Crowded Airwaves: Campaign Advertising in Elections*, pp. 113–148. Washington, DC: Brookings Institution Press.

Jacobson, Gary C. 2007. *A Divider, Not a Uniter: George W. Bush and the American People*. New York: Pearson Longman.

———. 2004. *The Politics of Congressional Elections*. New York: Pearson Longman.

———. 2000. Party Polarization in National Politics: The Electoral Connection. In John R. Bond and R. Fleischer (Eds.), *Polarized Politics: Congress and the President in a Partisan Era*. Washington, DC: CQ Press.

Jacobson, Gary C., and Samuel Kernell. 1981. *Strategy and Choice in Congressional Elections*. New Haven, CT: Yale University Press.

Jamieson, Kathleen Hall. 2006. *Electing the President 2004: The Insiders' View*. Philadelphia: University of Pennsylvania Press.

Jelen, Ted G. 1997. Culture Wars and the Party System: Religion and Realignment, 1972–1993. In Rhys Williams II (Ed.), *Culture Wars in American Politics: Critical Reviews of a Popular Myth*. New York: Aldine de Gruyter.

Jennings, M. Kent, and Richard G. Niemi. 1968. The Transmission of Political Values from Parent to Child. *American Political Science Review* 62(2): 169–184.

Johnston, Richard, Michael G. Hagen, and Kathleen Hall Jamieson. 2004. *The 2000 Presidential Election and the Foundations of Party Politics*. Cambridge, UK: Cambridge University Press.

Kahn, Kim Fridkin. 1993. Gender Differences in Campaign Messages: The Political Advertisements of Men and Women Candidates for U.S. Senate. *Political Research Quarterly* 46: 481–502.

Kaufmann, Karen M. 2006. The Gender Gap. *PS: Political Science and Politics* (July): 447–453.

———. 2004. The Partisan Paradox: Religious Commitment and the Gender Gap in Party Identification. *Public Opinion Quarterly* 68(4): 491–511.

———. 2002. Culture Wars, Secular Realignment and the Gender Gap in Party Identification. *Political Behavior* 24(3): 283–307.

Kaufmann, Karen M., James G. Gimpel, and Adam Hoffman. 2003. A Promise Fulfilled: Open Primaries and Representation. *Journal of Politics* 64(2): 457–476.

Kaufmann, Karen M., and John R. Petrocik. 1999. The Changing Politics of American Men: Understanding the Sources of the Gender Gap. *American Journal of Political Science* 43(3): 164–187.

Keith, Bruce E., David B. Magleby, Candice J. Nelson, Elizabeth Orr, Mark C. Westlye, and Raymond E. Wolfinger. 1992. *The Myth of the Independent Voter*. Berkeley: University of California Press.

Kelley, Stanley, Jr. 1983. *Interpreting Elections*. Princeton, NJ: Princeton University Press.

Kellstedt, Lyman A., John C. Green, James L. Guth, and Corwin E. Smidt. 1996. Has Godot Finally Arrived? Religion and Realignment. In John C. Green, James L. Guth, Corwin E. Smidt, and Lyman A. Kellstedt (Eds.), *Religion and the Culture Wars: Dispatches from the Front*. Lanham, MD: Rowman and Littlefield.

Kerbel, Matthew. 1995. *Remote Controlled: Media Politics in a Cynical Age*. Boulder, CO: Westview.

Kernell, Samuel. 1977. Presidential Popularity and Negative Voting: An Alternative Explanation of the Midterm Congressional Decline of the President's Party. *American Political Science Review* 71: 44–66.

Key, V. O., Jr. 1966. *The Responsible Electorate: Rationality in Presidential Voting 1936–1960*. Cambridge, MA: Harvard University Press.

———. 1961. *Public Opinion and American Democracy*. New York: Alfred Knopf.

———. 1955. A Theory of Critical Elections. *Journal of Politics* 17 (February): 3–18.

King, David C. 1997. The Polarization of American Parties and Mistrust of Government. In Joseph S. Nye, Jr., Philip D. Zelikow, and David C. King (Eds.), *Why People Don't Trust Government*. Cambridge, MA: Harvard University Press.

King, David C., and David Morehouse. 2004. Moving Voters in the 2000 Presidential Campaign: Local Visits and Local Media. In David Schultz (Ed.), *Lights, Camera, Campaign*. New York: Peter Lang.

Klein, Ethel. 1984. *Gender Politics*. Cambridge, MA: Harvard University Press.

Kohut, Andrew, John C. Green, Scott Keeter, and Robert C. Toth. 2000. *The Diminishing Divide: Religion's Changing Role in American Politics*. Washington, DC: Brookings Institution Press.

Kolodny, Robin. 1998. *Pursuing Majorities: Congressional Campaign Committees in American Politics*. Norman: University of Oklahoma Press.

Kousser, J. Morgan. 1996. Estimating the Partisan Consequences of Redistricting Plans—Simply. *Legislative Studies Quarterly* 21: 521–541.

Ladd, Everett Carll. 1999. *The Ladd Report*. New York: Free Press.

Lanoue, David J. 1991. The "Turning Point": Viewers' Reactions to the Second 1988 Presidential Debate. *American Politics Quarterly* 19: 80–95.

Lau, Richard R., and Gerald M. Pomper. 2004. *Negative Campaigning: An Analysis of U.S. Senate Elections*. Lanham, MD: Rowman and Littlefield.

Lau, Richard R., Lee Sigelman, Caroline Heldman, and Paul Babbitt. 1999. The Effects of Negative Political Advertisements: A Meta-Analytic Assessment. *American Political Science Review* 93(4): 851–875.

Layman, Geoffrey. 2001. *The Great Divide: Religious Cultural Conflict in American Party Politics*. New York: Columbia University Press.

———. 1997. Religion and Political Behavior in the United States: The Impact of Beliefs, Affiliations, and Commitment from 1980 to 1994. *Public Opinion Quarterly* 61: 288–316.

Layman, Geoffrey C., and Thomas M. Carsey. 2002a. Party Polarization and Conflict Extension in the American Electorate. *American Journal of Political Science* 46: 786–802.

———. 2002b. Party Polarization and Party Structuring of Policy Attitudes: A Comparison of Three NES Panel Studies. *Political Behavior* 24: 199–236.

Lazarsfeld, Paul, Bernard Berelson, and Helen Gaudet. 1948. *The People's Choice*. New York: Columbia University Press.

Lewis-Beck, Michael, and Thomas W. Rice. 1992. *Forecasting Elections*. Washington, DC: CQ Press.

Lewis-Beck, Michael, and Charles Tien. 2004. Jobs and the Job of President: A Forecast for 2004. *PS: Political Science and Politics* (October): 753–758.

Lichter, S. Robert, and Richard E. Noyes. 1995. *Good Intentions Make Bad News: Why Americans Hate Campaign Journalism*. Lanham, MD: Rowman and Littlefield.

Lijphart, Arend. 1997. Unequal Participation: Democracy's Unresolved Dilemma. *American Political Science Review* 91 (March): 1–14.

Lockerbie, Brad. A Look to the Future: Forecasting the 2004 Presidential Election. *PS: Political Science and Politics* (October): 741–743.

Lodge, Milton, Kathleen McGraw, and Patrick Stroh. 1989. An Impression-Driven Model of Candidate Evaluation. *American Political Science Review* 87: 399–419.

Lodge, Milton, Marco Steenbergen, and Shawn Brau. 1995. The Responsive Voter: Campaign Information and the Dynamics of Candidate Evaluation. *American Political Science Review* 89: 309–326.

Lodge, Milton, and Patrick Stroh. 1993. Inside the Mental Voting Booth: An Impression-Driven Model of Candidate Evaluation. In Shanto Iyengar and William J. McGuire (Eds.), *Explorations in Political Psychology*. Durham, NC: Duke University Press.

Lubell, Sam. 1952. *The Future of American Politics*. New York: Greenwood-Heinemann Publishing.

Lupia, Arthur, and Mathew D. McCubbins. 1998. *The Democratic Dilemma: Can Citizens Learn What They Need to Know?* New York: Cambridge University Press.

Maggiotto, Michael A., and James E. Piereson. 1977. Partisan Identification and Electoral Choice: The Hostility Hypothesis. *American Journal of Political Science* 21: 745–767.

Mansbridge, Jane. 1985. Myth and Reality: The ERA and the Gender Gap in the 1980 Election. *Public Opinion Quarterly* 49: 164–178.

Markus, George E. 1988. The Structure of Emotional Response: 1984 Presidential Candidates. *American Political Science Review* 82(3): 737–761.

Mattei, Franco. 2000. The Gender Gap in Presidential Evaluations: Assessments of Clinton's Performance in 1996. *Polity* 33(2): 199–228.

May, Ann Mari, and Kurt Stephenson. 1994. Women and the Great Retrenchment: The Political Economy of Gender in the 1980s. *Journal of Economic Issues* 28: 533–542.

Mayer, William. 2002. The Swing Voter in American Presidential Elections: A Preliminary Inquiry. Paper presented at the Annual Meeting of the American Political Science Association, August 29–September 1, Boston, MA.

Mayhew, David R. 1974. *Congress: The Electoral Connection*. New Haven, CT: Yale University Press.

McCleneghan, J. Sean. 1987. Impact of Radio Ads on New Mexico Mayoral Races. *Journalism Quarterly* 64: 590–593.

McDermott, Monika L. 1997. Voting Cues in Low Information Elections: Candidate Gender as a Social Information Variable in Contemporary United States Elections. *American Journal of Political Science* 41(1): 270–283.

McDonald, Michael P., and Samuel Popkin. 2001. The Myth of the Vanishing Voter. *American Political Science Review* 95(4): 963–974.

McPhee, William, and Jack Ferguson. 1962. Political Immunization. In William McPhee and Nathan Glaser (Eds.), *Public Opinion and Congressional Elections*. New York: Free Press.

Mendelberg, Tali. 1996. *The Race Card*. Princeton, NJ: Princeton University Press.

Miller, Roy E., David A. Bositis, and Denise L. Baer. 1981. Stimulating Voter Turnout in a Primary: Field Experiment with a Precinct Committeeman. *International Political Science Review* 2: 445–460.

Miller, Susan M., and L. Marvin Overby. 2007. "Party or Petition": Discharge Behavior in the Modern House. Unpublished manuscript, Department of Political Science, University of Missouri, Columbia.

Miller, Warren E. 1991. Party Identification, Realignment and Party Voting: Back to Basics. *American Political Science Review* 85: 557–568.

Miller, Warren, and Merrill Shanks. 1996. *The New American Voter*. Cambridge, MA: Harvard University Press.

Molyneaux, Guy. 2005. The Big Five-Oh. http://www.prospect.org/cs/ articles?articleId=8694.

Nagel, Jack H. 1988. Voter Turnout in New Zealand General Elections, 1928–1987. *Political Science* 40 (December): 16–38.

Nagel, Jack H., and John E. McNulty. 1996. Partisan Effects of Voter Turnout in Senatorial and Gubernatorial Elections. *American Political Science Review* 90(4): 780–793.

Nagourney, Adam. 2004. Baffled in Loss, Democrats Seek Road Forward. *New York Times*, November 7.

———. 2003. Political Parties Shift Emphasis to Core Voters. *New York Times*, September 11.

Nie, Norman H., Sidney Verba, and John R. Petrocik. 1979. *The Changing American Voter*, rev. ed. Cambridge, MA: Harvard University Press.

Niemi, Richard, and James Jennings. 1991. Issues and Inheritance in the Formation of Party Identification. *American Journal of Political Science* 35: 970–988.

Niemi, Richard, and Jane Junn. 1998. *Civic Education: What Makes Students Learn.* New Haven, CT: Yale University Press.

Nincic, Miroslav, and Donna J. Nincic. 2002. Race, Gender and War. *Journal of Peace Research* 39(5): 547–568.

Norpoth, Helmut. 2004. From Primary to General Election: A Forecast of the Presidential Vote. *PS: Political Science and Politics* (October): 737–740.

———. 1987. Underway and Here to Stay: Party Realignment in the 1980s. *Public Opinion Quarterly* 51: 376–391.

Norrander, Barbara. 1999. The Evolution of the Gender Gap. *Public Opinion Quarterly* 63: 566–576.

———. 1989. Ideological Representativeness of Presidential Primary Voters. *American Journal of Political Science* 33 (August): 570–587.

Overby, L. Marvin, and Jay Barth. 2003. Radio Advertising in American Political Campaigns. *American Politics Research* 34(4): 451–478.

Pacek, Alexander, and Benjamin Radcliff. 1995. Turnout and the Vote for Left-of-Center Parties: A Cross-National Analysis. *British Journal of Political Science* 25 (January): 137–143.

Page, Benjamin, and Robert Shapiro. 1992. *The Rational Public.* Chicago: University of Chicago Press.

Panagakis, Nick. 1989. Incumbent Races: Closer than They Appear. *The Polling Report,* February 27.

Panagopoulos, Costas, and Donald P. Green. 2006. The Impact of Radio Advertisements on Voter Turnout and Electoral Competition. Paper presented to the Challenges of Participatory Democracy Workshop, University of Southern California, January 24.

Patterson, Thomas E. 2002. *The Vanishing Voter: Public Involvement in an Age of Uncertainty.* New York: Alfred Knopf.

———. 1993. *Out of Order.* New York: Alfred Knopf.

Pedersen, Johannes T. 1978. Political Involvement and Partisan Change in Presidential Elections. *American Journal of Political Science* 22(1): 18–30.

Petrocik, John R. 2007. Party Coalitions in the American Public: Morality Politics, Issue Agendas, and the 2004 Election. In John C. Green and Daniel Coffey (Eds.), *The State of the Parties.* Lanham, MD: Rowman and Littlefield.

———. 2004. Hard Facts: The Media and Elections, with a Look at 2000 and 2002. In James Thurber and Candice Nelson (Eds.), *Campaigns and Elections American Style,* 2nd ed. Boulder, CO: Westview.

———. 1998. Reformulating the Party Coalitions: The Christian Democratic Republicans. Paper presented at the Annual Meeting of the American Political Science Association, Boston Marriot Copley Hotel, September 3–6.

———. 1996. Issue Ownership in Presidential Elections, with a 1980 Case Study. *American Journal of Political Science* 40: 825–850.

———. 1989. An Expected Party Vote: New Data for an Old Concept. *American Journal of Political Science* 33: 44–66.

———. 1987a. Realignment: New Party Coalitions and the Nationalization of the South. *Journal of Politics* 49 (May): 347–375.

———. 1987b. Voter Turnout and Electoral Preference: The Anomalous Reagan Elections. In Kay L. Schlozman (Ed.), *Elections in America*. New York: Allen and Unwin.

———. 1981a. *Party Coalitions: Realignment and the Decline of the New Deal Party System*. Chicago: University of Chicago Press.

———. 1981b. Voter Turnout and Electoral Oscillation. *American Politics Quarterly* 9 (April): 161–180.

———. 1974. An Analysis of Intransitivities in the Index of Party Identification. *Political Methodology* 1: 31–47.

Petrocik, John R., William L. Benoit, and Glenn J. Hansen. 2003–2004. Issue Ownership and Presidential Campaigning, 1952–2000. *Political Science Quarterly* 118(4): 599–626.

Petrocik, John R., and Thad A. Brown. 1998. Party System Structure and Electoral Realignments. In Birol Yesilada (Ed.), *Comparative Political Parties and Party Elites: Essays in Honor of Samuel J. Eldersveld*. Ann Arbor: University of Michigan Press.

Petrocik, John R., and William Perkins. 2003. Short-term Forces and the Partisan Bias of Turnout: House Elections, 1972–2000. Paper presented at the 2003 Annual Meeting of the American Political Science Association, Philadelphia, PA, August 27–31.

Petrocik, John R., and Daron Shaw. 1992. Nonvoting in America: Attitudes in Context. In William Crotty (Ed.), *Political Participation and American Democracy*. New York: Greenwood Press.

Piven, Frances F. 1985. Women and the State: Ideology, Power and the Welfare State. In Alice S. Rossi (Ed.), *Gender and the Life Course*, pp. 265–287. New York: Aldine.

Piven, Frances F., and Richard Cloward. 1988. *Why Americans Don't Vote*. New York: Pantheon.

Plutzer, Eric, and John F. Zipp. 1996. Identity Politics, Partisanship, and Voting for Women Candidates. *Public Opinion Quarterly* 60(1): 30–57.

Poole, Keith T., and H. Rosenthal. 2001. D-NOMINATE after 10 Years. *Legislative Studies Quarterly* 26: 5–29.

———. 1997. *Congress: A Political Economic History of Roll Call Voting*. New York: Oxford University Press.

Popkin, Samuel L. 1991. *The Reasoning Voter: Communication and Persuasion in Presidential Campaigns*. Chicago: University of Chicago Press.

Presser, Stanley. 1990. Can Changes in Context Reduce Vote Over-reporting in Surveys? *Public Opinion Quarterly* 54(4): 586–593.

Przeworski, Adam. 1975. Institutionalization of Voting Patterns, or Is Mobilization the Source of Decay. *American Political Science Review* 69: 49–67.

PS: Political Science and Politics. 2004. Election Forecasting Issue 37: 4.

PS: Political Science and Politics. 2001. Election 2000 Special: Al Gore and George Bush's Not-So-Excellent Adventure 34 (March): 9–48.

Putnam, Robert D. 2000. *Bowling Alone: The Collapse and Revival of American Community.* New York: Simon and Schuster.

———. 1995. Bowling Alone. *Journal of Democracy* 9: 65–78.

Rabinowitz, George, and Stuart E. Macdonald. 1989. A Directional Theory of Issue Voting. *American Political Science Review* 83: 93–122.

Radcliff, Benjamin. 1994. Turnout and the Democratic Vote. *American Politics Quarterly* 22 (July): 259–276.

Rahn, Wendy M., John H. Aldrich, Eugene Borgida, and John L. Sullivan. 1990. A Social-Cognitive Model of Candidate Appraisal. In John Ferejohn and James Kuklinski (Eds.), *Information and Democratic Processes.* Urbana: University of Illinois Press.

Rhode, David.W. 1991. *Parties and Leaders in the Postreform House.* Chicago: University of Chicago Press.

Robinson, Michael J., and Margaret Sheehan. 1983. *Over the Wire and On T.V.: CBS and UPI in Campaign 80.* New York: Russell Sage.

Rosenstone, Steven, and John Mark Hansen. 1993. *Mobilization, Participation, and Democracy in America.* New York: Macmillan.

Rosenstone, Steven, and Raymond Wolfinger. 1978. The Effect of Registration Laws on Voter Turnout. *American Political Science Review* 72: 22–45.

Sabato, Larry J. 1993. *Feeding Frenzy: How Attack Journalism Has Transformed American Politics.* New York: Free Press.

Sapiro, Virginia, and Pamela Johnston Conover. 1997. The Variable Gender Basis of Electoral Politics: Gender and Context in the 1992 US Election. *British Journal of Political Science* 27(4): 497–523.

Schlesinger, Joseph A. 1985. The New American Party System. *American Political Science Review* 85 (December): 1152–1169.

Schlesinger, Mark, and Caroline Heldman. 2001. Gender Gap or Gender Gaps? New Perspectives on Support for Government Action and Policies. *Journal of Politics* 63(1): 59–92.

Sears, David, and Nicholas Valentino. 1997. Politics Matters: Political Events as Catalysts for Pre-Adult Socialization. *American Political Science Review* 91: 45–65.

Seelye, Katherine Q. 2001. Ideas and Trends: From Selma to Florida; Election Reform, Meet Politics. *New York Times,* March 4.

Seltzer, Richard A., Jody Newman, and Melissa Voorhees Leighton. 1997. *Sex as a Political Variable: Women as Candidates and Voters in U. S. Elections.* Boulder, CO: Lynne Rienner.

Shapiro, Robert Y., and Harpreet Mahajan. 1986. Gender Differences in Policy Preferences: A Summary of Trends from the 1960s and 1980s. *Public Opinion Quarterly* 50: 42–61.

Shaw, Daron R. 2006. *The Race to 270.* Chicago: University of Chicago Press.

———. 1999a. A Study of Presidential Campaign Event Effects from 1952 to 1992. *Journal of Politics* 61: 387–422.

———. 1999b. The Effect of TV Ads and Candidate Appearances on Statewide Presidential Votes, 1988–96. *American Political Science Review* 93: 345–361.

Shea, Daniel M., and John Burton. 2003. *Campaign Craft.* New York: Praeger.

Shelley, Mack C., II, and Hwang-Du Hwang. 1991. The Mass Media and Public Opinion Polls in the 1988 Presidential Election. *American Politics Quarterly* 19: 59–79.

Sigal, Leon. 1973. *Reporters and Officials: The Organization and Politics of Newsmaking.* Lexington, MA: D.C. Heath.

Sigelman, Lee, and Malcolm E. Jewell. 1986. From Core to Periphery: A Note on the Imagery of Concentric Electorates. *Journal of Politics* 48(2): 440–449.

Silver, Brian D., Paul R. Abramson, and Barbara A. Anderson. 1986. The Presence of Others and Over-reporting of Voting in American National Elections. *Public Opinion Quarterly* 50(2): 228–239.

Smeal, Eleanor. 1984. *Why and How Women Will Elect the Next President.* New York: Harper and Row.

Stanley, Harold W., William Bianco, and Richard G. Niemi. 1986. Partisanship and Group Support over Time: A Multivariate Analysis. *American Political Science Review* 80(3): 969–976.

Steger, Wayne P. 2007. Who Wins Nominations and Why? *Political Research Quarterly* 60(1): 91–99.

Stimson, James. 2004. *Tides of Consent.* New York: Cambridge University Press.

Stone, Walter J., and L. Sandy Maisel. 1999. The Not-So-Simple Calculus of Winning: Potential U.S. House Candidates' Nomination and General Election Chances. Paper presented at the 1999 Annual Meeting of the American Political Science Association, Atlanta, GA, September 2–5.

Stonecash, Jeffrey M., Mark D. Brewer, and M. D. Mariani. 2003. *Diverging Parties: Social Change, Realignment, and Party Polarization.* Boulder, CO: Westview.

Sundquist, James L. 1983. *Dynamics of the Party System: Alignment and Realignment of Political Parties in the United States.* Washington, DC: Brookings Institution Press.

Taylor, Shelly, A. L. Peplau, and David O. Sears. 2000. *Social Psychology,* 10th ed. Upper Saddle River, NJ: Prentice Hall.

Teixeira, Ruy A. 1992. *The Disappearing American Voter.* Washington, DC: Brookings Institution Press.

————. 1987. Why Americans Don't Vote: Turnout Decline in the United States, 1960–1984. New York: Greenwood.

Tucker, Harvey J., and Arnold Vedlitz. 1986. Does Heavy Turnout Help Democrats in Presidential Elections? American Political Science Review 80(4): 1291–1298.

Tumulty, Karen, and Viveca Novak. 2003. Time, Sunday, May 25. http://www.time.com/time/magazine/article/0,9171,454487-2,00.html.

Valentino, Nicholas A. 2001. Group Priming in American Elections. In Roderick P. Hart and Daron R. Shaw (Eds.), Communication in U.S. Elections: New Agendas. Lanham, MD: Rowman and Littlefield.

Vavreck, Lynn, Constantine J. Spiliotes, and Linda L. Fowler. 2002. The Effects of Retail Politics in the New Hampshire Primary. American Journal of Political Science 46: 595–610.

Verba, Sidney, and Norman Nie. 1972. Participation in America: Political Democracy and Social Equality. New York: Harper and Row.

Verba, Sidney, Kay Lehman Schlozman, and Henry E. Brady. 1995. Voice and Equality: Civic Voluntarism in American Politics. Cambridge, MA: Harvard University Press.

WashingtonPost.com. 2004. www.washingtonpost.com/wp-dyn/content/article/2007/07/04/AR2007070401423.html.

Wattenberg, Martin P. 1990. The Decline of American Political Parties, 1952–1988. Cambridge, MA: Harvard University Press.

Wattenberg, Martin P., and Craig L. Brians. 1999. Negative Campaign Advertising: Demobilizer or Mobilizer? American Political Science Review 93: 891–899.

Welch, Susan, and John Hibbing. 1992. Financial Conditions, Gender and Voting in American National Elections. Journal of Politics 54: 197–213.

West, Darrell. 1983. Constituencies and Travel Allocations in the 1980 Presidential Campaign. American Journal of Political Science 27: 515–529.

Whirls, Daniel. 1986. Reinterpreting the Gender Gap. Public Opinion Quarterly 50: 316–330.

Wilcox, Clyde, Ted G. Jelen, and David C. Leege. 1993. Religious Group Identifications: Toward a Cognitive Theory of Religious Mobilization. In David C. Leege and Lyman Kellstedt (Eds.), Rediscovering the Religious Factor in American Politics. Armonk, NY: M. E. Sharpe.

Wilcox, Clyde, and Barbara Norrander. 2002. Of Moods and Morals: The Dynamics of Opinion on Abortion and Gay Rights. In Barbara Norrander and Clyde Wilcox (Eds.), Understanding Public Opinion, 2nd ed. Washington, DC: CQ Press.

Wlezien, Christopher, and Robert S. Erikson. 2004. The Fundamentals, the Polls, and the Presidential Vote. PS: Political Science and Politics (October): 747–751.

————. 2002. The Timeline of Presidential Election Campaigns. *Journal of Politics* 64: 969–993.

Wolfinger, Raymond, and Steven Rosenstone. 1980. *Who Votes in America?* New Haven, CT: Yale University Press.

Zaller, John R. 2003. *Studies in Public Opinions: Gauging Attitudes, Nonattitudes, Measurement Error and Change.* Ed. William E. Saris and Paul M. Sniderman. Princeton, NJ: Princeton University Press.

————. 1992. *The Nature and Origins of Mass Opinion.* New York: Cambridge University Press.

Zaller, John R., and Marc Hunt. 1994. The Rise and Fall of Candidate Perot: Unmediated versus Mediated Politics—part I. *Political Communication* 11(4): 357–390.

Zukin, Cliff. 1977. A Reconsideration of the Effects of Information on Partisan Stability. *Public Opinion Quarterly* 41(2): 244–254.

Index

Page numbers followed by *f* denote figures; those followed by *t* denote tables